CREATING VALUE WITH KNOWLEDGE

CREATING VALUE
WITH KNOWLEDGE _____

Insights from the IBM Institute
for Business Value

Edited by

Eric Lesser

Laurence Prusak

OXFORD
UNIVERSITY PRESS

2004

OXFORD
UNIVERSITY PRESS

Oxford   New York
Auckland   Bangkok   Buenos Aires   Cape Town   Chennai
Dar es Salaam   Delhi   Hong Kong   Istanbul   Karachi   Kolkata
Kuala Lumpur   Madrid   Melbourne   Mexico City   Mumbai   Nairobi
São Paulo   Shanghai   Taipei   Tokyo   Toronto

Published by Oxford University Press, Inc.
198 Madison Avenue, New York, New York 10016

www.oup.com

Oxford is a registered trademark of Oxford University Press

Library of Congress Cataloging-in-Publication Data
Lesser, Eric L.
Creating value with knowledge : insights from the IBM Institute for Business Value
/ edited by Eric Lesser and Laurence Prusak.
p.   cm.
Includes bibliographical references and index.
ISBN 0-19-516512-8
1. Knowledge management. I. Prusak, Laurence. II. Title.
HD30.2.L47 2003
658.4'038—dc21   2003051710

9 8 7 6 5 4 3 2 1

Printed in the United States of America
on acid-free paper

Foreword

Only five years ago, I received a telephone call from an executive search firm seeking candidates for a position of Chief Knowledge Officer (CKO). "Can you clarify for me what a Chief Knowledge Officer does," I inquired. There was a longish pause before the caller admitted with a nervous giggle, "I was hoping you could tell me."

Although today the caller and I might have a better idea about the role of CKO, there is still much mystery surrounding the field of knowledge management. In fact, the term is a kind of Rorschach test for managers, with some still entrenched in the belief that managing knowledge is just a new name for managing information—and information systems—and others comprehending that managing knowledge requires a deep understanding of human-to-human behavior and the workings of the mind.

How paradoxical, then, that a company whose existence depended on selling computers and related services should have sponsored so much research that ended up focusing on the psychology and sociology of knowledge as well as on computer facilitation. It is a tribute to the founders of this program that they were not encumbered by preconceptions about the nature of knowledge. It is a tribute to the IBM Corporation that once these pioneering researchers discovered that their paths in the wilderness led as much to face-to-face interactions as to technology-facilitated communications, the research sponsors continued their support.

This book is itself an embodiment of knowledge flows; an anthology is a "many to many" communication vehicle. The articles cover a range of topics from the most sophisticated technologically enabled knowledge flows to the most basic. The reader will be enlightened on issues as current as virtual work and as ancient as story-telling. In fact, the most remarkable characteristic of this collection, in addition to its grounding in human interactions, is its practicality. The volume addresses the question managers most seek to answer: What should I *do* to manage knowledge more effectively?

We have known for decades that knowledge constitutes the real competitive advantage of organizations. We are only just beginning to realize what that means in terms of daily decisions and routines. The authors in this volume have delved deeply into organizations to bring us some very promising courses of action.

Dorothy Leonard
Harvard Business School
February 2003

Acknowledgments

First, we wish to recognize the member organizations that have participated in our program over the past several years. These corporations and government agencies have opened their doors and allowed us access to conduct the research upon which this anthology is based. This work would not be possible without the personal and professional investment of our member community, which has contributed time, energy, and commitment to our program.

This anthology represents the accumulated insights of the IBM Institute for Business Value's Knowledge and Organizational Performance Forum (KOPF) and our affiliated researchers (more information about their backgrounds can be found in the list of contributors). Each has made significant contributions to the discipline of knowledge-based organizations. We sincerely thank each of them for their efforts and assistance in making this anthology come to life.

A special thanks to Judith Quillard, who, as our Member Services leader, edited many of the chapters of this book at the time of their original publication and provided important input into the overview sections of this book. Her eye for detail and language has helped all of us improve the quality of work and further bolstered our own personal standards.

We would like to thank many of the individuals who have worked for the KOPF over the last several years and helped make it the vibrant program it is today. In addition to the authors who appear in this book, Susan Allen, Yvette Burton, Kathleen Curley, Tony DiMarco, Joseph Horvath, Cynthia Kurtz, David Millen, David Mundel, Chris Newell, Sara Schecter, Joyce Sharon, Jason Slusher, David Smith, and Winny Wong have all made important contributions throughout our four-year history. Special thanks as well to Scott Smith, who has been an important supporter and friend of the KOPF over the last several years.

We would like to acknowledge the assistance of John Connolly, Randy Hancock, and Richard Bartolomeo from IBM in supporting this endeavor and helping us bring this book to fruition. We greatly appreciate the patience and support of our editor, Martha Cooley, at Oxford University Press. From the inception of the book to its completion, her assistance was invaluable throughout.

Finally, we thank our spouses, children, families, and significant others who have helped and supported us along the way. This book is a reflection of their contribution as well.

Credits

Chapter 7. Reprinted from *IBM Systems Journal,* Eric L. Lesser and John Storck, "Communities of Practice and Organizational Performance," Vol. 40, No. 4, 2001, pp. 831–841. Copyright © 2001 IBM Corporation. Reprinted with permission from IBM Corporation. All rights reserved.

Chapter 8. Reprinted from *Knowledge Management Review,* Michael Fontaine, "Keeping Communities of Practice Afloat: Understanding and Fostering Roles in Communities," Vol. 4, No. 4, September/October 2001, pp. 16–21. Copyright © 2001 Melcrum Publishing Limited. Reprinted with permission from Melcrum Publishing Limited. All rights reserved.

Chapter 9. Reprinted with permission from *Marketing Management,* published by the American Marketing Association, Eric Lesser and Michael Fontaine, "Learning from the Connected Customer: Enhancing Customer Web Sites with Community," November/December 2002.

Chapter 10. Reprinted from *IBM Systems Journal,* Salvatore Parise and John C. Henderson, "Knowledge Resource Exchange in Strategic Alliances," Vol. 40, No. 4, 2001, pp. 908–924. Copyright © 2001 IBM Corporation. Reprinted with permission from IBM Corporation. All rights reserved.

Chapter 11. Reprinted from *Ivey Business Journal,* Salvatore Parise and Lisa Sasson, "Leveraging Knowledge Management across Strategic Alliances," March/April 2002, pp. 41–47. Copyright © 2001 *Ivey Business Journal.* Reprinted with permission from *Ivey Business Journal.* All rights reserved.

Chapter 12. Copyright © 2001 by M. E. Sharpe, Inc. From *Journal of Management Information Systems,* Vol. 18, No. 1 (Summer 2001), pp. 95–114. Reprinted with permission.

Chapter 13. Reprinted from *Knowledge Management,* David Snowden, "Narrative Patterns: The Perils and Possibilities of Using Story in Organisations," July/August 2001, pp. 16–20. Copyright © 2001 Ark Group. Reprinted with permission from Ark Group. All rights reserved.

Contents

Contributors

Lisa C. Abrams is a Senior Consultant with the IBM Institute for Business Value. Her research has focused on social capital, knowledge sharing, trust on the Internet, and the linkages between trust and project performance. Her previous work experience has been in the publishing industry and the nonprofit sector. Lisa has master's degrees from the Columbia University School of International and Public Affairs and the Massachusetts Institute of Technology Sloan School of Management.

Stephen P. Borgatti is an Associate Professor of organizational behavior at Boston College's Carroll School of Management. He is the principal author of UCINET, the leading software package for social network analysis, and past president of INSNA, the professional association for social network researchers. Dr. Borgatti has published more than fifty journal articles in the area of social network theory and methodology. Dr. Borgatti earned his Ph.D. in mathematical social science from the University of California, Irvine.

Don Cohen is the Editor of *Business Value Directions,* the journal of the IBM Institute for Business Value. He previously was the Editor for *Knowledge Directions,* the journal for the IBM Institute for Knowledge Management. He is the coauthor (with Laurence Prusak) of *In Good Company: How Social Capital Makes Organizations Work* (Harvard Business School Press, 2001). Don earned his M.Phil. in English from Yale University.

Joseph Cothrel is Vice President of Research at Participate Systems, a provider of software and services for online community and collaboration. For more than a decade, Joe has conducted research on effective collaboration among customers, employees, and business partners. He has applied that research in work for almost 100 companies. Joe has been cited in publications including the *New York Times, Forbes,* and the *Wall Street Journal.* He holds an M.A. from the University of Michigan.

Rob Cross is an Assistant Professor at the McIntire School of Commerce (University of Virginia) and a former Senior Consultant with the IBM Institute for Business Value. He has consulted with over forty public and private organizations on issues related to social networks, organizational design, and knowledge management. Rob holds a doctorate from Boston University's School of Management and has published extensively in academic and practitioner publications.

Michael A. Fontaine is a Managing Consultant with the IBM Institute for Business Value. Michael's research has focused on enabling knowledge sharing through communities of practice, online communities, and collaborative environments. He has consulted to a number of government agencies on knowledge and collaboration issues. His previous work experience has been in retail operations management and music history. Mr. Fontaine is a frequent speaker on communities, collaboration, and knowledge management topics and has been published in a number of practitioner and trade journals. Michael holds an M.B.A. from Northeastern University.

John C. Henderson is the Richard C. Shipley Professor of Management and the Chair of the Information Systems Department at Boston University's School of Management. He also serves as the Director of the Systems Research Center at the school. Professor Henderson's research focuses on four main areas: managing strategic partnerships, aligning business and IT strategies, valuing IT investment, and knowledge management. He received his Ph.D. from the University of Texas at Austin.

Dorothy Leonard is the William J. Abernathy Professor of Business Administration at Harvard Business School, where she has taught since 1983. Her research, teaching, and consulting have focused on the management of knowledge and innovation, with particular emphasis on communication and human behavior. Author of *Wellsprings of Knowledge: Building and Sustaining the Sources of Innovation* and *When Sparks Fly* (with Walter Swap), she has published over 100 articles, book chapters, and field-based cases.

Eric L. Lesser is an Associate Partner with the IBM Institute for Business Value. Mr. Lesser oversees research initiatives at the Institute and has focused on knowledge strategy, communities, knowledge retention, and customer knowledge issues. He has consulted on knowledge and organization change issues in the financial services, transportation, government, and manufacturing industries. Mr. Lesser received his M.B.A. from Emory University.

Daniel Z. Levin is an Assistant Professor in the Management and Global Business Department of Rutgers Business School, Rutgers University. His research has focused primarily on knowledge transfer and organizational learning issues. Dr. Levin received his Ph.D. from the Kellogg Graduate School of Management at Northwestern University.

Nitin Nohria is the Richard P. Chapman Professor of Business Administration and chairs the Organizational Behavior unit at the Harvard Business School. His research interests center on leadership, human performance, and corporate renewal. Prior to joining the Harvard Business School faculty in July 1988, Professor Nohria received his Ph.D. in management from the Sloan School of Management, Massachusetts Institute of Technology.

Salvatore Parise is a Senior Consultant with the IBM Institute for Business Value. His research has focused on multilateral alliance structures, alignment between business strategy and alliance strategy, organizational learning, and knowledge management. He has consulted on strategy and alliances issues across a range of industries. Salvatore holds a doctorate from Boston University's School of Management.

Andrew Parker is a Senior Consultant with the IBM Institute for Business Value. His research has focused on social network analysis and the use of knowledge intermediaries in organizations. He has consulted on the use of social network analysis in the government and petroleum industries. He earned his M.Sc. from the London School of Economics.

Laurence Prusak, an independent researcher and consultant, is a former managing principal with IBM's Institute for Business Value. He has extensive research and consulting experience, within the United States and internationally, in helping organizations leverage and optimize their information and knowledge resources. He has co-authored several books, including *In Good Company: The Role of Social Capital in Organizations* (Harvard Business School Press, 2000), with Don Cohen; and *Information Ecology* (Oxford University Press, 1997), and *Working Knowledge* (Harvard Business School Press, 1997), with Thomas Davenport. He holds an M.A. in economic and social history from New York University.

Lisa Sasson is a Vice President of BrandEdge, a consulting firm focused on the health care industry. Previously she was a consultant with the IBM Institute for Business Value. Her research at the Institute focused on the use of knowledge intermediaries and strategic alliances. Lisa has a master's degree in international relations from Boston University.

Mimi Shields is a doctoral student at the Melbourne Business School. Previously she was a Research Associate in the Technology and Operations Management Group at Harvard Business School. She holds a master's degree in social psychology from Harvard University and has taught psychology and statistics at Harvard University, Harvard Business School, and the Harvard Extension School.

David J. Snowden is Director of IBM's Cynefin Centre, which focuses on research and consulting in the new area of pheunominological, or contextual, complexity. He was formerly the European Director of the Institute for Knowledge Management, where he pioneered the use of narrative techniques in knowledge management and decision support. He is a frequent speaker and author on a range of management topics and consults internationally at board level in both private and public organizations. His first book, *Complex Knowledge*, is due to be published in 2003. He holds a B.A. in philosophy from Lancaster University and an M.B.A. from Middlesex University.

John Storck is an Assistant Professor of Management Information Systems at Boston University, teaching in the M.B.A. program and the Master of Science in information systems program. His research activities focus on the nature of individual and group work in globally distributed organizations, with a particular emphasis on how communities of practice enhance knowledge diffusion and learning. He holds a D.B.A. from Boston University.

Walter Swap is a Professor of Psychology at Tufts University, where he chaired the Department of Psychology and was Dean of the College. His research interests include group dynamics, attitudes and attitude change, altruism, and creativity. He is the author of *When Sparks Fly: Igniting Creativity in Groups*, with Dorothy Leonard, and the editor of *Group Decision Making*, as well as the author of numerous articles in scholarly journals.

CREATING VALUE WITH KNOWLEDGE

Introduction

The mid-1990s saw the rise of an important movement: a recognition that organizational knowledge, in its various forms and attributes, could be an important source of competitive advantage in the marketplace. Books written at this time, such as Thomas Stewart's *Intellectual Capital*, Dorothy Leonard's *Wellsprings of Knowledge: Building and Sustaining the Sources of Innovation*, and Ikujiro Nonaka and Hirotaka Takeuchi's *The Knowledge-Creating Company: How Japanese Companies Create the Dynamics of Innovation*, illuminated how employees' ideas and experiences could be used to create more efficient, effective, and innovative organizations. While successful companies have always found ways to effectively create, share, and apply knowledge, the importance of competing based on one's knowledge has only recently been seen as a corporate imperative. Given the transformation of many companies from product manufacturers to value-added service providers, and technological advances that have both enabled and required firms to compete on a global scale, significant attention is being paid to this elusive, yet highly valued, asset.

As the knowledge management movement attracted attention in organizations, a number of the practitioners we knew through our consulting work began to make strides in this area. Indeed, many of them were speakers at the early knowledge management conferences and were often quoted in the business press regarding their efforts. These forerunners in the knowledge discipline, however, lacked access to two key ingredients: practical research that could take them to the next level of thinking and applying knowledge management practices, and a community of peers in which they could exchange ideas and share relevant insights.

The Beginnings of an Institute

Recognizing this need, we, along with a number of our colleagues, formed the IBM Institute for Knowledge Management (IKM) in 1998. IBM Global Services and Lotus Development (at the time a business unit within IBM and now part of its Software division) jointly sponsored the initiative. The focus of the Institute was to develop practical insights for member companies and our own consulting colleagues in the emerging discipline of knowledge management. The focus on practical learnings was critical to our mission. While we surely admire and use theoretical work in our research, we recognized that our insights needed to be based on a more practical understanding than was common in the knowledge research of the time. We all agreed that both robust theory and grounded practice were essential for any successful intervention in knowledge management.

A number of key decisions shaped the way we formed our Institute. Early on, we sought out membership from those organizations that already had knowledge management operations under way. From this initial critical mass of organizations, others soon followed. We decided to charge for our services, though not very much by most consulting or even research standards. It has been our experience that when research is provided for free, it tends to be discounted by clients as marketing or sales materials. We also solicited member input into the research planning process and required that organizations actively participate in at least one research project per year. This was done for several reasons. First, we wanted to do research that was relevant to members, and the only way to assure this was to work with them in choosing the subjects. Second, we wanted to design research projects that were feasible to do and that engaged people's attention. Finally, we (researchers and members) wanted to make a contribution to the practice of knowledge management. The researchers in the IKM, and many of our clients, were intrinsically motivated to contribute to the world's stock of knowledge on knowledge management.

We also wanted to make sure that the Institute was more than just a source for content. Part of our charter was to build a true sense of community among our company representatives. To this end, we created a number of face-to-face events to ensure that participants became acquainted with our research staff and with the other members in the consortium. We developed focused *Research Sessions* where individuals who were interested in a specific topic could come together for a day to help frame research directions, probe interim research findings, and have in-depth discussions with others facing similar issues. We also created *Member Forums*, two-and-a-half-day conferences that gave members the opportunity to learn about the results from research projects, listen to guest speakers, and exchange ideas about practices that worked (or did not work) from colleagues at other member organizations. As our members and staff have gotten to know each other over the last several years, the Member Forums have taken on an important role in bringing our community closer together—enabling members to make new connections, establish relationships, and develop the common context critical to effective knowledge sharing.

Emerging Research Themes

In reviewing our efforts since the Institute's early days, several themes emerge. It is useful to briefly discuss them, since they have substantial relevance in understanding the context in which the chapters in this book have been written. Perhaps the most pervasive theme, and one that is echoed in knowledge management practices throughout the world, is the shift in emphasis from the *individual* to the *group* as the unit of analysis when doing knowledge management projects.

As we delved deeper into how and what knowledge efforts were most effective in improving organizational performance, we found time after time that taking some form of group or social approach was immensely valuable. For example, it led us to look much more closely into *social capital*, a concept borrowed from sociology to indicate the value individuals, groups, and organizations could derive from their social networks. As we found from our research and experience, knowledge did not travel particularly well without the presence of important social factors such as networks, trust, and commonly held norms and values. Part I of this book focuses on a number of these social capital issues. Chapter 1 provides an overview of many of the issues that organizations face in creating and maintaining social capital. The authors believe that in increasingly complex and distributed work environments, the development of social capital can be easily stunted, ultimately making it difficult for a firm to take advantage of this important resource. The authors of chapter 2, recognizing the difficulty in building social capital in a virtual world, examine the role of technology in maintaining relationships beyond face-to-face encounters.

Our work in the area of social capital led us quite naturally to take a more extended look at two of its main components—trust and networks. The concept of trust proved to be a very valuable angle to understand how knowledge moves, or fails to move, within organizations. Many employees fail to share knowledge by being unwilling to do so, as much as they are often unable to do so due to infrastructure deficits. This unwillingness can have many causes, but a lack of generalized trust and reciprocity is an important factor. Little knowledge is ever shared, transferred, or codeveloped without trust that the engaged parties will be suitably rewarded and credited for their effort. And the extensive use of the Internet has only added layers of interesting, if vexing, questions on how to address issues of trust within a knowledge-rich environment. Chapter 3 reinforces the importance of trust in supporting effective knowledge sharing, highlighting the importance of both competence and benevolence in developing trustworthy relationships with others.

Our examination into how networks influence knowledge sharing led us to the application of *social network analysis*, a tool that had been developed by sociologists to understand interactions within and across different groups. Using social network analysis to better understand how knowledge travels within organizations has yielded a rich vein of insights that are highlighted in part II. In chapter 4, the authors dispel some of the commonly held assumptions about networks in organizations. For example, they believe that although networks are formed through individual relationships, the larger organizational context can have a significant impact on network development. Chapter 5 focuses on how four important drivers—awareness, access, engagement, and safety—influence how knowledge travels across informal networks. Finally, chapter 6 examines how social network analysis can be used as a diagnostic technique to better understand myriad organizational challenges, ranging from improving communication between functional organizations to identifying key knowledge-sharing roles and responsibilities.

A form of network, perhaps smaller and denser, is a *community of practice,* or interest. Many of our members were involved in some experiments, or new organization designs, applying this quite popular concept, and this provided us with a rich environment for our research. Knowledge "clumps" quite visibly in these communities, and they (as well as the larger networks) may well prove to be a fundamental building block for designing more knowledge-intensive organizations. Part III highlights some of our research in this area. Chapter 7 explains how communities of practice play a critical role in the development of social capital, providing employees with the opportunity to expand their connections, develop relationships, and establish common norms and values that can lead to improved knowledge transfer. Chapter 8 illustrates the importance of formal and informal roles within a community of practice. These roles, which range from planning community events to maintaining a community Web site, can help foster community participation and ensure that both individuals and organizations are making the most of their community investment. Finally, chapter 9 extends the notion of community to include customers. It focuses on how organizations are bringing together informal groups of customers via the Internet to exchange knowledge, build brand loyalty, and provide unique insights into product design and use.

Many of the early applications of knowledge management focused on knowledge within the organization. Yet we found that the diffusion of knowledge beyond organizational boundaries was also a critical issue faced by our members. Our work in the area of *knowledge and strategic alliances* has further reinforced the importance of a structured approach to understanding the opportunities and barriers to sharing knowledge with partners and outside stakeholders. As firms compete less on the strengths of individual products or businesses, and more on the ability to form and create value from relationships with outside parties, the need to manage knowledge across these entities has become a paramount concern. The chapters in part IV provide a number of important perspectives on the flow of knowledge between alliance partners. Chapter 10 focuses on the different types of knowledge that are shared within an alliance relationship, and how the knowledge exchanges between different partners can influence the development of a larger alliance strategy. Chapter 11 highlights how firms can apply knowledge management tools and techniques to identify potential alliance partners, negotiate successful arrangements, and more effectively maintain ongoing partnerships.

Finally, another important stream of research has focused on the use of narratives, or *storytelling,* as an important tool in communicating knowledge and retaining corporate memory. Much as we use stories to educate our children and ourselves about how the world operates, many of the same ideas can be applied to sharing knowledge within the workplace. A technique used since ancient times, storytelling has taken on a newfound importance as organizations look for ways to more effectively pass on experiential knowledge in time-pressed, information-congested environments. The chapters in part V discuss the applicability of storytelling in a number of settings. Chapter 12 examines the use of mentoring and storytelling in the context of venture capitalists sharing important learnings with newly minted entrepreneurs. Chapter 13 discusses a number of additional applications for using story techniques and underscores some of the potential dangers in underestimating the challenges and pitfalls associated with narrative-based approaches.

Moving Forward

At the beginning of 2002, having conducted research and worked closely with our member companies for the previous three years, we took a look at what we had accomplished. Over forty companies, representing eight countries and three continents, had participated in our member program. We conducted nine Member Forums and held numerous Working Sessions in locations across the United States and Europe. Researchers at the IKM had produced numerous books, articles, white papers, and practitioner toolkits on a variety of subjects, including communities of practice, knowledge intermediaries, narrative techniques, customer knowledge, social network analysis, knowledge and strategic alliances, and trust. At the same time, the program became part of a more comprehensive thought leadership group within IBM: The IBM Institute for Business Value.

We also recognized that much of our work went beyond examining how organizations could more effectively manage their knowledge. Rather, the primary thrust of our efforts was helping organizations use their knowledge to more effectively compete in the new economy. Therefore, in early 2003, we changed our name to one that we thought would better reflect our mission: The Knowledge and Organizational Performance Forum. We believe this name highlights our committment to helping organization achieve superior performance through the better use of knowledge.

The chapters in this book reflect the very rich and interesting issues and perspectives that have emerged from our interactions with our member companies over the last several years. Although we could incorporate only a small percentage of the work that we have produced into this anthology, we hope it provides an insight into our program and the learnings that have been created from it. We look forward to continuing to work with our growing member community and develop practical insights that will help to shape and guide the successful knowledge-based organization of the future.

PART I

SOCIAL CAPITAL

A question at the center of many knowledge management efforts is often a simple one: What motivates individuals to share what they know? At first glance, we find that such sharing behaviors are, in many cases, antithetical to the way individuals are educated and brought into the workforce. Many of us are educated in academic environments where sharing knowledge is viewed as "cheating," and our academic achievements are built up on individual, rather than collective, effort. When we move into the corporate world, our biases against knowledge sharing continue to be reinforced, as we are often measured and rewarded on the basis of achieving individually based targets. With much of this external reinforcement focused on the individual, it is little wonder that knowledge sharing is often perceived as an unnatural act.

To be successful in today's knowledge-intensive economic environment, however, one cannot simply work in isolation. For one thing, the overwhelming volume and complexity of information available today makes it impossible for any one person to stay on top of leading developments and trends. Further, competing across global markets forces managers to move beyond their spheres of local influence and effectively manage resources situated across multiple locations, time zones, and cultures. To complicate matters further, this need for coordination often stretches beyond formal boundaries of the organization, extending to a complex web of suppliers, alliance partners, and customers.

In today's rapidly changing environment, organizations still need to pay close attention to the development of personal knowledge, skills, and abilities (what is often referred to as *human capital*). At the same time, similar focus needs to brought to fostering connections among people and developing the trust, mutual understanding, and shared values and behaviors that bring people together and make cooperative action possible. We, and other researchers, refer to this as the *social capital* within an organization. A growing literature in the academic and business press, in addition to our own observations, suggests that the presence of social capital can produce a wealth of economic benefits at the individual, organizational, and even national level. Some of these benefits include reducing the amount of time and effort associated with finding new information, improving access to job opportunities and promotions, decreasing the transaction costs associated with developing contracts and monitoring their compliance, and, perhaps most important, facilitating the adoption of knowledge from one part of an organization to another.

In this part, chapter 1 suggests that the creation and maintenance of social capital is under fire within many organizations. The authors, Laurence Prusak and Don Cohen, state that in today's business environment, where workers have little sense of job security and migrate frequently from one organization to the next, the opportunities to build and maintain long-term relationships become limited. Also, the increasing number of "virtual workers" makes it difficult for individuals to have the spontaneous, face-to-face interactions that lead to increased levels of trust and common understanding. Further, the authors argue that many current management practices, such as assigning office locations on a day-to-day basis for mobile workers (otherwise known as "hoteling"), can limit the development of social capital. Prusak and Cohen have identified a number of organizations, such as UPS, Steelcase, SAS, and Russell Reynolds Associates, that recognize the importance of social capital and have adopted work practices that support its creation and maintenance.

While face-to-face interaction is often regarded as a critical component to the development of social capital, the fact remains that many employees need to develop social capital with colleagues who are not located on the same floor or within the same building. Whether they work across the street or halfway around the world, the ability to sustain social capital across employees from multiple time zones and cultural backgrounds remains critical to the success of sharing organizational knowledge. In chapter 2, Eric Lesser and Joseph Cothrel highlight the challenges associated with building social capital in a virtual environment and identify potential technologies that can help alleviate these problems. Through the creative use of tools such as instant messaging, expertise locators, collaborative spaces, and multimedia, individuals can build connections, relationships, and common context across time and space. Using an example of a virtual community of hardware retailers, Lesser and Cothrel show how technology can play an important role in maintaining the presence of social capital in between face-to-face interactions.

Chapter 3 focuses on a critical component of social capital: the importance of trust in enabling the successful transfer of knowledge between a knowledge seeker and a knowledge source. To understand this phenomenon, Daniel Levin, Rob Cross, Lisa Abrams, and Eric Lesser conducted a study of over 130 individuals across three major corporations. They found that two primary types of trust influence how knowledge gets shared across organizations: competence-based and benevolence-based. Competence-based trust is built on the premise that a knowledge seeker believes that a knowledge source is well versed in their subject matter. Benevolence-based trust is based on the assumption that the knowledge source will be willing to assist a knowledge seeker during a time of need. As these authors' study demonstrates, benevolence-based trust is important to sharing of all types of knowledge, whereas competence-based trust becomes more critical as the knowledge being transferred is more tacit, or experiential, in nature. They also dispel the notion that people who interact frequently are naturally disposed to sharing knowledge. Rather, it is the trust that is developed, through either frequent or infrequent interactions, that is the critical success factor in facilitating knowledge exchange.

The subject of social capital underlies many of the topics that are addressed in this book. When looking at the subject of communities of practice, we see that one of the benefits of communities is that they are valuable tools in promoting social capital within an organization. We also see the importance of social capital in managing knowledge across organizational borders, either through the development of relationships with alliance partners, or through the ability to build connections with, and across, individual customers. Social network analysis, another important component of our research agenda, represents an important and emerging method for helping organizations observe and measure various types of connections and relationships within organizations. Finally, the use of storytelling among employees represents one method of building the common context, or common understanding, necessary to create social capital, especially in organizations looking to preserve their organizational memory.

1

How to Invest in Social Capital

LAURENCE PRUSAK
DON COHEN

Every manager knows that business runs better when people within an organization know and trust one another—deals move faster and more smoothly, teams are more productive, people learn more quickly and perform with more creativity. Strong relationships, most managers will agree, are the grease of an organization. Business gets done without them, but not for long and not very well.

Scholars have given a name—*social capital*—to the relationships that make organizations work effectively. The term nicely captures the notion that investments in these relationships return real gains that show up on the bottom line. In fact, it all sounds pretty simple and straightforward. Managers need only get their people connected with one another and wait for the payback. Easy, right?

Wrong for two reasons. First, social capital is under assault in most organizations today because of rising volatility and overreliance on virtuality. More simply put, social capital is under assault because building relationships in turbulent times is tough—and tougher still with many people working off-site or on their own. Second, social capital is under assault because few managers know how to invest in it. Knowing that healthy relationships help an organization thrive is one thing; making those relationships happen is quite another.

For the past three years, we have explored managerial activities and techniques that constitute investments in social capital. Our research probably won't stun anyone with its originality—we have found that managers know more about social capital than most scholars—but we believe it is useful in its specificity. In the following pages, we will look at what managers can do to encourage connections among their people and enable trust to flourish. But first, a few words about the enemies of social capital: volatility and virtuality.

Volatile, Virtual Workplaces

These are volatile times. Disruptive technologies spawn new products and markets daily—or at least it feels that way—and organizations respond with constantly changing structures. Businesses used to review strategies annually; now strategy is on the table constantly. Mergers and acquisitions are at an all-time high, throwing companies together and tearing them asunder at an alarming rate.

These are virtual times, too. Most people used to work at the office from 9 to 5 every weekday. Now, aided by technology, work happens in every imaginable configuration of time and space. Telecommuters, virtual team members, and laptop-toting road warriors abound. Chances are, you are one yourself or have a slew of them working for you.

Luddites we are not. There are advantages to volatility and virtuality. Volatility spawns opportunity: for every company crushed by new technology, a new one is born. And virtuality gives employees flexibility, just as it gives companies the competitive weapon of being "out there" in the trenches.

But volatility and virtuality erode relationships—it's that simple—which is why managers must learn to invest in social capital. But how? The first answer is straightforward enough. Managers should stop doing things that destroy it. For a description of common ways companies trample on their social capital, see Box 1.1

Avoiding big mistakes is easy. Incremental, day-to-day investments in social capital are more daunting. They take time, energy, and focus—in a word, intentionality. We've grouped these practices into three categories: making connections, enabling trust, and fostering cooperation.

Making Connections

The companies we studied that valued social capital demonstrated a real *commitment to retention*. That is, they limited volatility by working hard to make sure their people stuck around. Relationships can only happen, and trust can only flourish, when people know one another.

A good example of a company committed to retention is SAS, whose turnover rate is below 4%—low for any industry and remarkable in a software company. SAS doesn't rely on high pay to keep its people. As Rob Cross, director of SAS's Advanced Technology unit, says, "Salary levels here are good but not extravagant. Money is not what draws people here."

What evidently does draw people to SAS and keep them there is a workplace that spills over, in a positive sense, into nonwork areas of their lives. As employees make use of the company's sports and recreation facility, its health care center (staffed with two full-time physicians), and its two on-site child care centers, they interact with one another in ways that deepen their collegial relationships and create a strong sense of community. A food plan, available as a negligible payroll deduction, encourages people to break for lunch with colleagues. The 300 pounds

BOX 1.1 Capital Offenses

Companies thrive when they have dense social networks, high levels of trust, and norms of cooperation. But management theory and practice are full of ways to undercut them. Here are some of the biggest social-capital destroyers we've seen:

Hoteling
A number of companies whose employees travel frequently have done away with the traditional "one person, one desk" approach. They assign office locations day-to-day to the employees who happen to be on-site. Hoteling, as the practice is called, may be an accountant's dream—it means less real estate is needed—but it drastically reduces employees' opportunities to form personal networks, develop trust, and learn the behaviors and values of the organization by observing people in action over time. It also eliminates opportunities for people to communicate their identities and connections with the organization through the artifacts displayed in personal work spaces.

Reengineering and Its Progeny
Reengineering, regardless of its original intent, evolved into a practice that valued efficient processes at any cost, and the idolatry of process efficiency is still with us. Yes, efficiency is important, but not at the cost of the breathing space and time that human connections—and thought—need in order to flourish.

The Leader as Superstar
Charismatic leaders sometimes accomplish extraordinary things, but elevating leaders to superstardom tends to negate the profoundly social nature of all work. No one person can be an organization. Ultimately, an emphasis on larger-than-life leadership detracts from trust, collaboration, and perceived fairness.

Hypocrisy
Hypocrisy is an obvious problem. One example is praising cooperation and knowledge sharing while promoting the wheeler-dealers who keep their cards close to their chests. Another is providing open, collaborative office space to everyone except senior managers (who "need" their privacy). When he was at Alcoa, U.S. Treasury Secretary Paul O'Neill provided an excellent example of how to avoid this second trap: he made senior managers the guinea pigs for open-space working before others at Alcoa's headquarters were asked to make the change.

of M&Ms the company lays out every Wednesday bring people together for snacks and knowledge-rich conversations. There is a company choir. These perks signal the company's acknowledgment that its people are human beings, not just workers. An even more important relationship builder (and volatility fighter) than these social benefits is the opportunity—backed by the resources—to do meaningful work, including the opportunity to stick with a project as long as it remains meaningful.

SAS invests in relationships by keeping the same crew around. And its investment approach is not to bind people with "golden handcuffs"—the kinds of economic incentives that keep people with mortgages in workplaces they may find demoralizing. SAS invests in ties that bind people more deeply and positively.

Connections (and retention) can also be bolstered by the quaint practice of *promoting from within.* UPS is a case in point. While the company must recruit a number of experienced technologists and other specialists from outside, the overwhelming majority of its senior managers have worked their way up through the ranks, and many have considerable experience in package sorting and delivery. Just as important, they have years of experience with one another. They have earned membership in durable corporate networks and communities where trust is developed and knowledge shared.

Connections also get made when companies simply help people to be in the same place at the same time. During the past decade, many companies have invested heavily in technologies that enable telecommuting, virtual teamwork, and heightened productivity on the road. But we would argue that *giving people time and space to bond in person* is also a form of investment. Social capital grows when team members meet face-to-face and work side-by-side. So it makes sense to encourage telecommuters and contractors not to be strangers to the office. In "Two Cheers for the Virtual Office" (*Sloan Management Review,* summer 1998), management researchers Tom Davenport and Keri Pearlson laud one consumer products company that discourages people from working at home until they've been with the organization for a year. That's how long it takes, at a minimum, for new employees to absorb the culture of a company and make connections with a meaningful variety of people.

It makes sense, too, to give far-flung teams the opportunity to convene in one place from time to time. Intranets and electronic meeting rooms can certainly help to maintain connections and foster knowledge sharing. But don't expect them to create a sense of community where one does not already exist. In fact, research has shown that most communities wither unless they're given the chance to meet periodically.

When it comes to social capital, allowing people to meet face-to-face is only half the battle if they talk only about work. Managers also need to *facilitate personal conversations.* That's why cafés, chat rooms, libraries, kitchens, and other social spaces are important. Sure, they promote knowledge exchange, but they also spur the discovery of mutual interests that support communities. Indeed, investments in those spaces legitimize informal conversation, signaling a company's belief in its value.

Some companies go beyond providing conversational space and help to provide icebreakers. Consider the Grand Rapids, Michigan, headquarters of Steelcase, a particularly open and attractive environment. Displayed on the walls are pictures of all the employees from the CEO on down, along with notes on their backgrounds, recent projects, and nonwork interests. People use whiteboards outside their work spaces to advertise what they're working on and invite comment.

Companies can also help people make connections by *fostering durable networks*. Fortunately, many networks come about naturally in organizations. Members are drawn together by their involvement and interest in a particular work domain. They engage with one another to share what they know, help one another accomplish tasks, and enjoy the satisfactions of membership in a group. UPS drivers in various areas around the country regularly meet for lunch in parks or cafés— for sociability and to exchange missorted packages, adjust workloads, and share information. These lunchtime meetings have developed informally, but the company recognizes and approves of them. "Our supervisor knows we meet here," said a driver who had met his coworkers for lunch at a suburban park outside Boston. "If he wants to talk to us together, he'll show up."

An organization's leaders can help such communities thrive. Modest financing to support meetings and newsletters or to pay part of the salary of a community leader can keep a group active while signaling corporate approval. For example, executives at the World Bank, beginning with the president, James Wolfensohn, have met with community leaders to recognize and praise their work. The bank now has more than 100 practice-based communities (called thematic groups) that share expertise; almost half of the employees belong to at least one of them.

One key to successful investment in community building is maintaining a light touch; heavy-handed efforts can be counterproductive. Etienne Wenger, a leading expert on "communities of practice" (self-selected, informal groups linked by shared expertise, passions, or goals), points out that too much funding can distort communities, causing them to focus excessively on pleasing their sources of support. In many companies, it may be enough for managers to understand where communities exist and to avoid harming them by disrupting contacts among members. Social network analysis provides one useful tool for identifying informal communities. This sociological technique has been around for more than two decades, but only very recently has it been used to make communities and networks visible and to highlight the key roles—such as thought leaders and social connectors—that generally emerge within them.

A more hands-on approach is warranted when two organizations are thrust together. An examination by British Telecom showed that human dynamics and interactions, not flawed business models, caused the failure of its merger with MCI. Trust, understanding, and equity are as important as strategic, technical, and financial issues in successfully bringing together two organizations with distinct cultures. Yet company after company makes the mistake of acting as if disparate groups of people could be welded together like machine parts.

Enabling Trust

No one can manufacture trust or mandate it into existence. When someone says, "You can trust me," we usually don't, and rightly so. But leaders can make deliberate investments in trust. They can give people reasons to trust one another instead of reasons to watch their backs. They can refuse to reward successes that are built on untrusting behavior. And they can display trust and trustworthiness in their own actions, both personally and on behalf of the company.

Most people seem to agree that trust is worth building in work teams and organizations. How else to explain the growing use of team-building events during off-sites? Anyone who has scaled a rock wall while a colleague far below held a safety rope knows that such exercises force people to experience, viscerally, the rewards of trusting others. But unless the team's workplace back at the office is also designed to engender and reward trust, the effects will quickly wear off. Such exercises can even be counterproductive if they highlight a hypocritical gap between the togetherness activity and the organization's real character.

Just as with community building, trust-building efforts can backfire if management is too heavy-handed. Not long ago, the business section of the *Boston Globe* published a letter complaining that the writer's boss, having become convinced of the value of connection and community at work, had instituted a weekly meeting during which everyone in the office was required to tell the group something about his or her personal life. This kind of coerced intimacy is as likely to damage trust as build it.

Most trust-building exercises probably help more than they hurt. But the conditions and connections that people experience day after day have far more influence on an organization's social capital than trust-building exercises do. That's why managers need to go beyond Outward Bound. We suggest several practices.

First, trust thrives where managers *give employees no reason to distrust*—where there is transparency and where employees have confidence in the rule of law. It's important to note that affability and pleasantness don't necessarily generate trust. Many of us have heard some version of this assessment of a manager. "He may not always be sweetness and light, but at least you always know where you stand." At Russell Reynolds Associates, an executive search firm we studied, trust levels are high but no one is coddled. It's understood that if a recruiter doesn't show continuous progress toward building a strong reputation in her particular area of focus, she won't be around for long. Says senior recruiter Riccardo Kustermann, "Everyone knows we have a 'grow or go' system. Promotion requirements are out in the open." Managers in other organizations often like to leave things ambiguous to give themselves wiggle room, and they often bend the rules for "special cases." But when rules are unclear or inconsistently enforced, people start getting paranoid. By coming up with rules you can live by, and then living by them, you invest in social capital.

Trust also grows out of trust—it is self-reinforcing—so one way to get it is to *show trust yourself.* We found that in companies that display trust, both toward employees and toward customers and suppliers, people are more likely to trust one another. By contrast, when managers display distrust, it can drive employees to become less trusting and less trustworthy. In *The HP Way*, David Packard describes working for General Electric in Schenectady, New York, in the 1930s, when "the company was making a big thing of plant security."

> GE was especially zealous about guarding its tool and parts bins to make sure employees didn't steal anything. Faced with this obvious display of distrust, many employees set out to prove it justified, walking off with tools or parts whenever they could. Eventually, GE tools and parts were scattered all around town, including the attic of the house in which a number of us were living.

Coincidentally, it was also at a GE plant that SAS's James Goodnight formed his strong opinions about creating a positive work environment. He hated seeing guards at every door, and he hated the rule that required employees to sign in every day. Today, in many companies, that kind of distrust extends well past the front doors. A recent survey by the American Management Association revealed that more than a third of responding employers conducted some form of electronic monitoring of employees' desktop computers.

The most important way in which companies display trust in their people is by trusting employees' judgment. Part of UPS's advantage in social capital stems from its leaders' support of distributed decision making, a policy that goes back at least as far as the 1950s, when George Smith was CEO. As he explained at the time, "It is considered desirable to have authority for decisions and actions as far down the line as possible, in keeping with the needs of the job, which have a better chance of being known where and when the needs occur." Similarly, Nordstrom is famous for the two rules of customer service its store employees must live by: (1) Use your own good judgment at all times; and (2) There are no other rules!

It's an axiom of management that if you want to see more of certain behaviors and outcomes, you must *send clear signals* that they are valued. One company we studied uses an annual Employee Relations Index survey to track trends in trust, communication, cooperation, and perceptions of fairness. Questions cover opportunities for advancement, cooperativeness of coworkers, openness and trust in the working environment, the degree to which good work is recognized, the accessibility of managers, and managers' receptiveness to new ideas. The survey gives the organization a way to measure its stock of social capital. And the very existence of the survey and the effort the company puts into addressing the problems show employees that these issues matter to management.

Even more important, *trust responds to rewards*. In particular, promotions to leadership positions act as powerful companywide signals; employee A's promotion over employee B shows which values, approaches, and ways of working are valued by management. When trustworthy individuals are promoted, the organization proves that trust succeeds. When untrustworthy individuals are promoted, everyone absorbs a noxious lesson: crime pays, and good citizens finish last.

BOX 1.2 What "Free Agent" Nation?

One of the most popular business buzzwords of the moment is "free agent." The idea is that each worker can be a company of one, porting his or her expertise, on a project-by-project basis, to wherever in the world it is needed. Techno-enthusiasts claim that the World Wide Web has opened the door to universal collaboration, that virtual firms will readily form to take advantage of emerging opportunities and dissolve when the work is done, that free agency is becoming the model of work and employment.

We are skeptical. These broad claims run counter to our observations of how people actually understand their shared tasks and come together to do work. The claims ignore the profoundly social nature of human beings and of almost all work. The fundamental socialness of organizations helps explain why, for instance, telecommuting, though an aspect of many people's work, is rarely the essence of *how* people work—despite the predictions of futurists that offices would be empty by the end of the twentieth century, with knowledge workers happily contributing their efforts from home.

The few places in the world where free agency seems to work only serve to underscore the point. Here we have in mind the creative ferment of Silicon Valley, where software engineers carry their expertise from place to place like bees pollinating a field of flowers. Would such freedom be possible without Silicon Valley's incredibly high social capital? On some level, the agents involved surely understand that their ability to work "independently" is dependent on the dense and durable networks in which they operate—is dependent, in fact, on their being socially tied into a physical community. Otherwise, how to explain that Silicon Valley has the highest real estate prices in the United States?

Fostering Cooperation

Organizations live by their norms and values. "The way things are done around here" and "what we care about" define organizational identity and functioning. Organizations with high social capital have strong norms of cooperation. When employees are faced with adversity or opportunity, their knee-jerk impulse is to pull together.

There's no better example than the people of Malden Mills, the Massachusetts-based Polarfleece manufacturer whose entire operation was destroyed by fire in 1995. What is best known about the incident is the extraordinary decision by owner Aaron Feuerstein to rebuild on the spot (many would have chosen that moment to relocate to a region where costs were lower) and to keep all employees on the payroll rather than lose them or allow them to lose their livelihoods. But just as amazing is that in the midst of the crisis, the workers of Malden Mills were on the scene giving their all, saving what could be saved and cleaning up the mess. This is social capital in action. And there are things management can do to bring about this kind of engagement.

First, it's vital to *give people a common sense of purpose*, which is a matter of good strategic communication and inspirational leadership. Take Johnson & Johnson. In its U.S. version, the company's well-known credo begins, "We believe our first responsibility is to the doctors, nurses, and patients, to mothers and fathers and all others who use our products and services." It goes on to describe employees as the second highest priority, followed by the community and then stockholders. J&J managers say this expression of purpose and values helps unite the employees of the organization's scattered companies.

By themselves, of course, mission statements posted on walls and Web sites have little value; they are always glowingly positive. But J&J's employees and customers saw the company credo tested in 1982, when cyanide hidden in Tylenol capsules killed seven people in the Chicago area. J&J moved rapidly to pull all Tylenol from store shelves—at tremendous expense and at the risk of increasing the public's fear of the brand. In times of adversity, noble goals and inspirational leadership can draw people together and give their work meaning beyond the need to earn a living.

BOX 1.3 Can You Have Too Much Social Capital?

Social capital isn't a business strategy, a marketing plan, or a substitute for either. It is not always even a good thing. Some companies have been damaged by high social capital that breeds what is often referred to as groupthink—a tendency not to question shared beliefs. A strong identification with a group sometimes leads people to support ideas that are narrow or wrong. Too much warm, fuzzy gemütlichkeit can prevent people from challenging one another with tough questions or discourage them from engaging in the "creative abrasion" that Dorothy Leonard describes as a source of innovation. Digital Equipment and Polaroid were known for collegiality, strong senses of employee membership, and humane management, but those aspects of their corporate cultures did not protect them from market misjudgments and strategic errors—and may have contributed to them.

In general, though, the effects of high social capital are overwhelmingly positive. Engagement, collaboration, loyalty, persistence, and dedication are important benefits. The firms we have studied closely—UPS, Hewlett-Packard, Russell Reynolds, SAS, and others—have made investments in social capital that enable them to attract and retain good people and that help people do their best work. None of these companies seems to face any imminent danger of an overdose of a good thing. And for the majority of companies we know, too much social capital is a remote worry indeed.

People feel they're "all in this together" when they have a financial stake in the outcome. That's why UPS managers *reward cooperation with cash.* The company allows all employees who have been with the company for 30 days, even part-time, to purchase stock. There are many other methods, short of sharing ownership, to reward teamwork and signal its importance. One of the ways in which IBM has changed over the past five years is that bonuses (often significant percentages of employees' remuneration) are much more dependent now on group and corporate performance and less dependent on individual performance.

Perhaps the most straightforward way to get people in the habit of cooperating is to *establish some rules* for doing so. At Russell Reynolds, recruiters starting searches must make five internal phone calls to get candidate suggestions before they call outside. This has the dual benefits of increasing the efficiency of the recruiters' efforts and forcing the consultants to get to know one another in ways they wouldn't in more self-reliant searches. Many companies, too, have established a rule governing outside conference attendance: an attendee is reimbursed for a trip only if he shares—during some internal event, typically a brown-bag lunch—what he has learned.

One last way of investing in social capital is as important as it is obvious: *hire for it.* Back in 1995, Herb Kelleher, CEO of Southwest Airlines, told the American Compensation Association how Southwest maintains its culture:

> Well, first of all, it starts with hiring. We are zealous about hiring. We are looking for a particular type of person, regardless of which job category it is. We are looking for attitudes that are positive and for people who can lend themselves to causes. We want folks who have a good sense of humor and people who are interested in performing as a team and take joy in team results instead of individual accomplishments.

Not long ago, Russell Reynolds Associates chose not to hire a very senior recruiter from another firm who unquestionably would have brought profitable connections with him. The individual clearly was not a team player, and management decided that the potential short-term advantages of hiring him were outweighed by the likely damage to the culture of collaborative peer relationships. The damage would have been caused not only by the recruiter's own behavior but by the signal that hiring a lone wolf for an important position would have sent to the rest of the organization.

Authenticity in Management

The three categories of investment we've explored here are, of course, mutually reinforcing and often overlapping. But for purposes of planning managerial interventions, we believe the categories sufficiently cover the waterfront. One last piece of advice: don't do any of this for the sake of appearances. Invest in social capital only to the extent that you believe in it.

Samuel Goldwyn is credited with a cynical joke: "The key for an actor is sincerity," he is supposed to have said, "because if you can fake that, you can fake anything." We suspect that in a company without authentic respect for social capital, none of the interventions we describe will succeed. Remember, we are talking about trust and relationships, and we human beings tend to know when someone is trying to manipulate our feelings about those core issues. No company can produce lasting social capital merely by going through the motions of team building. Organizations build trust over time; what they do day after day reveals what matters most to them. And social capital, because it represents the organic growth of trust, understanding, and loyalty, takes time to develop.

Former U.S. Secretary of Labor Robert B. Reich has spoken of a simple test he relies on when visiting a company for the first time: "I call it the 'pronoun test,' " he says. "I ask frontline workers a few general questions about the company. If the answers I get back describe the company in terms like 'they' and 'them,' then I know it's one kind of company. If the answers are put in terms like 'we' or 'us,' then I know it's a different kind of company."

Them as Has, Gets

Aaron Feuerstein, the Malden Mills owner, told an audience sometime after the fire that "a lot of the publicity I'm receiving is really not deserved. It is, rather, a sad reflection and commentary on our times." It's true: the social capital that used to be a given in organizations is now rare and endangered. But the social capital we can build will allow us to capitalize on the volatile, virtual possibilities of today's business environment.

In this chapter, we've stressed that building social capital can't be legislated or "managed" in any directive sense. It requires the kind of intervention that encourages natural development, that orients rather than orders, that provides nourishment rather than blueprints. Robert Putnam, in "The Prosperous Community" (*The American Prospect*, March 21, 1993), explained the process this way:

> Stocks of social capital, such as trust, norms, and networks, tend to be self-reinforcing and cumulative. Successful collaboration in one endeavor builds connections and trust—social assets that facilitate future collaboration in other, unrelated tasks. As with conventional capital, those who have social capital tend to accumulate more—them as has, gets.

Hobson Brown, Jr., president and CEO of Russell Reynolds, put it more simply. "Everything in this firm works," he told us, "because of social capital." In our organizations, just as in our neighborhoods and nations, our ability to recapture community and build social capital will determine our progress.

2

Fast Friends—Virtuality and Social Capital

ERIC L. LESSER
JOSEPH COTHREL

> *The new currency won't be intellectual capital. It will be social capital—the collective value of whom we know and what we'll do for each other. When social connections are strong and numerous, there is more trust, reciprocity, information flow, collective action, happiness, and by the way, greater wealth.*
> —James Kouzes, *The Leadership Challenge*

Social capital—the bonds between individuals in a group, organization, or society that constitute a valuable asset—has been getting increasing attention in today's business world. Once the province of sociologists, political scientists, and economic development specialists, social capital has emerged as an important discipline in management studies and organizational development. Management scholars have embraced social capital as a way of understanding and interpreting a variety of management phenomena, ranging from the development of high technology industry in Silicon Valley to the differentials in managerial pay and promotion rates. Recently published books by Wayne Baker, a professor at the University of Michigan, and Don Cohen and Laurence Prusak at the IBM Institute for Knowledge Management have further advanced the notion that both individual and organizational social capital can have a significant influence on enterprise performance.

One contributor to the growing importance of understanding and supporting social capital is the spread of computer-based communication technologies. These technologies have made companies more aware that social networks support formal organizational structures. As they put global networks in place, companies have learned that establishing an electronic connection does not ensure that a productive working relationship will result. The connections between virtual interaction and social capital in business organizations are just beginning to be explored. Will virtual interaction enhance—or endanger—the ties that bind us? In many ways, this argument parallels the debate about the impact of the Internet on communities and neighborhoods, about which Barry Wellman and Milena Gulia have written:

> The Manicheans on either side of this debate assert that the Internet either will create wonderful new forms of community, or will destroy community altogether.

. . . The statements of enthusiasm and criticism leave little room for the moderate, mixed situations that may be the reality.[1]

In organizations, too, new communications technology will neither destroy nor ensure healthy social capital. How can businesses achieve a balanced approach to these new media?

We survey the current thinking on social capital here, with an eye to the challenges organizations face in promoting its creation and preservation. We explore the ways virtual communication technologies help address these challenges, while introducing new challenges of their own. Finally, we examine a case from Ace Hardware Company as an example of how companies are using virtual technologies to create, maintain, and exploit their social capital.

Social Capital: A Key Ingredient in Today's Economy

What is social capital? Janine Nahapiet of Oxford University and Sumantra Ghoshal of the London Business School propose the following definition: Social capital is "the sum of the actual and potential resources embedded within, available through, and derived from the network of relationships possessed by an individual or social unit."[2]

Emerging trends in the business world have pushed social capital to the forefront of management thinking.[3] High on the list of trends is the migration towards a knowledge-based economy. As knowledge begins to supplant land, labor, and capital as the primary source of competitive advantage in the marketplace, the ability to create new knowledge, share existing knowledge, and apply organizational knowledge to new situations becomes critical. The presence (or absence) of social capital can affect an organization's capacity to replicate best practices, develop and maintain explicit knowledge repositories, or simply provide guidance and mentoring to less experienced staff. All of these capabilities relate directly to an organization's ability to exploit its knowledge.

Social capital also plays a critical role in an environment that is increasingly marked by mergers, strategic alliances, and joint ventures. As more and more resources that are critical to success lie outside organizational boundaries, establishing the right connections and relationships between relevant parties becomes both more important and more difficult. Identifying relevant subject matter experts, ensuring coordination between different firms, and building a sense of coherence among strangers (or even competitors) can all be daunting tasks, but accomplishing them is critical to successful collaboration. In the absence of social capital between alliance members, the likelihood of knowledge mismanagement increases. When knowledge critical to the success of the alliance becomes misused, misappropriated, misinterpreted, or is just plain missing, huge investments in resources, physical capital, and brand image may be jeopardized. One has only to look at the grim example of the Ford-Firestone tire situation to understand some of the problems that can result when knowledge breakdowns occur between companies that are dependent on one another.

As we have noted, increased reliance on computer-based communication as a tool to improve organizational effectiveness also makes understanding, developing, and using social capital important. As organizations try to tap into the knowledge and experience of individuals separated by time zones, geographies, and cultures, they have learned that there is more to building productive relationships than giving people the means of communication. They are also concerned, with some reason, about the potential negative impact of virtual tools on social capital, particularly in instances where face-to-face interactions are being replaced by virtual ones.

Challenges of Social Capital in Business Organizations

Nahapiet and Goshal further define social capital as having three dimensions:

- Individuals must perceive themselves to be part of a network (the structural dimension)
- A sense of trust and mutual obligation must be developed across this network (the relational dimension)
- The members of the network must have a common interest or share a common understanding of issues facing the organization (the cognitive dimension).

Challenges exist in each of these dimensions for organizations seeking to create, maintain, and exploit their social capital.

Structural Challenges

Connections made through face-to-face interactions are the best foundation for the development of social capital. A recent study showed that the level of trust that exists in virtual workgroups could be measurably improved by even a single face-to-face interaction at the beginning of the project.[4] But barriers of time, distance, and physical setting can make such interactions difficult to achieve. First, the number of connections an individual can create and maintain via face-to-face interaction is limited to the number of people at the physical locations he or she frequents. Further, tangible barriers including different floors or buildings, the absence of shared spaces where individuals can spontaneously interact, and common inhibitions associated with going outside of one's general sphere of influence can limit interaction among individuals. While examples of work environments specifically designed for collaboration and social connection exist—Alcoa's corporate offices and Oticon are examples—many of the buildings and spaces that people work in do not facilitate serendipitous encounters between coworkers.[5] Even where chance encounters can occur, the opportunity to have non-work-related conversations—a key element in building personal relationships—may be squeezed out by the time demands of the work day.[6]

Relational Challenges

In addition to these barriers to connection, other barriers get in the way of turning those connections into relationships of trust and mutual obligation. Corporate culture strongly influences an individual's ability to form trusting relationships with coworkers. A highly competitive, individualistic culture, for example, may actively discourage bonds of mutual obligation. Work processes and incentive programs that are excessively individualistic can create barriers as formidable as any wall or floor.

There may also be natural limits to the size of an individual's personal network. British anthropologist Robin Dunbar, whose work is highlighted in Malcolm Gladwell's popular book *The Tipping Point,* has argued that there is a natural limit to the number of people with whom a single individual can form stable relationships by means of direct personal contact. This number, 150, recurs so often in society—from the basic unit of military forces to the size of tribes and villages—that Dunbar's hypothesis merits serious attention.[7]

Cognitive Challenges

One of the biggest frustrations encountered in large organizations is the difficulty of ensuring that everyone is "reading off the same page." Varying interpretations of formal corporate communications and informal hints, tips, and messages make it dangerous to assume that any communication is received and understood with its core properties intact. Shared understanding is not guaranteed even when people are physically together, observing and discussing the same environment. But a shared environment and the opportunity to talk together go a long way toward building mutual understanding. For example, if two people simultaneously look at a defective part in a machine and can see, hear, smell, and feel the surrounding conditions, then the likelihood of their being able to identify a possible solution to the problem increases. Similarly, two people looking at the same spreadsheet can interact with one another to question assumptions, identify root causes implications, and determine alternative courses of action in ways that isolated individuals can not.

Written materials and, to some extent, the telephone, are not particularly useful in capturing environmental conditions and fostering the interaction that can make it easier to develop an accurate and shared understanding of the root causes of a particular situation. Xerox copier repair personnel found that standard manuals did little to help them diagnose problems. The complexity of the copiers and the influence of local environmental factors like temperature and humidity demanded a richer, more context-dependent approach than any manual could provide. Successful repair depended on being there and on sharing knowledge with other experienced repair people. Ultimately, the technicians discovered that discussion with their peers—not formal procedures—was most likely to produce the solutions required for repairing equipment in the field.[8]

How Virtual Interactions Address Social Capital Challenges

Face-to-face interactions are clearly vital for building social capital. Given the fact that face-to-face interactions are not always practical or possible, however, we must look for ways to build and leverage social capital virtually. Over the last several years, a number of technologies have emerged to help extend the reach of our relationships. A range of technologies relevant to each of the three dimensions of social capital can help sustain and perhaps increase the value that can be extracted from the development of relationships within an organization.

Structural Challenges

The chief benefit of computer-based communication is clearly the ability to help people make connections. In 1968, ARPANET pioneers J. C. R. Licklider and Robert Taylor predicted that computer networks would help individuals overcome the tyranny of location and the limitations imposed by the happenstance groupings in which human beings found themselves. Licklider and Taylor foresaw a day when these networks could foster "communities not of common location, but of common interest."[9] Although we sometimes debate the impact of these technologies in crossing boundaries, particularly with regard to hierarchy, the debate always focuses on the magnitude of the impact; there is no disagreement that an impact exists.[10]

Researchers who have explored virtual collaboration at Lucent Technologies note that:

> . . . Evolution of an affective bond often occurs through gradual escalation across opportunistic conversations, not necessarily related to work. Occasions for such encounters at a distance are limited by the intentional and formal nature of long distance communication. That is, a conference call with colleagues and superiors is not the ideal environment to probe for similarities with others that may form the basis for a deeper relationship.[11]

The findings suggest that the ease of use and relative informality of such tools as e-mail help break down the formal nature of long distance communication, making communication more frequent and therefore more conducive to development of relationships. But while "opportunistic conversations" can occur, e-mail, bulletin boards, and other traditional online tools do not support the chance encounters that some say spark real creativity in organizations.[12] Such capability has only recently appeared with instant messaging applications. Because these applications indicate when other members of the group or company are online, ad hoc interactions are possible among hundreds of people instead of the handful that might be encountered in the hallway of the typical office building on a given workday.

One of the biggest challenges for people in enterprises that extend across multiple locations is how to make connections with others having a specific expertise. Initial attempts to address this problem focused on the development of electronic "yellow pages" and the development of dedicated skill directories where individuals could provide data regarding their level of expertise on a variety of topics. While some of these initial efforts proved useful, many of them clearly did not achieve their desired results. Many of these systems relied upon generalized categories that were not relevant to those who were either classifying their skills or trying to locate a specific subject matter expert. Also, many systems were self-populating, relying on end users to make judgments about their own proficiency. Experience has shown that individuals are often poor judges of their own abilities. Further, many of these repositories required users to manually update their expertise profiles on a regular basis, which individuals often failed to do. As a result, the systems lost currency and value.

A new generation of expertise technologies incorporates "passive profiling" technologies that help address these issues. These systems use text-mining technologies to analyze the content in e-mail and other repositories to develop profiles of individual interests. Individuals can then review and modify these profiles and allow the system to update the profiles dynamically, based on additional content. These profiles allow individuals to query others in the organization and identify those willing and able to provide insight on a range of topics.

Other systems locate expertise through a question-and-answer format, rating systems, and a process for experts to "opt in" in specific topic areas. The software facilitates question routing and ensures that experts are not overwhelmed by requests for help. Like passive profiling systems, these technologies also refine themselves over time, since individuals have the opportunity to rate the responses they receive, and all users can view these ratings and can address questions specifically to an individual based upon them.

Relational Challenges

Connections are easy; relationships are hard. The problem of how best to foster relationships in virtual environments has attracted a significant amount of interest among both academics and business practitioners. The Internet age has given rise to a whole range of questions about how we evaluate the trustworthiness of others that we cannot see, and perhaps have never met. As Tim Berners-Lee, one of the founders of the modern-day Web, argues, "these (issues) have to do with information quality, bias, endorsement, privacy and trust—fundamental values of society, much misunderstood on the Web, and also highly susceptible to exploitation by those who can find a way."[13] Given the ease with which individuals can misrepresent themselves and their intentions to others in a virtual environment and the difficulty in ensuring compliance without traditional social reinforcement mechanisms, it would be only natural to expect individuals to surround themselves with barriers to guard against exploitation. Further, the public nature of many virtual conversations, such as discussion databases, can leave individuals exposed to attacks by others, many of them anonymous and not constrained by the norms and responsibilities of traditional social interactions. This form of attack, known as "flaming," can lower the level of social trust within a virtual environment and can inhibit the participation of individuals seeking more forthright relationships.[14]

In some respects, though, virtual technology provides new ways of communicating relationship-building social cues. We use situations where we can witness an individual's behavior in a public environment to evaluate the trustworthiness of another individual. In physical environments, this can sometimes be difficult. While we sometimes can see if an individual has adequately prepared for a team meeting, or if he or she has provided a helpful piece of information to a colleague who is struggling with a difficult problem, often these transactions occur away from the view of a larger audience. People may be hesitant, or unwilling to broadcast their altruism, or conversely, may actively try to conceal distrustful behavior. In a virtual environment, however, these transactions can be made visible by collaborative technologies. The most common of these are discussion forums or databases, and groupware. In these environments, everyone can see who contributed to threaded discussions, and can identify who has made explicit knowledge available for others to use.

Cognitive Challenges

Virtual communications compound the problems of ensuring that everyone has a common understanding of the background and context of a given situation. In the virtual world, a number of barriers make it difficult to ensure that each participant in a conversation has appropriate contextual clues necessary to developing mutual understanding and share knowledge. First, communicating across time and space often introduces cultural and linguistic differences that can hamper the best-intended discussions. Communicating with someone who is less familiar with your language can be difficult in a face-to-face setting; trying to do so without the benefit of facial expressions, gestures, and shared objects is harder. In addition, building common context in a virtual environment is made more difficult because the most commonly used forms of communication, the telephone and e-mail, primarily focus on using and isolating either our visual or auditory senses. These media are not particularly effective in sharing other sensory inputs that could provide additional assistance in transferring knowledge and developing common understanding.

Perhaps the biggest problem facing the development of social capital in a virtual environment is the difficulty associated with building a common set of assumptions and understandings. In physical settings, the interaction around common artifacts, or tools of the trade, makes it easier to develop reference points that everyone in a conversation can share. For example, when attempting to fix a broken piece of equipment, technicians working face-to-face all see the setting in which the equipment exists, sense the environmental conditions that could potentially affect the operation of the machine, and point to potential tools that they could use to solve the problem.

In a virtual world, building the common context necessary for effective knowledge sharing is significantly more difficult. The lack of environmental clues, compounded by the variety of assumptions that can be associated with cultural differences and language barriers, can significantly hinder the knowledge transfer process. A number of technologies can help overcome this barrier, however. Videoconferencing offers enough "face-to-face" interaction and environmental information to help build a joint view of a given situation. The classic example of the Virtual Teamworking project at British Petroleum underscores the importance of being able to visualize situations to improve decision-making in a remote environment.[15] Videoconferencing technology allowed members of globally dispersed teams to understand and solve problems together. Another important component of the Virtual Teamworking project was the use of shared "whiteboarding" technology, which allowed geographically separate individuals to jointly view and comment on a specific document. This ability to see changes made to a report or a presentation simultaneously can help ensure that everyone is literally "reading off the same page." While some of these technologies are considered difficult to use, increases in the availability of bandwidth within organizations and future refinements will make it easier for individuals to collaborate in real time shared environments.

Ace Hardware: Building and Exploiting Social Capital with Virtual Community

Leave it to a 75-year-old company to show how virtual interaction can help a company build and exploit its store of social capital. Ace Hardware's Commercial and Industrial Supply Community (ACIS) helps more than 300 dealers learn, problem-solve, and serve their large customer accounts better.

Social Capital in a Member Cooperative

Ace Hardware sells building materials, tools, paint, garden supplies, and a full range of other hardware products from more than 5,000 locations in the U.S. and 62 other countries. Ace is a member cooperative, unusual among retailers, though far from unique among hardware chains. Dealers voluntarily affiliate with the co-op to take advantage of Ace's volume pricing, and to benefit from Ace's national advertising, insurance policies, and training programs. The co-op distributes to its retailers from more than 20 wholesale warehouses. Dealers also receive dividends from the co-op's profits. Because they are part of a co-op, the relationship among members is a commercial one that is also characterized by bonds of trust and loyalty. Many members are second- or third-generation Ace dealers, whose relationship with the co-op is therefore personal and familial as well as commercial.

The neighborhood Ace hardware store is a familiar icon in America's cities and towns. Though most of these stores sell primarily to do-it-yourselfers, Ace also does a significant business selling to commercial and industrial (C&I) accounts like home improvement companies, hospitals, schools, and the like. In fact, many of those neighborhood stores serve C&I accounts out of "the back of the store" while also meeting the needs of residential customers.

In the competitive U.S. hardware market, C&I accounts have become increasingly important for local dealers, who can often serve these accounts more effectively than "big box" retailers like Home Depot. Serving these accounts requires its own set of knowledge and expertise, however, as well as different product lines. To build rapidly on its base of commercial and industrial expertise, Ace needed to exploit its best asset: the social capital that existed in its dealer network. The virtual community was built on already established ties of common experience, common aims, and personal acquaintance.

Building the ACIS Community

Some Ace dealers have served C&I accounts for decades. Others are new to the segment and are eager to climb the learning curve as quickly as possible. Helping these dealers connect and learn from one another is the primary objective of the ACIS community.

The heart of the ACIS program is an extranet site, ACENET 2000, an integrated set of message boards, online seminars, newsletters, and program materials relevant to the C&I hardware business. The message boards serve several purposes: one board, Merchandise Mart, allows dealers to discuss their experiences with different vendors and products. Another, Ask Tina, allows Tina Lopotko, the manager of the ACIS program, to answer dealer questions in a way that allows everyone to benefit from her answers. The Sourcing board enables dealers to ask for help in locating hard-to-find merchandise.

Online seminars are part of a program called "Coach's Corner." Anyone with expertise to share can be a "coach": a dealer, an Ace employee, even a vendor. In addition to sharing some prepared material, the coach is available to answer any questions the dealers might have.

A popular feature is the "Store of the Month." The home page of the ACIS site features the picture of a store being highlighted, along with whatever history the dealer wants to share. Because of the nature of the hardware as a family-run business, the histories shared online combine births and deaths, natural disasters, and the normal vicissitudes of life along with business events. Building trust and connection, the feature helps anchor business concerns in the similar and shared life experiences of the hardware dealers. In addition to being highlighted on the home page, the Store of the Month also has a message board where other dealers can share their common experiences or ask questions of the dealer being profiled.

The Role of Social Capital

The ACIS community is at once an effort to *build* social capital and to *exploit* it. It is an effort to exploit the social capital that exists in the organization to enable it to learn more quickly and evolve to meet the demands of the marketplace. This social capital wasn't created this year or this month: it has developed among members over many years, and has long been fostered and renewed in four face-to-face meetings every year. Yet, the ACIS online community is an effort to build that capital as well.

To understand how the ACIS builds social capital, it is necessary to examine the elements that constitute it. In his examination of the impacts of technology on social capital, Paul Resnick focuses on seven "productive resources" that develop in a social network over time:

- Communication paths
- Common knowledge
- Shared values
- Collective identity
- Roles and norms
- Obligations
- Trust[16]

These resources address the challenges of our three critical social capital dimensions. The first, communications paths, is structural, the next four mainly cognitive, and obligations and trust clearly relational. Online interaction in the ACIS community has an observable impact on each of these resources. As with any other networking initiative, the effort has expanded the communication paths that exist between dealers in the network. Not every dealer can attend face-to-face meetings. Interaction between meetings via telephone tends to occur among dealers who are already acquainted. Today, one third of the dealers in the ACIS community log on once a week, and virtually all of them visit at least once a month. The online community has enabled connections that would otherwise not have occurred.

Knowledge exchange is one of the stated goals of the ACIS effort, and the impacts are evident both in the conversations visible on the site, and the stories that dealers tell about problem-solving with their peers. A dealer in Bullhead, Arizona, for example, tells of his experience selling Ace brand paint to a casino operator. The casino operator said another vendor's product had a "direct-to-metal" ratio that indicated superior adhesion to metal surfaces. Unaware of such a ratio, the Ace dealer turned to the community for advice. Another dealer saw his question on the message board and suggested that he send a sample of the competitor's product to Ace's lab for analysis. The analysis showed that the competitors "direct-to-metal" rating was a marketing gimmick—the chemical composition of Ace's product actually made it a better choice for metal. The dealer won the contract, but the entire community benefited from the learning that resulted.

Unlike other forms of collaboration, online interactions in a community setting are public and very visible. They therefore serve as a continual reminder of the values that the community shares. On the "Merchandise Mart" board, dealers talk candidly about their experience with vendors and products. They compare notes with each other and in the process help Ace understand their needs better. By creating this forum, Ace shows it respects its dealers and takes their problems seriously. By using the forum, dealers demonstrate that Ace is a place where problems can be surfaced and resolved.

Ace understood that one of its challenges in expanding the C&I business was one of identity. Even today, any dealer can sell to C&I customers. There is no requirement to identify yourself as belonging to this group. In an organization like a co-op, where independence is a first principle, this is as it should be. Yet Ace recognized that much can be gained by forging a shared identity among C&I dealers with common goals. The C&I community has made that possible on a national scale.

What about mutual obligations? Though prizing their independence, dealers understand that support networks are a powerful asset. Yet communities become truly effective when a generalized trust prevails: that is, when members help other members without the expectation that the recipient will personally return the favor, expecting instead that someone will be there when the helper needs help. The "Sourcing Board" on the ACIS site provides a good example. Using the Sourcing Board, dealers ask for help when a customer requests an item that the dealer has never purchased before. With C&I accounts, good service often means going out of your way to find something your customer wants. The Sourcing Board helps dealers do this without expending extraordinary effort. A dealer in New York who helps a dealer in San Francisco is not necessarily looking for a response in kind, yet both dealers benefit from the community of generalized trust and generalized mutual assistance.

Long-time virtual community expert Lisa Kimball often points out that most groups—online or offline—are more productive when roles and norms are explicitly defined. It is a virtue of virtual groups, she says, that people accept that fact more readily in a virtual setting than a face-to-face gathering. For example, few hardware dealers would think of themselves as capable of "coaching" other dealers, no matter how experienced they might be. But through forums like "Coach's Corner," in which individual dealers and Ace personnel host discussions on topics in which they have expertise, the community recognizes that all of us have something to learn, and something to teach.

Finally, trust. Daniel McAllister has made a useful distinction between affect-based trust, which represents an emotional bond between people, and cognition-based trust, which represents a trust that an individual is reliable.[17] Both kinds of trust are clearly critical to organizations. While the conditions and interactions that foster affect-based trust are not clear, it does seem obvious that the shared history made visible in an online setting—a history of interactions among people that reveal, in different ways, expertise, responsiveness, reliability, and other aspects—provides a basis for cognition-based trust to grow.

The success of the ACIS community demonstrates how virtual interactions can build on and enhance the social capital that is so important for cooperation and knowledge exchange. We will continue to learn more about social capital and virtual interactions as we observe the progress of this and other online communities.

Notes

1 Barry Wellman and Milena Gulia, "Virtual Communities as Communities: Net Surfers Don't Ride Alone," in Marc Smith and Peter Kollock (eds.), *Communities in Cyberspace: Perspectives on New Forms of Social Organization* (London: Routledge, 2001), pp. 167–194.

2 Janine Nahapiet and Sumantra Ghoshal, "Social Capital, Intellectual Capital, and the Organizational Advantage," *Academy of Management Review*, vol. 23 no. 2, 1998, p. 243.

3 See Chapter 1 of Eric Lesser (ed.), *Knowledge and Social Capital* (Woburn, MA: Butterworth-Heinemann, 2000).

4 Elena Rocco, "Trust Breaks Down in Electronic Contexts But Can Be Repaired by Some Initial Face-to-Face Contact," *Proceedings of CHI '98* (New York: ACM Press, 1998).

5 For a more extensive description of the Alcoa and Oticon examples, see Don Cohen and Laurence Prusak, *In Good Company: How Social Capital Makes Organizations Work* (Cambridge, MA: Harvard Business School Press, 2001).

6 Elena Rocco, Thomas Finholt, Erik Hofer, and James Herbsleb, "Designing as If Trust Mattered," Collaboratory for Research on Electronic Work (CREW) technical report, University of Michigan, Ann Arbor, 2000.

7 Dunbar's argument is laid out in *Grooming, Gossip, and the Evolution of Language* (Cambridge, MA: Harvard University Press, 1996).

8 Julian Orr, *Talking about Machines: An Ethnography of a Modern Job* (Ithaca, NY: ILR Press, 1994).

9 J. C. R. Licklider and Robert W. Taylor, "The Computer and Communication Device," *Science and Technology* (April 1968), pp. 21–31.

10 David A. Owens, Margaret A. Neale, and Robert I. Sutton, "Technologies of Status Management: Status Dynamics in E-Mail Communications," *Research on Managing Groups and Teams*, vol. 3, 2000, pp. 205–230.

11 Rocco et al.

12 Cohen and Prusak, p. 143.

13 Tim Berners-Lee, *Weaving the Web: The Original Design and Ultimate Destiny of the World Wide Web* (New York: Harperbusiness, 2000), p. 206.

14 Anita Blanchard and Tom Horan, "Virtual Communities and Social Capital," in Eric Lesser (ed.), *Knowledge and Social Capital* (Woburn, MA: Butterworth-Heinemann, 2000), p. 299.

15 Thomas H. Davenport and Laurence Prusak, *Working Knowledge* (Cambridge, MA: Harvard Business Review Press, 1997), p. 19.

16 Paul Resnick, "Beyond Bowling Together: Socio-Technical Capital," to appear in John Carroll (ed.), *HCI in the New Millennium* (Reading, MA: Addison-Wesley).

17 D. J. McAllister, "Affect- and Cognition-Based Trust as Foundations for Interpersonal Cooperation in Organizations," *Academy of Management Journal*, vol. 38, 1995, pp. 24–59.

3

Trust and Knowledge Sharing:
A Critical Combination

DANIEL Z. LEVIN
ROB CROSS
LISA C. ABRAMS
ERIC L. LESSER

Introduction

"How can I encourage people to share what they know?" is a question often posed by mangers in today's knowledge-driven organizations. Much of the academic and business literature, and our own experience, suggests that having employees work together over an extended period of time can lead to successful knowledge sharing. Yet, there exists little systematic evidence about why this actually promotes effective knowledge transfer. Without understanding the linkage between regular, ongoing employee interactions (i.e., "strong ties") and effective knowledge sharing, managers are often left in the dark as to what they can do to foster valuable knowledge exchanges. Should they co-locate people in a common work area? Should they send people on "ropes courses" and ask them to discuss their innermost thoughts and feelings? Most of the research and advice in the marketplace provides little, if any, real guidance on these issues.

To obtain a more robust understanding of the issues related to personal relationships and knowledge sharing, we conducted a survey of 138 employees from three companies: a division from a U.S. pharmaceutical company, a division of a British bank, and a large group within a Canadian oil and gas company. All three groups were composed of people engaged in knowledge-intensive work where we anticipated a reliance on colleagues for information. We asked the respondents to consider a recent project they had worked on, and to rate the usefulness of the knowledge they received from those whom they had sought out for advice on that project. The results of the survey, which were similar across the three companies, identified some actionable recommendations for companies looking to share knowledge more effectively across their organizations.[1]

Trust: The Missing Link

This first part of the project set out to address a fundamental question: "Why do strong ties between co-workers appear to facilitate knowledge sharing?" Our study suggests that the magic ingredient that links strong ties and knowledge sharing is trust. In the business community, discussions about trust have typically been characterized by vague terminology, hand waving, and a frequently heard refrain of "it's all about the culture." However, given the importance of this topic, a more rigorous understanding of trust, its different forms, and its development is critical to the success of an organization's knowledge-sharing efforts.

The results from our study point to two specific types of trust that are instrumental in the knowledge-sharing process: benevolence-based trust and competence-based trust. When most people think about trust, they are typically thinking of its benevolence-based form—in which an individual will not intentionally harm another when given the opportunity to do so. However, another type of trust that plays an important role in knowledge sharing is competence-based trust. Competence-based trust describes a relationship in which an individual believes that another person is knowledgeable about a given subject area.

Either type of trust can exist independently. For example, I can trust that a co-worker knows the information I need (competence), but I may not trust that he will be forthcoming when I need it (benevolence). Conversely, there may be other people who I am confident will assist me (benevolence), but that do not possess the knowledge or skill I require (competence). Overall, we found that knowledge exchange was more effective when the knowledge recipient viewed the knowledge source as being both benevolent and competent.

With regard to our original question about the connection between frequent interactions and effective knowledge sharing, this study highlights an important conclusion: it is trust, not the presence of strong ties, *per se*, that leads to effective knowledge sharing. In fact, our survey also demonstrated a somewhat surprising result: the trust can develop even when there was only infrequent interaction between individuals ("weak ties"). Essentially, while trust can be created through frequent, ongoing communication, it can also form between people who do not converse with each other on a regular basis. Therefore, it is possible for effective knowledge sharing to occur in both strong-tie and weak-tie relationships as long as competence- and benevolence-based trust exist between the two parties.

Further, when we held the level of trust constant, survey respondents suggested that weak ties actually led to more valuable knowledge than strong ties. That is, people reported getting their *most* useful knowledge from trusted weak ties. This point may seem surprising at first, but conceptually it makes sense. Individuals with strong ties often have similar kinds of knowledge; they are aware of the same people, ideas, and concepts. However, individuals with weak ties are likely to have connections to different social networks and are exposed to different types of knowledge and ideas. Therefore, weak ties might be potentially more useful than strong ties in finding out answers because of the different perspectives and information that these people can bring to bear on a given problem. The key for effective knowledge transfer, though, is that these ties—whether strong or weak—need to be trusted ties.

Different Types of Knowledge Require Different Forms of Trust

The second key question examined in the study asked, "Does the nature of the knowledge itself affect the importance of trust in knowledge sharing?" Presumably, when knowledge is simple and straightforward (such as directions to an office location), one does not need a significant amount of competence-based trust in the knowledge source (although one may require benevolence-based trust to believe that the knowledge source is choosing to give accurate directions). However, when the knowledge required is more experiential, difficult to verify, or tacit in nature (e.g., how to negotiate the terms of a multi-million-dollar alliance), the knowledge seeker requires a relatively larger amount of competence-based trust in the provider of that knowledge.

Indeed, our results showed that competence-based trust had a major impact on knowledge transfers involving highly tacit knowledge. This is a significant finding, since much value-added knowledge found in organizations is often experiential and difficult to codify. For knowledge transfers involving codified knowledge, competence-based trust was less important. We also examined the importance of benevolence-based trust and found that it was significant in both explicit and tacit knowledge exchanges.

Making the Decision to Trust a Knowledge Source

Once we established that trust is a critical component in the knowledge-sharing equation, the next substantial issue to be addressed was, "What are the factors that a knowledge seeker uses to evaluate the trustworthiness of a knowledge source?" Previous studies have suggested that there are four factors that individuals may use to make this determination. These are summarized in Table 3.1.

We found that knowledge seekers relied on various factors to determine whether they felt an individual was trustworthy. These factors were different depending upon the type of trust (competence-based vs. benevolence-based) involved. As summarized by Table 3.2, three factors were important in determining competence-based trust: discretion, shared language, and shared goals. When evaluating benevolence-based trust, these same factors were viewed as important, plus two additional ones: strong ties and receptivity.

Table 3.1. Potential Attributes That Influence a Knowledge Seeker's Decision to Trust a Knowledge Source

Factor	Rationale	Attributes Examined
Demographic Similarity	Many business and communication experts have highlighted the importance of similar characteristics in fostering communication and the development of trust	• Gender • Age
Organizational Similarity	Elements of organization design such as formal structure, HR practices, and governance are likely to have a direct effect on trust in organizations	• Similar job function • Close physical proximity • Worked on same project • Relative position in hierarchy
Social Capital	Recent studies have suggested that the presence of an ongoing relationship between individuals has an impact on trust and knowledge sharing	• Strong ties between the knowledge seeker and knowledge source • Shared vision and goals • Shared language and terminology
Knowledge Source Behaviors	In addition to organization factors, individuals behaviors can have an impact on the decision to trust another person	• Availability (Does the source have free time and attention to devote to the knowledge seeker?) • Discretion (Is the knowledge source able to respect confidentiality?) • Receptivity (Is the knowledge source a good listener?)

Table 3.2. Significant Attributes That Influence a Knowledge Seeker's Decision to Trust a Knowledge Source

Attribute	Definition	Significant Impact on Competence-Based Trust	Significant Impact on Benevolence-Based Trust
Common Language	The extent to which the knowledge source and seeker understand each other and use similar jargon and terminology	Yes	Yes
Common Vision	The extent to which a knowledge source and seeker have shared goals, concerns, and purpose	Yes	Yes
Discretion	The extent to which a knowledge source is viewed as keeping sensitive information confidential	Yes	Yes
Receptivity	The extent to which a knowledge source is a good listener	No	Yes
Strong Ties	The extent to which the knowledge seeker and knowledge source frequently converse with each other and have a close relationship	No	Yes

Trust: Implications for Organizations

The results of the study underscore that trust, or lack of it, can have serious implications for organizations. While managers often scratch their heads trying to figure out the value of the "soft stuff" associated with knowledge management, our study clearly highlights the importance of trust in enabling effective knowledge sharing. As a result, promoting an environment in which employees have the opportunity to develop both competence- and benevolence-based trust needs to be a central part of an organization's knowledge management agenda.

The study also highlights that when it comes to knowledge sharing, trusting people's benevolence consistently matters, while trusting their competence is even more important when the knowledge is difficult to codify. For individuals to take advantage of experiential, or tacit knowledge, they must believe that the knowledge source is both willing to help and well versed in their particular discipline. Finding people who are willing to assist others, and are "knowledgeable" about a particular subject can be difficult, especially in large, dispersed organizations where individuals do not have the opportunity to get to know others involved in the same type of work. Also, individuals themselves may be reluctant to let others know about their expertise, either because they do not believe that their knowledge is relevant or they simply do not want to bring attention to themselves. Individuals have several options to make others aware of their expertise including: participating in informal communities of practice, answering questions posed on internal discussion boards, presenting during brown-bag lunches and training classes, and mentoring junior employees. By engaging in these types of activities, individuals have the opportunity to display their experience and engender competence-based trust with their co-workers.

Finally, a significant implication of this study is that managers can affect the extent to which trust is developed among employees. Below are some actions that managers can take to help build trust among individuals:

- *Create a common understanding of how the business works:* One area where managers can have an impact is the development of a common context, or common understanding among employees regarding the nature and goals of the work. Several of the factors that were significant in building benevolence- and competence-based trust, such as shared language and goals, relate to the importance of building a shared view of how work gets accomplished, how it is measured and ultimately rewarded. Creating this common understanding can make it easier for employees to focus on mutually held goals and values, and reduce the amount of time and effort spent on individual issues and motivations.
- *Demonstrate trust-building behaviors:* Another area where managers can influence the level of trust is the modeling and recognition of trust-building behaviors, such as receptivity and discretion. Employing active listening skills and encouraging employees to air their concerns in an atmosphere where their issues will not be improperly disclosed can build trust between managers and employees. For example, as the newly appointed CEO of Mat-

tel, Robert Eckert said one of his most important early actions was to eat lunch in the cafeteria as often as possible, allow employees to ask him questions anonymously, and listen carefully to the tone and words that people used in conversation with each other.[2] All of these practices helped him develop a strong rapport with his new co-workers and raised his level of perceived trustworthiness.

- *Bring people together:* Managers may have some discretion in determining the physical locations in which people work together. Our study highlights that while frequent interactions do not always build trust, bringing people together can spur the conversations that can signal an individual's benevolence. Therefore, managers need to consider how they can create both physical and virtual spaces where people can easily interact with one another. While it may be impossible for team members who are located in different sites to work together consistently in the same room, managers should think about ways to bring people together, especially early in the project lifecycle, and then periodically in the future to recharge the relationships and maintain their connections. Further, organizations can leverage tools such as collaborative spaces and instant messaging to make it easier for team members to communicate with one another when they cannot be physically co-located.

Conclusion

Fostering knowledge sharing is more than simply putting people together in a conference room or sending them on experiential learning programs. It is about creating an environment in which people are able to discern whether their colleagues are both knowledgeable and willing to extend their knowledge to the benefit of others. Without building a sense of competence- and benevolence-based trust between the knowledge seekers and sources, firms will find it difficult to take advantage of perhaps their most valuable resource: their employee know-how. While trust is negotiated by people firsthand, managers can play a substantial role in creating the conditions through which trust is developed and fostered.

Notes

1 The detailed results from this survey are available in two reports published by the IBM Institute for Knowledge-Based Organizations: "The Strength of Weak Ties You Can Trust: The Mediating Role of Trust in Effective Knowledge Transfer" (March 2002) and "Why Should I Trust You? Antecedents of Trust in a Knowledge Transfer Context" (May 2002). The authors of both papers are Daniel Z. Levin (Rutgers University), Robert L. Cross (University of Virginia), and Lisa C. Abrams (IBM Institute for Knowledge-Based Organizations).

2 "First Person: Where Leadership Starts," *Harvard Business Review*, November 2001, page 53.

PART II

SOCIAL NETWORK ANALYSIS

In 2002, IBM acquired PriceWaterhouseCoopers Consulting (PWCC), effectively doubling the size of its consulting division and creating one of the largest management consulting practices in the world. During the early stages of integration, a number of formal efforts were designed to ensure that clients would be presented with a unified organization that would draw from the best capabilities of each firm. These efforts involved jointly staffed teams and addressed many of the key operational issues faced by the new organization, including business development, staffing, incentives, and methodologies.

Soon after the closing of the deal, a senior consultant from PWCC's knowledge management practice contacted us to gain a better understanding of how knowledge management consulting was done at IBM and how the Institute could assist her in selling and delivering work. When we received her initial message, we realized that she had been a colleague of ours at a previous consulting firm. Although we had not spoken in several years, we were able to quickly catch up and share our insights about the new opportunities we were facing. Soon after we had reconnected, my reunited colleague and I were able to introduce each other to members of our respective consulting practices through a number of conference calls, further widening the number of connections between practitioners across the two organizations. Within a week, these new connections led to several business opportunities that were approached by teams composed of members from both entities. From a single conversation, many new connections resulted that led to a greater awareness of capabilities and skills, as well as the potential for future sales.

This story illustrates an important point: while the formal efforts that were undertaken to integrate the two firms were essential, the importance of informal social networks as a vehicle for knowledge sharing cannot be overstated. Both our research and experience have shown us the strength and speed of informal networks in finding individuals with specific knowledge, exchanging ideas and insights, providing access to job information, and deciphering cultural norms and values. Yet we find that despite their importance, organizations spend little, if any, time helping to foster and maintain social networks. This is despite the fact that many of the realities of today's business environment—such as downsizing, increased employee mobility between companies, and the rise of "virtual employees" who are no longer colocated in an office—have the potential to significantly erode these networks. Much like wireless phone networks, insufficient social network connections can lead to "drops" and distortions that can prevent organizations from sharing knowledge, especially in time-constrained environments.

To better understand how social networks operate, we have conducted a significant research effort focused on understanding social networks and their impact on organizations. Most of the work in this area, led by Rob Cross, a professor at the University of Virginia and a former IBM colleague, and Andrew Parker of the KOPF, has applied techniques used by sociologists for decades, to increase the visibility and gain better insight into the dynamics of network formation and operation. Social network analysis uses survey data and graphics software to examine the types of connections made by individuals and to depict these connections in a way that is easy to visualize and compare.

In chapter 4, Rob Cross, Nitin Nohria, and Andrew Parker suggest that many managers hold basic preconceptions about informal networks that prevent them from taking advantage of this very important channel. Among the ideas they demystify is that informal networks are random entities that come together independent of any sort of intervention that managers or organizations have power to influence. The authors argue that there are, in fact, numerous actions that can be taken to encourage individuals from different groups to form and sustain valuable connections. Further, they believe that networks are not just made of gregarious, outgoing individuals who actively seek out others. Rather, networks are developed through conscious behaviors that can be taught or encouraged, even among people who are more comfortable in front of a computer terminal than in a face-to-face conversation. They also suggest that simply increasing communication, for communication's sake alone, can prove to be counterproductive. Instead, organizations should focus on helping individuals know "who knows what" and make it easier for knowledge seekers and knowledge sources to come together to form their own connections.

The importance of making knowledge visible is highlighted in chapter 5, in which Rob Cross, Andrew Parker, Laurence Prusak, and Stephen Borgatti highlight four critical dimensions that influence how knowledge is shared across a network. The first relates to the concept of knowledge *awareness*—how do individuals become aware of the knowledge, skills, and abilities of others within a particular group? Just building awareness, however, is not enough to ensure successful collaboration. Another dimension they highlight is *access*—can the knowledge seekers actually obtain the time and attention they need from someone to get their question addressed? In today's hectic work environment, the ability to get time with an expert, who may be deluged by requests from all directions, may prove to be more arduous than actually finding the person in the first place.

Another critical knowledge dimension is *engagement*—the extent to which the knowledge source is willing to work with the knowledge seeker to help focus the seeker's questions and think through the problem-solving process. Rather than simply providing the knowledge seeker with documents, successful knowledge sharing often occurs when the knowledge seeker and source engage in a dialogue. This interaction often provides the right level of contextual background and tacit knowledge sharing that leaves the knowledge seeker confident in his or her ability to apply the newfound knowledge. Finally, the issue of *safety* comes into play. Does the knowledge seeker feel comfortable that his or her questions or ideas will not be ridiculed by the knowledge source? In many organizations, just the notion of asking a question of someone higher in the organizational hierarchy may indicate a lack of knowledge that could be considered a sign of weakness or insecurity.

Using network analysis techniques, the authors are able to show that people view their networks differently according to each of these dimensions. While people may be very aware of the skills of others in their group, they may find that certain people are bottlenecks to knowledge sharing because they do not have the time to help others or an interest in doing so. Further, people may be willing to help but are hampered by measurements or corporate cultures that prevent individuals from speaking up or collaborating with others. By looking at these dimensions, organizations can be more targeted in their interventions to better support knowledge sharing across their informal networks.

In chapter 6, Rob Cross, Stephen Borgatti, and Andrew Parker focus on the different types of problems that social network analysis can help diagnose. Having worked with many firms, the authors have found social network analysis to be particularly valuable in promoting collaboration within important groups, such as senior management teams. For example, looking at the knowledge-sharing patterns between senior executives can highlight the extent to which they collaborate on cross-functional initiatives, or whether the group leader is engaging only a select number of opinions before making decisions.

Another situation where network analysis can prove valuable is in highlighting the communication patterns across functional, hierarchical, and geographic boundaries. Used for this purpose, network analysis can reveal individuals who play critical knowledge-sharing or "broker" roles within their organizations. This can be especially important, since these individuals are often not recognized for these activities and can create significant problems if they leave the organization. Similarly, network analysis can illustrate the presence of a strong dependence on a limited number of people to connect separate groups. These limited connections can result in a potential knowledge "bottleneck" that can prevent the groups from working effectively together.

Finally, network analysis can be an important tool in evaluating the level of integration between merged or restructured groups. Looking at the knowledge-sharing patterns prior to the integration can identify central individuals who need to be targeted to ensure a smooth transition, and highlight peripheral people who need to be better connected to the larger group. In addition, comparing the groups prior to and then again after the changes can help determine whether the group has changed its knowledge-sharing behaviors as the result of the organizational change.

Social network analysis can provide us with a unique picture of how we interact with our colleagues. Like viewing a world through a different camera lens, it can allow us to see things that we perhaps take for granted in our day-to-day work interactions. In addition, social network analysis lets us focus on issues that may have escaped our first glance, or represent challenges in a new light. Social network analysis gives managers a new set of tools that can provide more analytic rigor to the elusive challenge of trying to harness the power of informal collaboration. By applying these techniques, organizations have a greater opportunity to create more effective, targeted solutions to their knowledge challenges.

4

Six Myths about Informal Networks—
and How to Overcome Them

ROB CROSS
NITIN NOHRIA
ANDREW PARKER

Over the past couple of decades, management innovations have pushed companies toward the ideal of the "boundaryless" organization. On the inside, delayering, reengineering and the rise of cross-functional teams have pushed decision making and accountability downward and made functional boundaries more permeable, increasing the flow of information in the process. On the outside, joint ventures, alliances and supply-chain integration have blurred borders between companies.

As a result of these changes, formal reporting structures and detailed work processes have a much diminished role in the way important work is accomplished. Instead, informal networks of employees are increasingly at the forefront, and the general health and connectivity of these groups can have a significant impact on strategy execution and organizational effectiveness.

Informal networks often, for example, provide the glue that holds together cross-functional process-improvement initiatives, alliances and mergers. They can also be significant contributors to new-product development; in the pharmaceuticals industry, for instance, the type of informal network known as a community of practice is critical to reducing drug development costs and to the more rapid introduction of new products. In addition, informal networks are important sources of job satisfaction and retention. Many employees today join and commit to local sets of relationships while feeling no particular allegiance to the corporation as a whole.

Many corporate leaders intuitively understand these facts—put an org chart in front of any executive today and he or she will tell you that the boxes and lines only partially reflect the way things are done in the organization—but few spend any real time assessing or supporting informal networks. Their very invisibility as formal organizational entities, combined with the absence of clear ownership, are major reasons for this neglect. And because they do not receive adequate resources or executive attention, these groups are often fragmented and their efforts disrupted by management practices or organizational-design principles that are biased in favor of task specialization and individual rather than collaborative endeavors.

Informal networks—also known as social networks—are especially important in knowledge-intensive sectors, where people use personal relationships to find information and do their jobs. This fact is supported by our own research and that of many others. One researcher who looked at this question for more than a decade, just to give one example, found that engineers and scientists were roughly five times as likely to turn to friends or colleagues for information as to impersonal sources.[1] Despite the explosion of information that is accessible through the Internet and databases, people still rely heavily on their networks for help with their work.

Because of the increasing importance of relationships in the workplace, we initiated a research program two years ago to determine how organizations can better support work occurring in and through informal networks of employees. Working with a group of Fortune 500 companies and government agencies, we assessed more than 40 networks in 23 organizations. In all cases, the networks provided strategic and operational benefits by enabling members to collaborate effectively.[2] We discovered, however, that executives had to make counterintuitive shifts in their thinking if they truly wanted to promote the health of these groups. In almost every organization we studied, management's decisions to intervene in a network were based on myths—deeply held assumptions—about what would, and wouldn't, make them more effective.

We saw that executives believed broadly in six myths about social networks. In the course of our work, we helped managers understand the myths and how they were misguided at best and harmful at worst. We also helped them operate according to reality checks; in other words, to find alternative ways of intervening in informal networks for the greater good of the organization. Senior managers who can separate myth from reality, and act accordingly, stand a much better chance of fostering the growth and success of these increasingly important organizational structures. We'll review each assumption in turn to explain how and why that is true.

Myth: To Build Better Networks, We Have to Communicate More

Executives often assume that communication of any and all kinds—even pure socializing—is the essence of an informal network. As a result, they commonly conclude that uniting fragmented networks or developing sparse ones is simply a matter of more and better communication. Their thinking usually changes when they are asked, "Do you, yourself, want to attend more meetings or receive more e-mail?" Most executives cringe at the thought and start to see that more communication in a world of information overload is not the solution.

Extend the thought, and it's clear that the quantity of communication in any situation has no necessary bearing on its quality. It's easy to prove this by asking people two different questions and then mapping the resulting networks: With whom do you routinely communicate? and To whom do you typically turn for information to do your work? (These maps can appear forbidding to the unini- tiated. For help in demystifying them, see Box 4.1.) In our research, we found that answers to these questions yield very different diagrams. When the diagram of information seekers (second question) is subtracted from the diagram of com- municators (first question), a web of people who say they are communicating but aren't exchanging useful information often comes to light.

Reality Check: To Build Better Networks, Focus on Who Knows What

Managers should resist the tendency to equate communication and socializing with network building. They are better served by distinguishing between the ac- tual achievements of a network—what it has done or is currently doing—from its potential accomplishments. To do that, they must shift the question from Who is currently obtaining information from whom? to Who knows what? Answers to the second question will show fruitful connections that might be made in the future; the result of this analysis should be a network that can leverage its mem- bers' expertise in the face of new problems or opportunities.[3] This was the case in a recent merger between two financial institutions, where managers developed an awareness of who had unique skills and expertise at each organization. Such understanding is critical to the success of any merger involving knowledge- intensive organizations.

Beginning with who knows what also gives managers ways of building net- works that can complement efforts based on assessments of current flows of in- formation. Thus if they find that a network is sparse, they might apply technical solutions such as skill profiling to help employees search for expertise in the or- ganization. (Skill profiling requires employees to record their expertise and expe- rience in a central, searchable database, updating their file as new projects yield new skills or knowledge.) Companies can also leverage HR practices to improve awareness of who knows what. For example, they can bring together newcomers and experienced hands by scheduling lunches for that express purpose. Or the knowledge and skills of new people can be advertised by creating "baseball cards" that can be posted in common areas.

Companies may also benefit by changing staffing practices. One professional services firm attempts to have its people work on a project in another office at least once a year. The relationships that result from this practice benefit the firm as a whole by building connections between offices. They are often critical to the firm's ability to win new contracts and to deliver high-quality service on existing ones. The relationships help employees accomplish more than they could if they had to rely solely on their own expertise or that of local colleagues.

BOX 4.1 How to Read a Network Diagram

Information collected from social network surveys can be used to create network diagrams that illustrate the relationships between members of a group. This example shows the flow of information within a globally dispersed product-development team.

Subgroups
Groups within a group often arise along the lines of location, function, hierarchy, tenure, age or gender. In this case, the team is split by function; very little information is being shared among the three groups. Moreover, connections in marketing and finance are sparse, while the manufacturing subgroup is tightly knit. That can be a good thing or a bad thing. Perhaps the manufacturing people have developed communication practices that the team as a whole could use to its benefit. It's also possible that those people rely on one another so heavily that they are preventing integration. Only follow-up interviews can reveal which scenario is true.

Peripheral People
Some people are only loosely connected to a network; a few may be completely isolated—members in theory but not in practice. In this network, no one goes to Carl for information, and Kevin is out of the loop entirely. As is true with central people, the diagram alone doesn't say anything about the value of peripheral people. Such outsiders often turn out to be underutilized resources, and integrating them can be critical to a network's effectiveness and efficiency. Of course, sometimes people are isolated for good reason: They lack the skills, social and otherwise, for the job. By identifying peripheral people, network analysis enables appropriate developmental action to be taken.

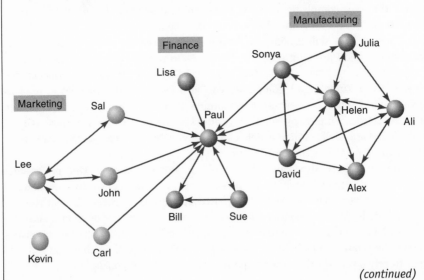

(continued)

Lines and Arrows

Each line indicates an information link between two people; arrows represent the direction of the relationship (incoming arrows show that the person is a source of information; outgoing, that the team member seeks information from the linked party). Thus Helen has two-way relationships with each member of the manufacturing group but limited or no contact with marketing and finance.

Central People

Network diagrams make clear who the most prominent people within a group are. On this team, nine people rely on Paul for information. His colleagues in finance come to him, but so do people in marketing and manufacturing. Paul himself does not reach out to people outside of finance. The diagram alone can't tell us if Paul's impact is positive or negative. If the group is overly dependent on him, he may be a bottleneck, slowing the flow of information and holding up decisions. On the other hand, people like Paul often play a very positive role in a network—providing not only valuable information but also cohesion—and would render the group much less effective if they left the company.

By working with networks that start from what people know, managers can intervene to sustain informal groups without adding the burden of more and potentially useless communications.

Myth: Everyone Should Be Connected to Everyone Else

In the course of our analysis, we frequently found that executives jumped to the conclusion that more connections within a network must always be better. However, in networks of any size it is not possible for everyone to be connected to everyone else, nor is it desirable. Rather than leading to improved collaboration and problem solving, an indiscriminate increase in connectedness can be a drag on productivity, as people get bogged down maintaining all their relationships.

Reality Check: People Should Be Connected When a Strategic Payoff Is Likely

Instead of trying to develop a fully integrated network, managers will find it more fruitful to invest in developing and maintaining relationships that have strategic value. A tool called *social network analysis* can be applied to make clear where such critical junctures exist within the organization. (For a brief look at this tool, see Box 4.2.)

We found, for example, that many organizations were not getting the kind of cross-boundary collaboration they needed to take advantage of new opportunities. Mapping the pattern of information flow (or, more frequently, lack of flow) across

BOX 4.2 Conducting a Social Network Analysis

The most important managerial tool available for assessing patterns of relationships in informal networks is called social network analysis. By making critical patterns of interaction visible, *social network analysis* helps managers give informed answers to such questions as: Does information flow smoothly within a given network? Do functional departments or business units collaborate appropriately in taking their services to market? Is the collective expertise within a network being leveraged effectively? The result of such probing is likely to be improved collaboration at strategic junctures within an organization. Managers can carry out a social network analysis by following six steps:

Pick The Right Group
Although social network analysis can be applied to any group—from one consisting of a few people to an entire organization—it's best to focus on those that are strategically important. Examples include top leadership networks, groups operating in cross-company partnerships and alliances, teams involved with new-product development, and networks of people who cross core work processes. In general, groups that cross physical, functional or hierarchical boundaries are good targets for improvement.

Ask the Right Question
Social network analysis can be used to find out a variety of things about the groups in an organization. Companies are usually most interested in the flow of information within a network (the overarching question, then, is, Who do you seek information from to help you do your work?) or in the interdependent nature of certain tasks (the question shifts to, Who do you rely on for input to complete your work?). Other questions can provide valuable information about networks that exist on the basis of trust, career advising, and even energy (when you interact with so-and-so, how does it affect your energy level?).

Design the Survey
In addition to questions about the network itself, the survey should include demographic questions about the respondent's time in the organization and in the group; it should also ask about geographic location, organizational function and gender. Answers to such questions can indicate impediments to the network's ability to surmount various boundaries. To reassure people about confidentiality, the survey should explain how the results will be used. Finally, it's advisable to keep the time needed to complete the survey to no more than 20 minutes; Web-based survey tools make this easier to accomplish. After 20 minutes, survey fatigue tends to set in.

Collect the Data
The quality of a network analysis is highly dependent on getting a survey response that lands in the 80% to 100% range. If a key person is omitted from the network because he or she did not complete the survey, the analysis will be

(continued)

badly skewed. To ensure a high rate of response, a strong project sponsor must be willing to send several e-mail messages reminding people to complete the survey.

Inducements such as movie tickets, lotteries for prizes or time off can also help persuade people to respond. Note that network data can also be collected by analyzing e-mail or phone logs, and even through personal observation. But surveys are generally preferred because they can be used to ask targeted questions.

Analyze the Data

Once the data have been collected, they can be viewed using a variety of network-drawing packages. (These can be obtained easily by searching the Web and can range in price from free to thousands of dollars.) Similarly, network analysis software is available that can derive metrics from the data; for example, it can show through quantitative analysis who the central people are in a given network. On its own, the drawing software will reveal the overall pattern and key players of a small group, but quantitative analysis is especially important for analyzing larger networks.

Share the Results

Although much can be learned from interpreting the data, the full value of the analysis will be realized only after the results have been shared with the group or with executives who have a good awareness of the group. (Depending on the terms set out in the survey, names can be disclosed or kept confidential.) Sharing information provides a powerful stimulus to collective sense making and problem solving. Network information, then, is both a valuable diagnostic tool and an agent of change.

functional barriers revealed where management should make efforts to promote strategically valuable collaboration. Defining these critical junctures in networks allows managers to take a targeted approach to improving collaboration. It's much easier to bring about change in this manner than to attempt it through broad, top-down mandates designed to get everyone working together, or through a full-scale organizational-learning intervention or by altering an entire organization's incentive schemes.

Consider how a focus on targeted collaboration based on strategic needs played out at a commercial bank. The sponsor of the project asked us to assess the network of the bank's top 62 executives; his goal was to create a more fluid leadership group so that employees in the organization could more effectively tap into their colleagues' expertise to respond to new lending or fee-based opportunities. He knew that such opportunities were often overlooked by his employees simply because they did not know that the organization had expertise to address them.

As we engaged in analysis of the network, we discovered that 49% of all pairs of individuals within the real estate lending division had collaborative relationships. In stark contrast, only 10% of all pairs in which one person was a member of the real estate division and the other a member of the commercial lending division were collaborating. Needless to say, given the organization's strategic initiative to integrate service offerings for key customers, this lack of collaboration was a real problem. Similarly, we found a lack of integration between the risk assessment unit and the lending divisions (collaboration with real estate, 7%; with commercial, 8%), despite the institution's recent restructuring to integrate risk assessment into the lending processes earlier in order to reduce rework and cycle time on loan applications.

As a result of the analysis, the bank made several policy and procedural changes. It established sales goals to ensure cross-selling between the commercial and real estate lending divisions. It required lending teams to include a credit analyst in the proposal stage. These and other changes had the desired effect: the cost of booking loans declined as time and energy spent on low-quality loans diminished, and revenues increased as a result of cross-selling to existing accounts.

Myth: We Can't Do Much to Aid Informal Networks

Many executives were either taught in business school or decided as a result of their own experiences that it's not possible to do much about the informal parts of an organization.[4] At the root of such thinking is the pervasive belief that network patterns are exclusively the result of personal relationships. Personality differences, executives say, are the reason some networks exist and others fail to form; thus two groups are not integrated because they are made up of "different kinds of people," and two other networks exist because of a feud between two managers. While such dynamics can be important, systemic forces create network patterns as frequently as personality clashes.

Reality Check: Informal Networks Can Be Aided by Changing the Organizational Context

When executives do attempt to promote collaboration, they usually turn to a technical solution. In fact, most of the organizations we work with have a more than adequate but underused technical infrastructure which includes such elements as skill-profiling technologies and tools that allow people to work together in different locations. Rather than relying heavily on technology, managers should consider how changes in four areas of organizational context can improve collaboration in informal networks.[5]

The first area of context to consider is the organization's formal structure. To intervene in networks, managers must understand how the formal structure impedes group effectiveness. For example, in organizations with a strong top-down culture, informal networks themselves tend to closely mirror the prevailing pattern of hierarchy; as a result, they lack the flexibility to respond effectively to new opportunities. Some degree of empowerment is necessary in these situations if flexible networks are to evolve. In other cases, informal networks can be heavily constrained by functional or departmental boundaries as leadership, job design, information systems and performance-management practices promote collaboration within units but not between them. Creating time and space for cross-unit collaboration is a critical leadership challenge in these settings. A pharmaceutical organization in our study does this by building cross-functional projects into its annual budgeting and planning processes. By bringing together expertise on different drug compounds, the organization has become more efficient and realized new market opportunities.

Work management practices constitute a second important element of organizational context. The natural unit of work for a group is one of the most powerful levers available to managers who want to develop a network's effectiveness. In contrast to off-site events or team-building exercises, the development of relationships in this context occurs in the pursuit of organizational objectives and so is comparatively inexpensive.

Managers should be creative in thinking through ways to carve out assignments that can lead to effective collaboration. Several consulting firms, for example, have begun to put two or more people on projects even when it might be more efficient to have only one person involved for a longer period of time; they have found that the value of the relationships that develop outweighs the costs associated with starting up and marketing more projects. Morale is higher and turnover lower in such settings, and the consultants build stronger personal networks that they can tap into on future projects.

Employee management practices are a third area of organizational context affecting collaboration. Human resource decisions, which become institutionalized to the point of being taken for granted, often have long-lasting effects on collaborative activity. In addition, executives can take a range of actions that promote collaboration, from hiring people who have demonstrated collaborative practices to rewarding people for collaborative efforts. (Paradoxically, companies often use critical-incident techniques that require job candidates to describe actual scenarios in which they were collaborative; yet the same companies admit that they base hiring decisions purely on individual expertise.) Managers often have the latitude, at a minimum with targeted rewards, to formally recognize collaborative behaviors. Such recognition can be a powerful signal about what kind of work is valued by the company.

Finally, cultural values that prize individual accomplishment over collaborative endeavors and behavioral norms that keep people from sharing ideas until they are fully formed can result in sparse network patterns. Who is publicly praised in most organizations? The person who took a risk or overcame the odds to achieve something, or the one who involved others in solving a problem? Typically, the hero is noticed and networks suffer, often invisibly, as a result. Leaders can change that culture over time by publicly acknowledging collaborative work, rewarding those who go out of their way for others, and promoting such people along with the rainmakers.

The key for managers is to begin the process by defining the collaborative behaviors that have strategic importance; only then will they be able to reward people appropriately. For example, the managers of a technology company we worked with were concerned about the "not invented here" syndrome so prevalent among engineers. The organization had world-class expertise, but social network analysis revealed that people rarely reached out to colleagues outside their project teams. One step executives took to begin correcting the problem was asking—in every project review, update or planning meeting—who people on the team had contacted on the outside and what the team's plans were for continuing to leverage outside experts.

Myth: How People Fit into Networks Is a Matter of Personality (Which Can't Be Changed)

It's commonly held that people who are good networkers fit a stereotype: They are extroverted, social and aggressive in the pursuit of their goals. The view that personality determines who is and who isn't likely to be an important member of a group contributes to the idea that little or nothing can be done to improve the effectiveness of informal networks. After all, executives often say to us, it's not really possible to change someone's personality.

Reality Check: How People Fit into Networks Is a Matter of Intentional Behaviors (Which Can Be Influenced)

We have mapped personality scales such as the Myers-Briggs test on our social network analyses and found that the link between someone's personality and his or her position in a network is not as strong as one might think.[6] Even highly introverted people can, and often do, have robust personal networks. Managers should focus less on personality and more on the behaviors of people who wind up at the center of networks.

From our interviews with people in networks, we discovered that those who occupy pivotal positions do things differently from those who stay on the margins. Central people don't focus exclusively on getting tasks done; they also consider how to build relationships and get others involved in the work. In fact, because they realize the future value of relationships, they take the time to systematically build their own networks. Such people often include relationship building as a critical part of their professional development plans and always seem to have lists of people they are trying to meet or planning to call.

Network patterns, then, are a product of intentional behaviors rather than entrenched personality characteristics—and, in contrast to personality traits, behaviors can be taught or encouraged. Managers can take specific steps to leverage the expertise of peripheral network members, for instance, by having them work with better-connected colleagues and by having them answer requests for information directly (so that others will come to recognize what they know and will turn to them in the future). People can also be trained to learn how to assess, develop and support their own networks. (When executives thoroughly analyze their own networks, they often uncover a variety of biases; that is, they find that they turn only to people in the same function or in the same geographic location or of the same gender, and that they generally fail to reach down in the hierarchy, where the best information usually resides.) Thus network development can be embedded in an organization's routines by making it a critical component of orientation practices, professional development plans, learning exercises and staffing initiatives.

Myth: Central People Who Have become Bottlenecks Should Make Themselves More Accessible

People at the center of an informal network often work long hours at a grueling pace. Their very work ethic has, in fact, made them essential to the network's effectiveness, and they often feel that they must work harder and be more available, if necessary, to keep it running smoothly. What such people fail to understand, however, is that they frequently become bottlenecks who slow down the whole group.

Reality Check: Central People Who Have become Bottlenecks Should Shift Burdens for Providing Information and Making Decisions to Others in the Network.

More accessibility and harder work on the part of pivotal people is not the solution. To understand why, consider what we learned by examining a global network of 218 people within a technology organization. The executive running this group had six direct reports (managing principals) based in various regions of the world; the rest of the organization reported to these people. One managing principal had 51 people indicating that they came to him for critical information to get their work done and another 48 saying they would be more effective in their work if they were able to communicate more with him. In short, the manager was working at his limits but had become a bottleneck for the group. His immediate world was one of fast decisions and action—things always felt like they were happening at an incredible pace—and he had no idea he was slowing down the group. It was not until we sat down with him and showed him the network analysis and results of our interviews that he became aware of how he was obstructing opportunities and holding up projects. He quickly determined that he could shed responsibility for owning certain information and decisions. As a result, he freed up his own time for efforts that drew on his expertise, and the network itself was less constrained by him.

Although this is an extreme example, we have consistently seen this pattern in a wide range of networks. Senior managers can intervene to correct the problem by reallocating information domains (that is, who's responsible for what information) and changing decision rights (allowing others to make decisions).

People often become central to a network because they know things that bridge different parts of the organization. But such people have to give up on the losing battle of trying to answer everyone's questions. Rather, they should learn to point people toward others in the network with the expertise to provide answers. Such action not only opens up the bottleneck, it also draws in peripheral people to the center of the network.

Defining a busy executive's information domains and considering ways to real-locate ownership of them can usually be done in a couple of hours, even over lunch. Start with the executive's role in directing the substance of meetings held during the previous month. In addition, it can be helpful to review the subject lines of e-mail messages from the same time period. These quick exercises almost always allow people to identify categories of informational requests that others in the group could own more productively.

Clarity about who gets to make decisions is an even bigger problem than how information flows in informal networks. People frequently let opportunities pass because they feel that the cost of getting a simple decision approved is excessive. Even worse, members of newly formed groups often don't know where to turn to get a decision made. They end up trying to get an audience with some busy executive, which only slows the process down. It also adds an element of risk: The organization can become too reliant on one decision maker, someone who is frequently too far removed from day-to-day issues to be able to make a well-informed decision.

The same analysis used on informational requests can be applied to decision categories. Again, many categories can be delegated. For example, travel approvals can easily be handled by an administrative employee or with a policy (a travel budget for each person, for example). Less routine decisions can also be effectively distributed to the experienced people in a network.

Myth: I Already Know What Is Going on in My Network

Executives often claim that they have a good understanding of who is in their network and how it operates. As far as their immediate circle goes, that is usually true, but it is false when applied more broadly to include all the people they interact with or manage. As a way of getting them to consider that next level, we ask, "When and how have you had your perception tested?" They usually can't answer. Studies show, in fact, that managers often have a limited under-standing of the networks around them.[7]

Reality Check: Those Who Are Most Adamant in Asserting That They Know Their Network Are Usually the Farthest Off Base

By virtue of their position in the hierarchy, managers are frequently far removed from the day-to-day work that generates an organization's informal structure and so may have a limited picture of relationship patterns. The problem is compounded by the fact that most executives do little to systematically assess and support informal groups. They spend vast sums of money for new information systems or to implement better and faster financial-reporting practices but seem less inclined to make the investments that would give them a clear picture of how work is getting done within their organization. That's usually because executives are bound by myths about informal networks and don't realize the potential of social network analysis to map important networks and the interventions that might emerge from this perspective.

In today's knowledge-intensive environment where organizations have been significantly restructured, creating healthier informal networks is a critical job of managers and executives. Collaboration across organizational boundaries is required, as people seek out innovative solutions to increasingly complex and interconnected problems. The key point for managers overseeing informal networks is that, contrary to conventional wisdom, such groups can be supported in ways that produce strategic and operational benefits for the whole organization.

Acknowledgments We would like to thank Larry Prusak and Steve Borgatti for comments on aspects of this work.

Notes

1 G. Simmel, *The Sociology of Georg Simmel* (New York: Free Press, 1950); M. Granovetter, "The Strength of Weak Ties," *American Journal of Sociology* 78 (May 1973): 1360–1380; T. Allen, *Managing the Flow of Technology* (Cambridge, Massachusetts: MIT Press, 1977); R. Burt, *Structural Holes* (Cambridge, Massachusetts: Harvard University Press, 1992); E. Rogers, *Diffusion of Innovations*, 4th ed. (New York: Free Press, 1995); J. Lave and E. Wenger, *Situated Learning: Legitimate Peripheral Participation* (Cambridge, England: Cambridge University Press, 1991); J. S. Brown and P. Duguid, "Organizational Learning and Communities of Practice: Toward a Unified View of Working, Learning and Innovation," *Organization Science* 2 (January–February 1991): 40–57; J. E. Orr, *Talking about Machines* (Ithaca, New York: Cornell University Press, 1996); and E. Wenger, *Communities of Practice* (Oxford: Oxford University Press, 1998).

2 Our work with these networks was designed to test several relational and structural models of knowledge creation and sharing in social networks. We typically tested each empirical model in two to four organizations in order to generalize findings beyond a single network analysis (the prevalent mode in the scholarly literature). Just as important, we sought to develop managerial applications of social network analysis, a goal that has not been a central concern of the field. To do that we engaged with each company in four- to six-hour problem-solving sessions in which we fed back results of our assessments to executives and facilitated brainstorming sessions to develop insight into applications of social network analysis. Further, where possible, we conducted follow-up network assessments or in-depth interviews (or both) to get a true understanding of the impact of interventions in support of informal networks.

3 This notion was drawn from scholarly research on transactive memory in groups. For a review, see R. Moreland, L. Argote and R. Krishnan, "Socially Shared Cognition at Work: Transactive Memory and Group Performance," in *What's Social about Social*

Cognition? ed. J. Nye and A. Brower (Thousand Oaks, California: Sage, 1996): 57–85. Other researchers have since begun to apply social-network techniques to further expanding this notion: S. Borgatti and R. Cross, *A Social Network View of Organizational Learning* (Washington, D.C.: Academy of Management Proceedings, 2001); and R. Cross, A. Parker, L. Prusak and S. Borgatti, "Knowing What We Know: Supporting Knowledge Creation and Sharing in Social Networks," *Organizational Dynamics* 30(2): 100–120.

4 Part of this problem also seems to stem from the focus on communities of practice and strong arguments that they must be left alone to emerge. We would suggest that forces we identify also affect the ability of a community to emerge effectively in a given organizational context.

5 For much more depth on these ideas. see R. Cross and A. Parker, "Toward a Collaborative Organizational Context: Supporting Informal Networks in Knowledge Intensive Work," working paper 43, University of Virginia, Charlottesville, Virginia, November 2001.

6 Other scholarly studies have found only slight relationships between personality characteristics and network position; however, these studies are rare and have not been replicated as this is an emerging area for management scholars. See A. Mehra, M. Kilduff and D. J. Brass, "The Social Networks of High and Low Self-Monitors: Implications for Workplace Performance."*Administrative Science Quarterly* 46 (March 2001): 121–146; and R. S. Burt, J. E. Jannotta and J. T. Mahoney, "Personality Correlates of Structural Holes," *Social Networks* 20 (January 1998): 63–87.

7 D. Krackhardt, "Cognitive Social Structures," *Social Networks* 9 (June 1987): 109–134; D. Krackhardt, "Assessing the Political Landscape: Structure, Cognition and Power in Organizations," *Administrative Science Quarterly* 35 (June 1990): 342–369; and T. Casciaro, "Seeing Things Clearly: Social Structure, Personality and Accuracy in Social Network Perception," *Social Networks* 20 (October 1998): 331–351.

5

Knowing What We Know: Supporting Knowledge Creation and Sharing in Social Networks

ROB CROSS
ANDREW PARKER
LAURENCE PRUSAK
STEPHEN P. BORGATTI

So the call came in late on Thursday afternoon and right away I wished I hadn't answered the phone. We had received a last-second opportunity to bid on a sizable piece of work that the Partner on the other end of the line really wanted to pursue. I had no clue how to even begin looking for relevant methodologies or case examples, so my first move was to tap into my network to find some relevant info and leads to other people or databases. And I relied pretty heavily on this group over the next couple of days. Seth was great for pointing me to other people and relevant information, Paul provided ideas on the technical content of the project while Jeff really helped in showing me how to frame the client's issues in ways that we could sell. He also helped navigate and get buy-in from the client given his knowledge of their operations and politics. . . . I mean the whole game is just being the person that can get the client what they need with [the firm's] resources behind you. This almost always seems to mean knowing who knows what and figuring out a way to bring them to bear on your client's issue.

—Anonymous Interviewee

The way in which this manager relied on his network to obtain information and knowledge critical to the success of an important project is common and likely resonates with your own experience. Usually when we think of where people turn for information or knowledge we think of databases, the Web, intranets and portals or other, more traditional, repositories such as file cabinets or policy and procedure manuals. However, a significant component of a person's information environment consists of the relationships he or she can tap for various informational needs. For example, in summarizing a decade worth of studies, Tom Allen of Massachusetts Institute of Technology (MIT) found that engineers and scientists were roughly five times more likely to turn to a person for information than to an impersonal source such as a database or a file cabinet. In other settings, research has consistently shown that who you know has a significant impact on what you come to know, as relationships are critical for obtaining information, solving problems, and learning how to do your work.

Particularly in knowledge-intensive work, creating an informational environment that helps employees solve increasingly complex and often ambiguous problems holds significant performance implications. Frequently such efforts entail knowledge management initiatives focusing on the capture and sharing of codified knowledge and reusable work products. To be sure, these so-called knowledge bases hold pragmatic benefits. They bridge boundaries of time and space, allow for potential reuse of tools or work products employed successfully in other areas of an organization, and provide a means of reducing organizational "forgetting" as a function of employee turnover. However, such initiatives often undervalue crucial knowledge held by employees and the web of relationships that help dynamically solve problems and create new knowledge.

As we move further into an economy where collaboration and innovation are increasingly central to organizational effectiveness, we must pay more attention to the sets of relationships that people rely on to accomplish their work. Certainly we can expect emerging collaborative technologies to facilitate virtual work and skill profiling systems to help with the location of relevant expertise. However, as was so poignantly demonstrated by reengineering, technology alone can only accomplish so much in the pursuit of business performance. Improving efficiency and effectiveness in knowledge-intensive work demands more than sophisticated technologies—it requires attending to the often idiosyncratic ways that people seek out knowledge, learn from and solve problems with other people in organizations.

With this in mind, we initiated a research program to determine means of improving employees' ability to create and share knowledge in important social networks. In the first phase of our research, we assessed the characteristics of relationships that 40 managers relied on for learning and knowledge sharing in important projects. In the second phase, we systematically employed social network analysis to map these dimensions of relationships among strategically important networks of people in various organizations. Working with a consortium of Fortune 500 companies and government organizations, we developed empirical support for relational characteristics that facilitate knowledge creation and sharing in social networks as well as insight into social and technical interventions to facilitate knowledge flow in these networks.

Supporting Knowledge Creation and Sharing in Social Networks

In the first phase of our research we asked 40 managers to reflect on a recent project that was important to their careers and indicate where they obtained information critical to the project's success. As can be seen in Figure 5.1, these managers overwhelmingly indicated (and supported with vivid stories) that they received this information from other people far more frequently than impersonal sources such as their personal computer archives, the Internet, or the organization's knowledge management database. And we found this in an organization that most industry analysts heralded as a knowledge management exemplar because of its investment in technology. This is not to say that the firm's leading-edge technical platform and organizational practices for capturing, screening, and

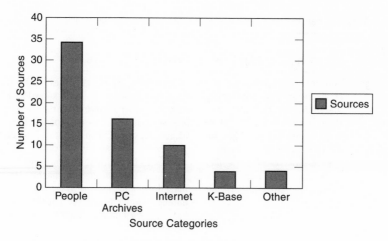

Figure 5.1 Sources of important information.

archiving knowledge were not helpful. Just to point out that "impersonal" information sources were primarily leveraged only after the managers had been unsuccessful in obtaining relevant knowledge from colleagues (or when directed to a point in the database by a colleague).

We also asked the managers to identify the people most important to them in terms of information or knowledge acquired for that project, and had them carefully describe these relationships. Four features emerged that distinguished effective from ineffective relationships: (1) knowing what another person knows and thus when to turn to them; (2) being able to gain timely access to that person; (3) willingness of the person sought out to engage in problem solving rather than dump information; and (4) a degree of safety in the relationship that promoted learning and creativity. An in-depth review of these dimensions is beyond our scope here; however, a summary of these relational features and representative quotes can be found in Table 5.1.

The managers we interviewed indicated that these four dimensions were key characteristics of relationships that were effective for acquiring information, solving problems, or learning. In contrast, they also recounted numerous times when learning or knowledge sharing did not happen because of one of the above dimensions not existing in the relationship (e.g., someone knew what they needed to know, but did not make himself or herself accessible). Further, a separate quantitative study demonstrated that these dimensions consistently predict whom people seek out for informational purposes, even after controlling for such features as education or age similarity, physical proximity, time in organization; and formal hierarchical position. With the importance of these four relational characteristics established, the second step of our research was to use social network analysis to map information flow as well as these relational characteristics among strategically important groups to improve knowledge creation and sharing.

Table 5.1 Relational Qualities That Promote Effective Knowledge Sharing

Relational Dimensions	Impact on Knowledge Seeking	Representative Quote
Knowledge	Knowing what someone else knows (even if we are initially inaccurate and calibrate over time) is a precursor to seeking a specific person out when we are faced with a problem or opportunity. For other people to be options we must have at least some perception of their expertise.	"At [Company X] we had access to background information and you know lots of case studies and approaches that were really well written up. I had no experience though of actually applying this approach on an engagement. So what was specifically useful to me was to talk with Terry who I knew had done several of these engagements. He helped me work some of the content in the database into a workable approach. I was lucky I knew him and could leverage some of his experience . . ."
Access	However, knowing what someone else knows is only useful if you can get access to their thinking in a sufficiently timely fashion. Access is heavily influenced by the closeness of one's relationship as well as physical proximity, organizational design, and collaborative technology.	"I have gotten less frustrated the more I have worked with him because I know how to get ahold of him. It took me a while to figure out that he was a phone guy and not an e-mail guy. And I have also learned how to ask him for help and what I can expect. It was important to learn what I could rely on him for and how to get his attention to make the relationship, which was initially frustrating, an important one for me . . ."
Engagement	People who are helpful in learning interactions actively think with the seeker and engage in problem solving. Rather than dump information, these people first understand the problem *as experienced by the seeker* and then shape their knowledge to the problem at hand.	"Some people will give you their opinion without trying to either understand what your objectives are or understand where you are coming from or be very closed in their answer to you. [She] is the sort of person who first makes sure she understands what the issue is. I have been around people who give you a quick spiel because they think they are smart and that by throwing some framework or angle up they can quickly wow you and get out of the hard work of solving a problem. [She], for all her other responsibilities and stature within the firm, is not like that."
Safety	Finally, those relationships that are safe are often most effective for learning purposes. Being able to admit a lack of knowledge or to diverge in a conversation often results in creativity and learning.	"[He]" is always looking for the positive spin on something. I mean even if he thinks that is garbage and if he really thought that, he would make this known but in a positive way. So he might say 'Well I think we might be a little off track on that and here's why' and then say why and of course there is learning that comes from that."

Social Network Analysis

Social network analysis (SNA) provides a rich and systematic means of assessing informal networks by mapping and analyzing relationships among people, teams, departments, or even entire organizations. Though managers are often adamant that they know their organization, studies are showing that they have different levels of accuracy in understanding the networks around them. By virtue of their position in the hierarchy, managers are frequently far removed from the day-to-day work interactions that generate an organization's informal structure, and so may have a very inaccurate understanding of the actual patterns of relationships. And the potential for inaccurate perceptions is only increased by our transition into a world of virtual work and telecommuting, where employees are engaged in work relationships increasingly invisible to superiors. Social network analysis can provide an X-ray of the way in which work is or is not occurring in these informal networks.

Mapping Information Flow among Executives

We conducted a social network analysis of executives in the Exploration and Production Division of a large petroleum organization. This group was in the midst of implementing a distributed technology to help transfer knowledge across drilling initiatives and was also interested in assessing their ability as a group to create and share knowledge. As a result, we were asked to conduct a social network analysis of information flow among the top 20 executives within the Exploration and Production Division. As can be seen in Figure 5.2, this analysis revealed a striking contrast between the group's formal and informal structure.

Three important points quickly emerged for this group in relation to sharing information and effectively leveraging their collective expertise. First, the social network analysis identified mid-level managers who were critical in terms of information flow within the group. A particular surprise came from the very central role that Cole played in terms of both overall information flow within the group and being the only point of contact between members of the production division and the rest of the network. A facilitated session with this executive team revealed that over time Cole's reputation for expertise and responsiveness had resulted in his becoming a critical source for all sorts of information. Through no fault of his own, the number of informational requests he received and the number of projects he was involved in had grown excessive, which not only caused him stress but also frequently slowed the group as a whole, because Cole had become a bottleneck.

The social network analysis also revealed the extent to which the entire network was disproportionately reliant on Cole. If he were hired away, the efficiency of this group as a whole would be significantly impacted as people in the informal network re-established important informational relationships. Of course, people would find ways to reconnect to obtain necessary information. However, the social network diagram made it very clear that if Cole left, the company would lose both his valuable knowledge and the relationships he had established that in many

Formal Organizational Structure of Exploration and Production Division

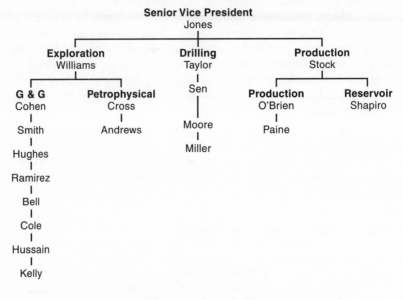

Informal Organizational Structure of Exploration and Production Division

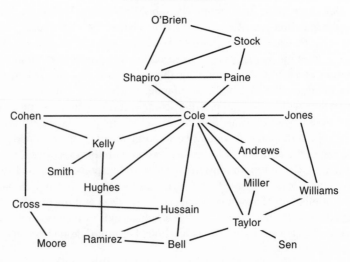

Figure 5.2 Formal vs. informal structure in a petroleum organization.

ways were holding the network together. As a result, a central intervention that came from this analysis was to reallocate many of the informational requests coming to Cole to other members in the group. Simply categorizing various informational requests that Cole received and then allocating ownership of these informational or decision domains to other executives served to both unburden Cole and make the overall network more responsive and robust.

Just as important, the social network analysis helped to identify highly peripheral people who essentially represented untapped expertise and thus underutilized resources for the group. In particular, it became apparent that many of the senior people had become too removed from the day-to-day operations of this group. For example, Figure 5.2 reveals that the most senior person (Jones) was one of the most peripheral in the informal network. This is a common finding. As people move higher within an organization, their work begins to entail more administrative tasks that make them both less accessible and less knowledgeable about the day-to-day work of their subordinates. However, in this case our debrief session indicated that Jones had become too removed, and his lack of responsiveness frequently held the entire network back when important decisions needed to be made. In this case, the social network diagram helped to make what could have been a potentially difficult conversation with this executive non-confrontational, and resulted in more of his time being committed back to the group.

Finally, the social network analysis demonstrated the extent to which the production division (the subgroup on the top of the diagram) had become separated from the overall network. Several months before this analysis, these people had been physically moved to a different floor in the building. Upon reviewing the network diagram, many of the executives realized that this physical separation had resulted in loss of a lot of the serendipitous meetings that occurred when they were co-located. In this case, the executives decided that they needed to introduce more structured meetings to compensate for this recent loss of serendipitous communication (and they also adopted an instant messaging system to promote communication).

Beyond Information Flow

In addition to mapping information flow, we also use social network analysis to assess the relational characteristics of *knowledge, access, engagement,* and *safety* among a group. Sometimes, if we have only mapped an information network and find that certain people are not as connected as they should be, it is difficult to tell what to do. Simply proposing more or better communication is the oldest consulting recommendation in the book—and no one today really needs more meetings. By analyzing the dimensions of relationships that precede or lead to effective knowledge sharing, we can offer more precise ways to improve a network's ability to create and share knowledge. For example, if it is discovered that the *knowledge* network is sparse, it might make sense to consider a skill profiling system or new staffing practices—technical and social interventions designed to help a network know what it knows. In contrast, if the *access* network is sparse, then it might make sense to consider peer feedback or technical means of connecting distributed workers (e.g., video conferencing or instant messaging) to make sure that people within the network have access to each other in a timely fashion.

Throughout our research we have found organizations employing various practices to promote these relational dimensions in important networks. We have summarized some of these initiatives in Box 5.1 and now turn to specific case examples where we used social network analysis to assess these relational dimensions.

Knowledge Dimension: Do We Know What We Know? Other people can only be useful to us in solving problems if we have some awareness of their expertise. Even if we are wrong, our initial perception will determine whether and how we turn to them for information when faced with a new problem or opportunity. The managers we interviewed in the first phase of our research reported that people they turned to for information provided a critical extension to their own knowledge when the manager had at least a semi-accurate understanding of her or his contact's expertise. As a result, assessing this relational knowledge of "who knows what" at a network level provides insight into the potential for members of a network to be able to tap others with relevant expertise when faced with a new problem or opportunity.

Supporting New Product Development

For example, we analyzed a network of immunologists in a Fortune 250 pharmaceutical company. By virtue of effectively integrating highly specialized knowledge in the drug development process, this group of people held the potential to provide strategic advantage to the organization. However, they also dealt with many impediments to effective collaboration, in that they were dispersed across five geographic sites and four hierarchical levels and attempting to integrate very different kinds of expertise. One telling view of this network emerged when we mapped the *knowledge* relation to get a better understanding of who understood and valued other people's expertise in this group.

What we found was that the *knowledge* network was very sparse compared with others that we had seen, indicating that an impediment to this group effectively creating and sharing knowledge was that they did not know what each other knew. Two characteristics of this group seemed to result in the sparse pattern. First, the group was physically dispersed, which precluded serendipitous interactions that help people learn colleagues' expertise and skills. Second, the group housed deep specialists who often struggled to find overlap with their colleagues. Stories emerging in interviews indicated that even when there were opportunities to incorporate each other's expertise, this was often not done, because one group of specialists did not know enough about what another group did to be able to "see" a way to involve them in projects.

Conducting the social network analysis provided several intervention opportunities. A facilitated session with leaders allowed them to assess and discuss the relative isolation of the specialties, as well as more pointed concerns about certain

BOX 5.1 Initiatives Promoting Knowledge Sharing in Human Networks

Knowledge Dimension: Do we know what we know?
- British Telecommunication's global effort to expand product lines and services was hampered because all of its six industry sectors were acting as silos. Employees in one industry sector were not aware of the knowledge and expertise of employees in the other sectors. To overcome this lack of awareness, they introduced virtual communities of practice that were connected through the Knowledge Interchange Network (KIN). This increased awareness of experts via the distributed technology and improved cross-sector collaboration.
- IBM Global Services, the management consulting division of IBM, has a strategic drive to ensure that the best expertise is brought to bear on client projects. To help employees better understand "who knows what" in this complex and distributed workforce, they have adopted Tacit Systems EKG profiling system. This technology actively mines e-mail (that the employees permit the system to assess) and distributed databases to categorize kinds of knowledge that are being requested/shared and by whom. Though limited to electronic communications, the system is then able to generate and make available a profile of an employee's expertise that others in the organization can then seek out as necessary.
- Recently the World Bank made a strategic decision to reposition itself away from being a lending organization to being a provider of knowledge and services (a "Knowledge Bank"). In order for its employees to meet the needs of its member organizations, it was necessary to increase awareness of the expertise throughout the organization. A critical step in this process has been to hold regular Knowledge Fairs, where people from each department and/or thematic group set up booths which inform others of their expertise. This helps to increase people's awareness of the experience of employees throughout the Bank.

Access Dimension: Can we access what we know in a sufficiently timely fashion?
- Alcoa, the world's leading producer of aluminum, wanted to improve access between its senior executives. When designing their new headquarters they focused on open offices, family-style kitchens in the center of each floor and plenty of open spaces. Previously, top executives would only interact with a couple of people in the elevator and those they had scheduled meetings with. Now, executives bump into each other more often and are more accessible for serendipitous conversations. This change in space has increased general accessibility as well narrowed the gap between top executives and employees.
- Shearman & Sterling, a top New York law firm, wanted to make its attorneys more accessible to each other in order to use the full expertise of staff on client cases. They implemented Same Time, an instant messaging system, throughout the organization. This quickly began to overcome barriers of physical distance that often precluded serendipitous interaction. It also allowed

(continued)

eys to send messages to each other while simultaneously being on conference calls with opposing counsel. The increased accessibility of their attorneys meant that the firm's human capital could be more effectively used.

- IBM Global Services has incorporated knowledge creation, sharing and reuse measurements into performance metrics. Performance metrics and incentives, particularly at the executive rank, have driven collaborative behavior into the day-to-day work practices of executive networks. Further, knowledge sharing has been incorporated into personal business commitments, which are required for certification and affect promotion decisions. This encourages employees at all levels to be collaborative with and accessible to each other.

members' expertise not being tapped while other members appeared to be bottle-necks in sharing information. As a result of the discussion around this social network, various changes were made to the group's operations. First, a variety of internal projects—ranging from process improvement to a project tracking data-base—were jointly staffed with people from various locations. This forced people to work together and so begin to develop an appreciation of each other's unique skills and knowledge. Second, several new communication forums were created—including weekly status calls, a short update e-mail done weekly and a project tracking database that helped each person keep up to date on what other members of the group were doing. Finally, some simple changes in project management practices and restructuring of the project leaders' responsibilities helped people to connect around them.

Facilitating Merger Integration

In another scenario we assessed the top leadership network of a Fortune 250 organization (i.e., top 126 executives of this conglomerate). This was an organization that had grown by acquisition over the course of several years, with the strategic intent that acquired companies would combine their expertise in developing and taking to market new products and services. The chief executive officer (CEO) of this organization had become acutely aware of the need to create a leadership network that knew enough of what others in the conglomerate knew to be able to combine the appropriate resources in response to new opportunities. As there was some evidence that this was not happening, he asked us to conduct a social network analysis of his top executives across these acquired organizations.

Mapping information flow among these executives showed that there was only limited collaborative activity in pockets of the organization, and that in general this lack of collaboration was a product of people not knowing what other people knew. In fact, we found that the problem was so significant that a key executive would not only indicate that he or she did not know what a specific person in another division did, but also that the executive did not even know what that division did. Despite alignment of the organization's formal structure, this lack of collective awareness of "who knows what" was having a significant impact on the organization's ability to execute strategically.

Two interventions were undertaken to begin helping to integrate this group. First, on a technical front, a customized technology was introduced for this group that combined a skill-profiling system with a new collaborative environment where executives posted project information. This system was quickly used, as the CEO pushed people into adopting it and also made it the primary forum by which these executives began to get information they needed to run their business. In addition, action learning sets were employed on internal projects. People from across these divisions were staffed together on small teams that each attacked a given project, but did so with reflective exercises, as the point of the initiative was both to solve problems for the company and to create connections across the executive team.

Creating Awareness of "Who Knows What"

Overall, we are finding that it is important for organizations to pay attention to how strategic networks of employees develop an understanding of their collective knowledge. In more staid times, working relationships developed as a product of interaction over longer time periods. This is not so in today's business environment. Given the rapid turnover many companies experience today, it is important to find ways to help people become better connected so the organization can get the true benefit of their expertise more quickly. This is often a process that can be improved by focusing on the way that new people are brought into a group. Generally what most organizations do when hiring a new person is to hold orientation courses that teach the person about the computer system, benefits and, perhaps, some homilies about the culture and history of the company. It is rare to find practices that teach the group what the newcomers know. This is a critical shortcoming in increasingly project-based work, where people will be brought into the center of the network primarily as a result of what other people understand about their expertise and so how to tap them when new problems or opportunities arise.

However, knowingly or unknowingly, some organizations we worked with were employing different mechanisms that built this awareness of "who knows what." For example, on a technical front many organizations are implementing skill-profiling systems or corporate yellow pages. On an organizational front, organizations such as the World Bank have organized their employees into thematic groups that have Help Desks whom anyone connected with the organization can contact. The individuals staffing the Help Desks are able to route people to others within the thematic group who have expertise on a particular subject. Other companies and government organizations have regular Knowledge Fairs where teams, communities or departments can set up a booth and distribute information about the expertise that they have. Although this has limited scope, it has proven effective in increasing awareness of the projects and knowledge activities taking place within the different departments and communities of the organization.

Access Dimension: Can We Access What We Know in a Sufficiently Timely Fashion?
Of course knowing that someone else knows something of relevance does little
good if we cannot gain access to their thinking in a timely fashion. Critical issues
on which we may turn to others for help or advice often require turnaround
within increasingly tight time frames. As with the *knowledge* dimension, we have
found it helpful to map the *access* relation at a network level to understand who
is able to reach whom in a sufficiently timely fashion.

Assessing Access in a Global Consulting Practice

We conducted a network analysis of the global consumer goods practice within a
major consulting firm. One of the more telling networks in this analysis was the
diagram reflecting who was sufficiently accessible to whom among this group of
46 people spread through Europe and the U.S. Despite the entire practice reporting
to one overall partner and being subject to a common strategy, performance measurement, and reward practices, we found significant clustering in the network
when we assessed who was accessible to whom. The social network analysis of
accessibility showed three tightly knit groups rather than one integrated network—two in North America and one in Europe—that were all highly centralized
around different partners. In fact, only three employees served to bridge these
fiefdoms, and these were not the people in charge of the group. Rather, they had
been through rotating work assignments and so developed relations with many
others in the network.

A first intervention for this organization was reconsidering staffing practices to
help integrate people from the different locations on both client projects and internal initiatives. A key concern lay with developing relationships throughout the
overall practice to improve knowledge sharing and the location of relevant expertise for both sales efforts and client engagements. Further, increasing overall connection within the network also reduced the extent to which the practice was
exposed by the potential for any of these three central people leaving. In this and
many other examples, we have consistently found that a network view makes it
clear that, should certain central people in a network leave, they take more than
just what they know—they also fundamentally affect the connectivity of the entire
group.

The two groups in the U.S. represented another challenge for management. It
turned out that the majority of people in these two groups not only had offices in
the same building, but also were interspersed along the same corridor. What we
discovered in interviews was a political problem that had emerged and resulted
in tensions between two subgroups. While management had suspected there were
problems, the visual representation of the network diagram clearly showed the
extent to which these issues were impeding the ability of the overall group to
effectively leverage the expertise of its members. Various steps were taken to help
resolve the problem including: executive coaching, revised performance management practices, and an extensive off-site planning session and organizational development (OD) interventions to help the group integrate.

Accessibility after a Transition to Teams

Reorganizations often shift the location and concurrently the accessibility of specific expertise. For example, we worked with one commercial lending organization in a transition from a functional to a team-based structure. To minimize inefficiencies resulting from cross-functional hand-offs in the commercial lending process, the organization shifted to a team-based structure that colocated lenders, analysts, and servicers in industry teams. Before the transition, these groups had been housed together on different floors and so were able to tap into each other's functional knowledge with relative ease. With the redesign, it was far more difficult for inexperienced people to learn the basics of their function and also for experienced lenders and analysts to engage in collaborative problem-solving efforts on the more creative aspects of commercial lending (e.g., structuring a specific transaction).

Social network analysis showed that four months after the transition to teams, several key people had become significantly overburdened, as they were heavily sought out by both their past functional colleagues as well as their new team members. In particular, we found that the people who were reputed experts in their area were tapped for advice to such an extent that they were falling behind on their own work. While in the functional department these interactions were more controlled and observable, in the team-based environment it was difficult for management to see how instrumental these opinion leaders really were to the success of the whole system. In fact, from a cursory review of their individual performance metrics (e.g., loans serviced or loans booked) these people experienced a fairly significant decline in productivity. Further, the longer hours that these people were working, in tandem with declining individual performance metrics that influenced their bonus calculations, served to undermine their own morale. As a result of these findings, several steps were taken—such as new staffing practices, better orientation materials (to help bring new people up to speed more effectively), and a reallocation of tasks within teams.

Managing Accessibility

Through the course of our research we have found that many organizations struggle with the notion of accessibility as people increasingly work from diverse locations. By and large, most solutions that companies considered were technical in nature and included such things as e-mail, asynchronous and synchronous collaborative environments, video conferencing, and instant messaging. However, we generally find that organizational design considerations and cultural norms are the more powerful indicators of who is accessible to whom.

Performance management systems promoting individualistic behaviors seem to be one of the primary drivers of sparse, disconnected networks. Further, though more of a trait of organizational culture, we often find that hierarchy has a marked impact on who is able to access whom. Again, this is a telling indicator for organizations trying to become more flexible and effective at information sharing.

Some organizations have taken interesting steps to promote access across hier-archy, such as making knowledge sharing a part of the mission or code of ethics. At Buckman Laboratories, all associates are empowered to speak with any asso-ciate at any level, and this is supported by a communication technology that gives each employee access to all other employees. Others are beginning to turn to creative uses of physical space to promote both intentional and serendipitous in-teractions among high-end knowledge workers. For example, Chrysler has gone full circle (from dispersion back to co-location) by recently bringing all the people involved in new car development into one building so that they can have face-to-face access to each other.

Engagement Dimension: How Do We Improve Engagement in Problem Solving? One of the most interesting findings from our interviews with the forty managers in the first phase of our research was the importance of the person sought out for infor-mation being willing to cognitively engage with the information seeker. People who were willing to engage in problem solving helped seekers to create knowledge with sufficient understanding and clarity that they could take action on it. And when we say engaging in problem solving, we do not mean a significant time investment on the part of the person sought out. Rather, we mean a simple two-step behavior whereby those contacted for information first ensured that they understood the other person's problem, and then actively shaped what they knew to the problem at hand. In short, these people taught rather than dumped infor-mation on the seeker—a behavior that if developed among a network can improve the effectiveness with which people learn from each other.

Integrating Specialized Expertise in Problem Solving

We conducted one network analysis of a specialist group supporting the internal knowledge management efforts of a global computer manufacturer. This group of 18 people was a virtual team that had been formed to combine expertise in both the technical and organizational/strategic aspects of knowledge management. While members of the group claimed to know and have access to each other's expertise, a quick review of the *engagement* network showed that in fact the group was having little success in integrating their expertise. Rather, what became ap-parent was a strong split in the network because of unique skill bases.

Despite people technically knowing at a high level what the skills and knowl-edge of people in the other discipline were, there were only two connections be-tween the two groups on the *engagement* relation. This clustering was a significant concern, as it is in engagement in problem solving that true learning takes place and people effectively integrate specialized expertise in projects—rather than just doing what they know or have done before. Interviews revealed that each group's depth of specialization and the fact that they were virtual and so had little slack, face-to-face time to interact made it difficult for them to find common ground. Aside from the leader of the group, who had experience with both subgroups, there was little common language or occupational values that existed between the two subgroups.

Several organizational learning interventions have been undertaken in this group to help build engagement and trust. As always, a key component of these interventions has been the use of various network diagrams in facilitated sessions to help the group create common awareness and make sense of productive and unproductive dynamics. Further, a shift in performance measurement was made to encourage joint problem solving and de-emphasize individual project metrics. While in the midst of these initiatives, the group plans to periodically assess the *engagement* network and intervene as appropriate to improve their operations over time.

Supporting Engagement of Specialists in New Product Development

In another scenario, we conducted a network analysis of 78 members of a drug development community of practice. The community, which was geographically dispersed across eight sites in the U.S. and Europe, included people from the drug discovery stage all the way to clinical development. The analysis indicated that within this highly dispersed community there were many people who did not know each other. It also became apparent that, although the people within each functional unit engaged with each other on matters relevant to the community, there was little engagement between the functions. This was a critical problem for this group, given the need to combine unique expertise to effectively develop and market a specific drug.

Further, the network proved to be highly centralized around a few individuals. The six most central people resided in the main U.S. site. Although they had many connections to people within the site, they did not engage as often with community members in the European locations. There were also several people who were totally disconnected from the group, which resulted in their skills and expertise being lost to the community. In this instance, a new collaborative technology was introduced that had both synchronous and asynchronous features. Second, different project management practices and a new role within the community were initiated to help bridge functional areas of expertise. Finally, the network diagrams were used to convince management to support staged face-to-face forums focusing on specific problems. These forums helped the different functional areas find common ground, while solving problems critical to the success of a project.

Engagement in Human Networks

Overall, as with the access dimension, we found that many of the things organizations were doing that had an impact on engagement were technical in nature and included synchronous technologies such as VP Buddy, Same Time, or white boarding applications that allow for dispersed engagement in a common problem. In many ways, instant messaging does seem to support the serendipitous kinds of interactions that are lost when employees are not co-located. However, there are limitations in the ability of these applications to richly convey knowledge across media that provide relatively few cues in comparison to face-to-face interactions. Videoconferencing for visual interaction between people in different locations does seem to help. This has been particularly important at British Petroleum, where experts have been able to assist technicians who are working on oil rigs thousands of miles away.

British Petroleum is also unique in its recognition of the importance of engagement in problem solving early in projects where learning from others' experiences can have a disproportionate impact on the trajectory and success of a project. For example, BP has instituted a peer review process in its drilling initiatives as an effective way to tap into others' knowledge. Before engaging in any significant task, the individual or group invites peers to provide input. Because the focus is performance, those with the most relevant knowledge and recent experiences are tapped to participate. Through this peer review process not only is performance on the task at hand improved, but also people become much more aware of the unique skills and abilities of others. This creates a natural reason for meeting and developing the needed norms of reciprocity and trust that make engagement and sharing of expertise a natural process.

Safety Dimension: How Do We Promote Safety in Relationships? Finally, the managers we interviewed in the first phase of our research indicated that safe relationships offered certain advantages in problem solving. First, they provided more learning, as people were not overly concerned about admitting a lack of knowledge or expertise. Asking someone for help often requires that the seeker have some degree of trust in the person sought out for information. Such trust often shapes the extent to which people will be forthcoming about their lack of knowledge, as defensive behaviors can knowingly and unknowingly block learning in critical interactions. Second, several of the managers indicated that in more safe relationships they could be more creative. An important feature of these relationships was that they were more willing to take risks with their ideas and felt that this often resulted in more creative solutions.

Safety Promotes Learning in High-End Knowledge Work

Social network analysis provides us with a means of understanding the extent to which information and knowledge seeking is a safe behavior in important groups. For example, we assessed the safety network in the information resources group supporting a key research and development function of a Fortune 500 manufacturing organization. This group of 34 people was composed of two organizational units that had recently been merged under one leader. The *safety* network represented an interesting point of intervention here because, unlike many networks we have seen, the *knowledge, access,* and *engagement* networks were all very well connected, whereas the safety network was not.

Interestingly enough, the *safety* network split into two groups that reflected the two departments that had been merged several months before this analysis. This is a common finding in both restructuring and merger scenarios. We often have found that communication networks (i.e., network diagrams developed from asking people who they typically communicate with) form quickly in restructuring or merger scenarios. However, what simply assessing communication patterns obscures is the time and effort that must be put into developing trust among a group, if we truly want people to learn from each other. Safety is important and highly predictive of who is sought out when one engages in problem solving and so exposes a lack of knowledge or allows someone else to shape the course of a solution. Relationships that are safe, and therefore useful for deeper levels of knowledge sharing and true learning, take time to develop.

In this specific network analysis, there were two interesting points. First, two people who were low in the hierarchy had become important ambassadors between the groups. Several amusing anecdotes were discovered in our interviews, whereby people that were senior in this group often went to these more junior people when they needed information from a colleague in the other subgroup. A light-hearted but very effective intervention was created by using these anecdotes along with the network diagram in a facilitated session debriefing the overall group. Playfully illuminating the way in which members of each group had stereotyped the other, and the inefficiencies that this caused, resulted in a productive discussion of a potentially charged issue.

Second, there were different levels of safety between the two groups. In part this seemed to be a product of the physical environment, as the more tightly connected group had all worked in an open space environment that allowed frequent, face-to-face communication. We also found that leadership style differed in the two groups before the restructuring. In general, creating a greater degree of safety within networks of relationships is often a product of leadership style and organizational (or sometimes occupational) culture. The behaviors that leaders exhibit and those they reward shape the extent to which people will be forthcoming about their lack of knowledge on various topics. This varied widely by organization. In some, safety was never considered a concern, because it was an accepted norm to doggedly seek out the most relevant knowledge for the success of a given project. In others, safety was a critical concern, and employees were very cautious about exposing a lack of knowledge.

Just as important, our interviews indicated that relationships need time and some space (physical, cognitive and social) to develop a sense of safety. Although communication technologies such as e-mail are helpful in maintaining relationships, when creating relationships we have found that it is important to increase the opportunity for face-to-face interactions between people. For example, though often chided, organizations that have instigated a program of brown bag lunches find that this process is effective for the development of safe relationships between people. One organization we worked with encouraged face-to-face contact by monthly meetings between different groups of researchers. These meetings consisted of a discussion session in the morning and a working session in the laboratory in the afternoon and allowed for a free flow of ideas within the context of a real working environment.

A Combined Network View and Organizational Learning

In addition to looking at each of the networks individually, it is also instructive to assess the dimensions cumulatively to get a better understanding of a network's underlying learning potential. In doing this, we can analyze networks where pairs of relationships exist (e.g., both *knowledge* and *access*) or networks where all of the relationships exist (e.g., *knowledge, access, engagement,* and *safety*). For example, we conducted a social network analysis of 38 employees constituting the telecommunications consulting practice of a Big Five accountancy. We first assessed the *knowledge* network to better understand who in this network of people indicated that they knew and valued other's expertise. Though relatively sparse, we found that the *knowledge* network showed a healthy, integrated pattern without distinct subgroups. However, the network diagram took on added life when we also considered the *access* network, where each person rated his or her colleagues on the extent to which they were accessible in a timeframe sufficient to help solve problems. Ultimately, both *knowledge* and *access* relations must be present for information sharing in a group to be effective. By combining the networks from these two questions, we had a view of the potential of a person to obtain information from others when faced with a new problem or opportunity.

Several things were interesting in this network. First, we noticed a fairly marked decline in the number of connections among the group in comparison to the *knowledge* network. While many central people remained central, several people higher in the hierarchy shifted out to the periphery of the network. As people move higher in an organization, their work begins to entail more administrative tasks, which makes them both less accessible and less knowledgeable about the day-to-day work of their subordinates. What network analysis affords in this picture is an opportunity to assess whether those in positions of formal authority are sufficiently central to the flow of knowledge, as well as to identify those people that truly are influential knowledge brokers in the group.

The third question asked of the 38 consultants was who in the group they could count on to actively engage in problem solving. When the *engage* network was added we were assessing a network where a line was drawn between two people *only* if all three dimensions of a relationship existed (knowing what the other knows, having access to their thinking and being willing to engage in problem solving). With the addition of the engagement network, we found a significant decrease in connections, which is not trivial in terms of the network's ability to solve problems. As outlined in the initial interviews, it is often those people who are willing to engage in problem solving who help both create actionable knowledge (rather than information overload) and ensure that we are solving the right problem. The final question we asked of this consulting practice determined with whom each person felt safe discussing work-related issues. With the incorporation of the *safety* network there is very little change. This is because the *safety* network in this group was the densest of all the networks. Ultimately, this was a sound indicator of the culture of this group for knowledge creation, and is obviously not a place we would look to intervene. It is also important to note that based on our experiences, a dense safety network is not typical.

Interventions from a Combined Network View

Analyzing the combined network (i.e., *knowledge* + *access* + *engagement* + *safety*) provides a great deal of insight into who is critical as well as who is currently less utilized within a group in terms of knowledge creation and sharing. Understanding who is central to a group indicates people who might either be bottlenecks or highly valued knowledge resources upon whom the group is reliant. Only interviews providing an in depth understanding of a network can tell, but these people do pose interesting questions to management. Has the group become too reliant on these people should they decide to leave? Are these people hoarding information and so are bottlenecks in terms of the group's knowledge creation and sharing activities? In contrast, should these people be rewarded for the somewhat invisible role they play in supporting a group from a knowledge perspective?

If we discover that people are central in these networks for legitimate reasons, management has an opportunity to begin acknowledging the work that these people do for the group. In the words of one of the people central in the telecommunications practice, "I spend about an hour and a half every day responding to calls and other informational requests . . . [and] . . . none of that time gets seen in my performance metrics." Network analysis makes such interactions that are critical to a group visible, thus providing an opportunity for management to acknowledge these people and the critical role they play. For example, management might choose to better support knowledge creation and sharing by offering central people such things as:

- Monies for efforts that might stimulate knowledge flow in a group via face-to-face meetings, or to purchase technologies such as groupware.
- Cognitive and social space to allow room for both individual and collective creativity and bonding to occur.
- Executive focus such as rewarding or promoting network-enabling people to both acknowledge their efforts and signal the importance of this kind of work to others within the organization.

In addition to central or core individuals, we also find it important to better understand why some people are peripheral in these networks. It might be that people in these positions do not know what we thought they knew when hired. In these cases they are peripheral for a legitimate reason and so reflect development or re-staffing opportunities. Alternatively, it might be that these people are peripheral because they are relatively new and the organization's assimilation processes do little to help them integrate into a network of colleagues. The important feature of this combined network view is that we can isolate why people are peripheral. Being peripheral because one is inaccessible is a different coaching process than if one is not considered safe.

Finally, on a more conceptual level, the combined network view offers unique purchase on the elusive concept of organizational learning. Some have claimed that an organization has learned when, through its processing of information, its range of potential behaviors has changed. Thus, if we are interested in promoting an organization's ability to react to new opportunities, we need to account for the ways in which people in networks become able to leverage each others' knowledge. Changes in the knowledge, access, engagement, and safety relationships underlying a network's future information processing behavior provide one means of both descriptive and prescriptive traction on organizational learning. Organizations have often been claimed to be path-dependent or constrained by what they know. Such notions as absorptive capacity, core rigidities, or architectural knowledge have been claimed to lead to this path dependence over time. While critically important, this work has often been done at a level of abstraction that makes interventions questionable. In contrast, the combined view of these networks provides some idea as to precisely whose knowledge is primarily responsible for what a group is likely to learn over time.

Conclusion

A critical resource embedded within organizations is the knowledge that workers bring to work on a day-to-day basis. However, aside from human resource policies targeted to the attraction, development, and retention of identified valuable workers, there has been little effort put into systematic ways of working with the knowledge that is embedded in social networks. Given the extent to which people rely on their own knowledge and the knowledge of their contacts to solve problems, this is a significant shortcoming. By introducing social network analysis to understand how a given network of people create and share knowledge, we are able to make these interactions visible and so actionable.

In applying these ideas in various organizations, we have found it particularly important to identify points of knowledge creation and sharing within an organization that hold strategic relevance. Typical domains yielding benefit include senior management networks, communities of practice and collaborative initiatives such as new product development, R&D units, or joint ventures and alliances. It is particularly fruitful to map collaborative relationships that cross boundaries of some form. Such boundaries might be hierarchical, functional, geographical, or even organizational, as in joint venture or merger and acquisition scenarios. Understanding how knowledge flows (or more frequently does not flow) across these various boundaries within an organization can yield critical insight into where management should target efforts to promote collaboration that has a strategic payoff for the organization.

Selected Bibliography

Much of the emphasis on organizational knowledge today (at least in terms of practice) is focused on efforts to capture, screen, store and codify knowledge. To get a more popular view of what many organizations are doing under the rubric of knowledge management we suggest some of the following publications: T. Davenport & L. Prusak, *Working Knowledge* (Boston, MA: Harvard Business School Press, 1998); C. O'Dell & C. J. Grayson, *If Only We Knew What We Know* (New

York, NY: Free Press, 1998); T. Stewart, *Intellectual Capital: The New Wealth of Organizations* (New York, NY: Doubleday, 1997); and R. Ruggles, "The State of the Notion: Knowledge Management in Practice," *California Management Review*, 1998, 40(3), 80–89.

Of course, our own perspective is that knowledge embedded in human networks is too often overlooked in these initiatives. Two streams of literature heavily influenced our thinking here. First is the rich ethnographic evidence accumulating within the situated learning and community of practice traditions. This work is making clear the large degree to which people learn how to do their work not from impersonal sources of information but through interactions with other people. Some important work in this tradition includes: J. S. Brown & P. Duguid, "Organizational Learning and Communities-of-Practice: Toward a Unified View of Working, Learning and Innovation,"*Organization Science*, 1991, 2(1), 40–57; J. Brown & P. Duguid, *The Social Life of Information* (Cambridge, MA: Harvard Business School Press, 2000); J. Lave & E. Wenger, *Situated Learning: Legitimate Peripheral Participation* (Cambridge, UK: Cambridge University Press, 1991); J. Orr, *Talking about Machines* (Ithaca, NY: Cornell University Press, 1996); and E. Wenger, *Communities of Practice* (Oxford, UK: Oxford University Press, 1998).

The second stream of literature influential in our thinking came from the social network tradition, which has also shown, with very different methods, the extent to which information that affects what we do largely comes from other people. Some important works on how social networks influence information flow and diffusion in networks include: G. Simmel, *The Sociology of Georg Simmel* (New York, NY: Free Press, 1950); R. Burt, *Structural Holes* (Cambridge, MA: Harvard University Press, 1992); M. Granovetter, "The Strength of Weak Ties," *American Journal of Sociology*, 1973, 78, 1360–1380; T. Allen, *Managing the Flow of Technology* (Cambridge, MA: MIT Press, 1984); P. Monge & N. Contractor, "Emergence of Communication Networks," forthcoming in F. Jablin and L. Putnam (Eds.), *Handbook of Organizational Communication*, 22nd ed. (Thousand Oaks, CA: Sage); and E. Rogers, *Diffusion of Innovations*, 4th ed. (New York, NY: Free Press, 1995).

Note

1 Total sources exceed the number of interviews because several respondents indicated more than one critical source of information. In this case, prior material included computer or paper files or archives that the interviewees had used in prior projects.

6

Making Invisible Work Visible: Using Social Network Analysis to Support Strategic Collaboration

ROB CROSS
STEPHEN P. BORGATTI
ANDREW PARKER

Over the past decade, significant restructuring efforts have resulted in organizations with fewer hierarchical levels and more permeable internal and external boundaries. A by-product of these restructuring efforts is that coordination and work increasingly occur through informal networks of relationships rather than through channels tightly prescribed by formal reporting structures or detailed work processes. For example, informal networks cutting across core work processes or holding together new product development initiatives are not found on formal organizational charts. However, these networks often promote organizational flexibility, innovation, and efficiency as well as quality of products or services by virtue of effectively pooling unique expertise. Supporting collaboration and work in these informal networks is increasingly important for organizations competing on knowledge and an ability to innovate and adapt.

Unfortunately, critical informal networks often compete with and are fragmented by such aspects of organizations as formal structure, work processes, geophic dispersion, human resource practices, leadership style, and culture. This is particularly problematic in knowledge-intensive settings where management is counting on collaboration among employees with different types of expertise. People rely very heavily on their network of relationships to find information and solve problems—one of the most consistent findings in the social science literature is that who you know often has a great deal to do with what you come to know.[1] Yet both practical experience and scholarly research indicate significant difficulty in getting people with different expertise, backgrounds, and problem-solving styles to effectively integrate their unique perspectives.[2] Simply moving boxes on an organizational chart is not sufficient to ensure effective collaboration among high-end knowledge workers.

Movement toward de-layered, flexible organizations and emphasis on support-ing collaboration in knowledge-intensive work has made it increasingly important for executives and managers to attend to informal networks within their organi-zations. Performance implications of effective informal networks can be significant as the rapidly growing social capital tradition has indicated at the individual, team, and organizational levels.[3] Yet while research indicates ways managers can influ-ence informal networks at both the individual[4] and whole network levels,[5] exec-utives seem to do relatively little to assess and support critical, but often invisible, informal networks in organizations.[6]

Over the past eighteen months, we have conducted research to determine how organizations can better support work occurring in informal networks of employ-ees. Working with a consortium of *Fortune 500* companies and government agen-cies, we assessed collaboration and work in over 40 informal networks from 23 different organizations. In all cases, the networks we studied provided strategic and operational value to the embedding organization by enabling employees to effectively collaborate and integrate disparate expertise. The first goal of our re-search was to better define scenarios where conducting a social network analysis (SNA) would likely yield sufficient benefit to justify the investment of time and energy on the part of the organization. A second goal of our work was to develop generalized insight into analyses that were informative and actionable for prac-titioners.

Assessing and Supporting Informal Networks

Put an organizational chart in front of most any employee and they will tell you the boxes and lines only partially reflect the way work gets done in their orga-nization. Informal relationships among employees are often far more reflective of the way work happens in an organization than relationships established by po-sition within the formal structure. However, these informal relationships are often invisible or at least only partially understood by managers—a problem that is growing with de-layering of organizations, virtual work, and globalization. While managers often think they understand the networks around them, studies show that they can vary widely in the accuracy of their network perceptions.[7] As out-lined by Krackhardt and Hansen: "Although managers may be able to diagram accurately the social links of the five or six people closest to them, their assump-tions about employees outside their immediate circle are usually off the mark."[8]

Social network analysis can be an invaluable tool for systematically assessing and then intervening at critical points within an informal network. Of course, social network techniques have been around for some time. The idea of drawing a picture (called a "sociogram") of who is connected to whom for a specific set of people is credited to Dr. J. L. Moreno, an early social psychologist who envisioned mapping the entire population of New York City.[9] Cultural anthropologists inde-pendently invented the notion of social networks to provide a new way to think about social structure and the concepts of role and position,[10] an approach that culminated in rigorous algebraic treatments of kinship systems.[11] At the same time, in mathematics, the nascent field of graph theory began to grow rapidly, providing the underpinnings for the analytical techniques of modern SNA.[12] The new methods were particularly embraced in sociology, where relational theoretical perspectives had been important since the dawn of the field.[13]

Today, the scholarly discipline is growing in the field of management as researchers have clearly demonstrated the extent to which informal networks pervade and affect life and work within organizations.[14] A particularly important line of inquiry in this work has been to understand forces influencing the emergence of informal networks within organizations.[15] Through such work we have learned that communication is likely to occur in homophilous[16] relationships and have evidence of the role of similarity between people in increasing the likelihood of communication.[17] At the same time, we have also learned that design of an organization can have a strong influence on the pattern of informal networks via formal structure,[18] physical proximity,[19] and nature of the task.[20]

This and other research has begun to help us think about means of assessing and supporting informal networks within organizations. Yet while clearly informing the field of management, the majority of this work is found in academic outlets often inaccessible to practitioners due to the technical nature of the publications and network terminology employed. In addition, these pieces intend to advance science and so do not as a matter of practice make clear to managers the ways in which network analysis can be applied to organizational issues. While the outcomes of such research might influence decision makers in terms of policy variables, a more contextualized perspective is needed to help practitioners apply network analysis to their specific organizational concerns.

At the most rudimentary level, we have found that visually assessing the pattern of relationships that hold a certain group together can reveal a number of interesting and actionable points. For example, identifying people that are highly central in networks (and so disproportionately impact a group by controlling information or decision making) can help a manager consider how to reallocate informational domains or decision-making rights so that the group as a whole is more effective. Alternatively, understanding who is peripheral in a network and crafting ways to engage these people is also an important means of ensuring that expertise resident in a given network is being effectively utilized. Particularly in high turnover situations, it is increasingly important to get people connected more and more quickly so that they are productive for an organization. Furthermore, assessing junctures in networks that are fragmented across functional or hierarchical boundaries (or detecting sub-groups) can be particularly informative for social or technical interventions that help to integrate disparate groups.[21]

While social network information can be obtained in a variety of ways, the most pragmatic means in organizational settings is typically through surveys. Very informative social network diagrams can be generated from 10–15 minute surveys assessing information or knowledge flow among members of a group. In this process, the first step is to identify an informal network where effective collaboration and knowledge sharing has a significant impact on the organization's operations or strategy. Often, these groups do not appear on a formal organizational chart, yet their ability to collaborate and pool disparate expertise is critical to the current and future success of an organization. As a result, in the first stages of an SNA it is often important to push executives beyond groups defined by the formal organizational chart to those that might cross functional or hierarchical boundaries (e.g., new product development, communities of practice, or top leadership networks). These groups often go unrecognized and unsupported even when their interactions underlie organizational capabilities or support strategically important innovation.

Conducting a social network survey is a straightforward process of obtaining a list of all people in the defined network and simply asking all members of the group to characterize their relationship with each other. In this process, it is important to ensure that the kinds of relationships measured are appropriate for the task at hand and not unnecessarily inflammatory. Organizations are very different in their tolerance for disclosure of various kinds of social relations. In some, we have been asked to map relationships of trust and power, while in others we have been asked to disguise names on all relationship diagrams (including more innocuous ones such as who works with whom). One of the most powerful ways to apply SNA as a diagnostic tool and a catalyst for change is to put people's names on a network diagram and make the diagram available to all group members as a basis for dialogue. However, such diagrams can be sensitive, depending on the kinds of network questions asked and the culture of the specific organization. As a result, we pay considerable attention to shaping the questions asked so that they are helpful to the specific issue an organization is grappling with while at the same time not unnecessarily disruptive to existing relationships.

As a guide, we have outlined several important relationships and reasons for targeting these relationships in the Appendix. The primary focus of our research lay with establishing applications of SNA as a diagnostic tool for managers attempting to promote collaboration and knowledge sharing in important networks. Through this process, we found SNA uniquely effective in:

- promoting effective collaboration within a strategically important group;
- supporting critical junctures in networks that cross functional, hierarchical, or geographic boundaries; and
- ensuring integration within groups following strategic restructuring initiatives.

Promoting Effective Collaboration within a Strategically Important Group

SNA can be a very effective tool for promoting collaboration and knowledge sharing within important groups such as core functions of an organization, research and development departments, and strategic business units. For example, in one global consulting organization, we worked with a highly skilled group that was commissioned to provide thought leadership and specialized support to the organization's knowledge management consultants. This group was composed of people with either advanced degrees or extensive industry experience in strategy and organizational design or technical fields such as data warehousing or information architecture. By integrating these highly specialized skill sets, leadership of the consultancy felt the firm could provide a holistic knowledge management solution that would differentiate it from competitors focusing on solely technical or organizational solutions. However, the partner leading this group felt intuitively that the team was not leveraging its abilities as effectively as possible and asked us to conduct an SNA of information flow within the group.

Our analysis confirmed the partner's intuition. As shown in the top half of Figure 6.1 the information-sharing network revealed not one group at all, but two distinct sub-groups. Interestingly enough, the network had become divided on precisely the dimension it needed to be connected, as it was the group's unique skill sets that turned out to account for the fragmentation of this network. The group on the left side of the network was skilled in the "softer" issues of strategy or organizational design, often focusing on cultural interventions or other aspects of organizations to help improve knowledge creation and sharing. The group on the right was composed of people skilled in "harder" technical aspects of knowledge management, such as information architecture, modeling, and data warehousing.

Over time, members of these two sub-groups had gravitated to each other based on common interests. These people often worked on projects together and just as importantly shared common work-related interests in terms of what they read, conference attendance, and working groups within the organization. The problem was that each sub-group had grown to a point of not knowing what people in the other sub-group could do in a consulting engagement or how to think about involving them in their projects. Thus, even when there were opportunities in client engagements to incorporate each other's skill sets, this was often not done because neither group knew what the other knew or how to apply their skill sets to new opportunities. This was despite the fact that the group's strategic charter was to integrate these unique skill sets and that all aspects of formal organizational design supported this mission (e.g., reporting structure, common performance metrics and incentives).

Conducting the SNA provided several intervention opportunities. A lengthy facilitated session with this group allowed them to assess and discuss the relative isolation of the two specialties as well as more pointed concerns about certain members' expertise not being tapped while other members appeared to be bottlenecks in sharing information. As a result of the discussion around this social network, various changes were made to the group's operations. First, a variety of internal projects—ranging from white papers to development of a project-tracking database—were jointly staffed with one person from each group. This forced people to work together and so begin to develop an appreciation of each other's unique skills and knowledge. Second, the partner implemented mixed revenue sales goals so that each of the managers was accountable for selling projects that included both a technical and an organizational component. This also forced people to find ways to integrate their approaches to addressing client problems. Finally, several new communication forums were created—including weekly status calls, a short update e-mail done weekly, and a project-tracking database that helped each person keep up to date on what other members were doing.

Pre-Intervention

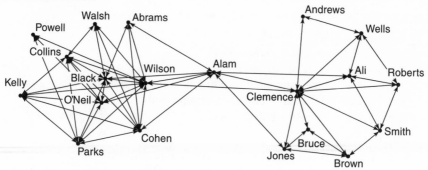

Post-Intervention (Nine Months Later)

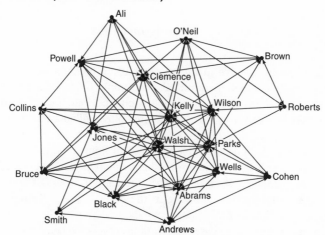

Figure 6.1 Information sharing with an expert consulting group (names have been disguised at the request of the organization).

The result of these interventions was significant. Over the course of the next several months, the group began to sell more work that integrated technical and organizational skills. Importantly, this integration often proved to differentiate the consultancy from their competition in the sales process. Further, as can be seen in the bottom half of Figure 6.1, a network analysis conducted nine months later revealed a well-integrated group that was sharing information much more effectively.

In this case, the underlying problem was that each sub-group had grown to a point of not knowing what the other group knew (and so how to even consider integrating their expertise in projects). As a result, the interventions undertaken focused on helping to develop this awareness and not simply implementing a collaborative technology or group process intervention that ultimately would not have addressed the underlying need to create an awareness of each other's expertise. Other common factors fragmenting networks include:

- hierarchical leadership style;
- physical dispersion and virtual work;
- politics resulting in sub-groups;
- "not invented here" mentality resulting in networks with dense sub-groups only weakly connected to other sub-groups; and
- workflow processes or job descriptions that overload specific roles and slow the group.

Each of these issues demands a different set of interventions; however, social network analysis, combined with some interviews, makes these interactions visible, allowing for a diagnosis and an appropriate solution.

Supporting Critical Junctures in Networks That Cross Boundaries

SNA can also be an effective means of pinpointing breakdowns in informal networks that cross functional, hierarchical, geographic, or organizational boundaries (e.g., merger or acquisition scenarios, new product development or top leadership networks). People within these networks must often collaborate effectively for the organization to benefit despite the fact that they may reside in different physical locations and/or be held accountable for different financial and operational goals. SNA provides insight into collaborative behavior within and across boundaries that can yield a similar purchase on performance improvement opportunities as process mapping did for reengineering in the early 1990s.[22] Reengineering generally focused on "hand-offs," decision points, and the "white space" in organizational charts to improve efficiency of work processes. Today, concern has shifted to innovation that often requires critical collaboration within and between functional units, divisions, and even entire organizations. Network analysis provides us with the means to understand where collaboration is and is not occurring.

Collaboration across Functional Boundaries

For example, we mapped the relationships of one *Fortune 500* organization's top 126 executives to assess collaboration across divisions. This was an organization that had grown by acquisition over several years with the primary intent that acquired companies would combine their expertise in developing and taking to market new products and services. The CEO of this organization had become acutely aware of the need to create a leadership network that was able to recognize opportunities in one sphere of the network and know enough of what others in the conglomerate knew to be able to combine the appropriate resources in response to these opportunities. As there was some evidence that this was not happening, we were invited to come in and conduct an SNA of his top executives both within and across these acquired organizations.

While various network diagrams were generated in our assessment, the most insightful view came from a simple table demonstrating collaborative activity among this network of executives. Table 6.1 outlines the percentage of collaborative relationships that existed within and between each specific division (out of 100% possible in each cell). Looking at the table provided an opportunity to learn from practices within one division and apply these practices in others where the work of each division required similar levels of collaboration. Similarly, we were also able to determine which of the merged organizations (termed divisions in Table 6.1) had integrated well with other divisions. For example, a quick review of Table 6.1 shows that Divisions 3 and 4 had a relatively high degree of collaboration, whereas Divisions 1 and 7 had minimal contact.[23]

This simple summary of collaborative activity within and between divisions provided a great deal of insight into the inner-workings of the organization. The company had acquired various organizations with the intent that they collaborate in bringing their offerings to market. However, the SNA showed that there was only limited collaborative activity in pockets of the organization. Various reasons existed for this. In some settings, members of the executive team were not sure what a given division did and so did not know how to even think about involving them in their projects. In others, cultural barriers restricted people from seeking information outside of their own division. In some, the complementarity of product offerings that was presumed when an acquisition was made did not exist. As a result, different interventions were applied as appropriate throughout the network; however, it was the view of collaborative activity afforded by the SNA that allowed the organization to intervene appropriately at these strategic junctures.

Throughout the organizations we worked with in our research we found this kind of cross-boundary view powerful for identifying points where collaborative activity is not occurring due to organizational boundaries and providing a more targeted approach to interventions. It is important to recognize that it is often not the case that you want high collaborative activity among all departments within an organization. People have a finite amount of time to put into developing and maintaining relationships. With network analysis, we can begin to take a portfolio approach to considering the constellation of relationships that is worth investing

Table 6.1 Collaboration across Merged Divisions within a Conglomerate

	Div. 1	Div. 2	Div. 3	Div. 4	Div. 5	Div. 6	Div. 7	Div. 8
Division 1	33%							
Division 2	5%	76%						
Division 3	11%	18%	45%					
Division 4	2%	11%	21%	38%				
Division 5	6%	7%	12%	6%	75%			
Division 6	7%	2%	13%	7%	2%	76%		
Division 7	1%	3%	16%	6%	8%	2%	36%	
Division 8	10%	2%	9%	6%	3%	10%	0%	90%

time and energy to develop and maintain. For example, in the disguised scenario outlined above, it was not critical that Division 1 be tightly connected to all other divisions to help the organization meet strategic objectives. To provide strategic value to the organization, Division 1 really only needed to be well connected to Divisions 3, 5, and 6. Thus, rather than engage in a company-wide initiative to improve collaboration, more targeted and ultimately more successful interventions were employed to facilitate collaboration at specific junctures.

Mapping the pattern of information flow (or, more frequently, lack of flow) across functional barriers can yield critical insight into where management should target efforts to promote collaboration that will provide strategic benefit. Quite often, initiatives attempting to promote collaboration and learning take a cultural perspective and usually struggle with the enormity of the task at hand. In contrast, we have found that by targeting junctures in networks that hold strategic relevance for an organization, it is much more feasible to intervene where investments in collaboration yield strategic payoff for the organization. Moreover, by tracking changes in networks over time, management and network participants have a very real way of assessing the impact of interventions on both the informal network and organizational effectiveness.

Collaboration across Hierarchical Boundaries

Another type of critical boundary within organizations is not functional but hierarchical. Across the various companies in our research, we have seen very different network patterns in relation to hierarchy. Some organizations' informal networks are very similar to, and thus obviously constrained by, the organization's hierarchy. Others are more fluid and seem to place less of a constraint on whether employees follow the chain of command to obtain information. What is good or bad depends on the kind of work the organization does; however, it is interesting diagnostically to see the extent to which hierarchy conditions information flow and knowledge exchange in a given organization. Just as we analyzed collaboration across divisional boundaries in the conglomerate noted above, we can also assess collaboration and information sharing across hierarchical levels within an organization.

Alternatively, we can assess how those in positions of formal authority are embedded in larger networks within their organization. For example, we were asked to map the top leadership network of a commercial bank. However, rather than just mapping the top nine members of the management team, we looked at information-seeking and sharing behaviors among the top 62 executives of this organization (SVP level and above) to understand how this network was collaborating. One particularly informative view came from assessing the pattern of relationships *among* the top nine executives and then *between* these executives and the overall top 62 executives in the institution. By pulling out the top nine executives and mapping the flow of information among these executives, we could assess the extent to which this group was effectively collaborating as a decision-making body. Further, by considering this group in the context of the larger network of 62 people, we could also see the extent to which the executive team tapped into the larger leadership network for informational purposes or communicated decisions effectively back to this group. Figure 6.2 shows a simplified graphic portrayal of this network that identifies connections between the CEO and the remaining executives in both the executive leadership team and the bank's functional departments. In this diagram, the direction of the arrows reflects whom the CEO seeks out for information or advice and the numbers beside the arrows reflect the number of people in each department that the CEO turned to.

Diagnostically, these kinds of views are important along two fronts. First, by looking at a completed diagram showing the same relationship patterns for all members of the top management team, we can get a sense of how information tends to enter and leave this group. The bulk of information that managers use

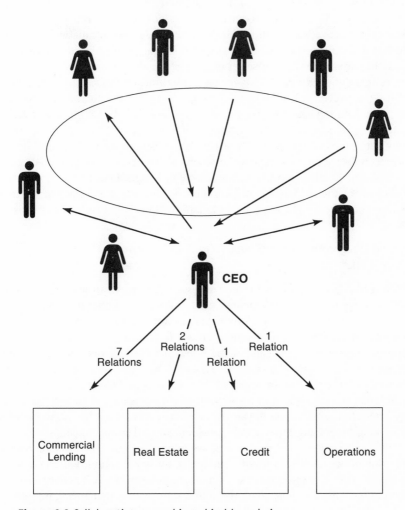

Figure 6.2 Collaboration across hierarchical boundaries.

to make decisions comes from meetings and conversations. SNA provides a way to better understand the way in which teams might be biased in critical decisions by virtue of the kinds of information received in discussions with others. Which members of the executive team seem to reach out to various functional areas (and so likely best understand issues and concerns of these groups)? Is the executive group seeking information from (or at least listening to) these people? Are certain functional departments more sought out than others (thereby potentially representing biases in information this group relies on for strategic decision-making)? Given the strategic importance of the decisions that a top management team makes, understanding their sources and usage of information can provide critical insight into ways to improve their effectiveness. This of course also holds for other groups such as new product development initiatives or process redesign efforts where one hopes that the teams are effectively reaching out to relevant and balanced sources of information prior to making critical decisions.

In terms of executive development, these kinds of views can also be highly effective in uncovering potential biases in a single person's network. A long-standing finding in communication research is that people tend to interact with people that are similar to themselves on a set of socially important attributes, such as race, gender, and age.[24] This makes communication easier and often more satisfying; however, it is also a source of bias in what executives learn and think is important. In the example above, it was apparent that the CEO heavily attended to and was influenced by the concerns of the commercial lending group where he spent the bulk of his career. In private conversations after reviewing this diagram, he reflected on what he felt were ineffective tendencies in his own decisions over time due in large part to the biased way he sought information from others. As a result of the SNA of his organization, he made more concerted efforts to balance whom he sought out for information within and outside of the bank.

Ensuring Integration within Groups Following Strategic Change Initiatives

SNA can also play a powerful role in assessing the health of informal structure after a change has been implemented such as an internal restructuring or acquisition. It is well known that performance does not always improve as anticipated even when technically sound solutions are implemented. Frequently, this problem is attributed either to a misalignment somewhere in the organization's formal structure or to a failure of leadership. However, we have consistently found that a lack of social, technical, or organizational support provided to strategically important informal networks is at least as important a predictor of failure. Very often, large-scale change initiatives impair the effectiveness of established networks while at the same time doing little to help development of new relationships.

SNA can be a very useful means of assessing the impact of strategic restructuring initiatives on the informal structure of an organization. For example, we conducted an SNA of the global telecommunications practice of a major consulting organization. This firm was going through a significant restructuring initiative to combine the expertise of several groups into one industry practice in order to compete more effectively with other major consulting organizations. By combining smaller practices into one global network, partners felt that the firm would be better able to provide the best and most directly relevant expertise for both sales initiatives and consulting engagements. Further, significant efficiency benefits were anticipated as consultants would be able to leverage the work of others in this practice rather than continually starting from scratch.

Of course, deriving these strategic benefits hinged on this group's willingness and ability to share information and leverage each other's expertise. Almost a year after the initial restructuring, the partner leading the practice had become increasingly concerned that the overall group was not integrating as effectively as it should. However, aside from some surface-level indicators of this problem based on sales and billable hour metrics, he had no true understanding of his practice's integration or where to begin in terms of corrective action. The practice was globally distributed and of such size that he had never even had the opportunity to meet many of the people. To get a better understanding of this network, he invited us in to conduct an SNA.

Our SNA revealed fragmentation of the network and provided some useful insights and information to work with in helping integrate his practice. What we immediately noticed was significant clustering in the network despite the entire practice reporting to one overall partner and being embedded within a common organizational context (i.e., strategy, performance metrics, technical infrastructure). As can be seen in Figure 6.3, we found three tightly knit sub-groups rather than one integrated network—two in North America and one in Europe. In fact, apart from the partner, only a handful of hierarchically lower-level employees served to bridge these sub-groups because they had developed relationships when staffed on projects together.

A first intervention for this partner was to use the network diagram to create common awareness of the lack of integration among the leaders of this practice. One of the more important benefits of SNA is that it helps to make visible, and therefore actionable, ways that work is occurring within organizations. We have worked with global groups ranging up to almost 300 people with only three or four levels of hierarchy. Clearly, the span of control combined with the physical dispersion of such groups makes it close to impossible for any one person or group of people to know what is going on or how executive decisions are affecting the work and effectiveness of these networks. SNA provides a snapshot for executives that can be used to gain agreement on what problems need to be addressed in such a distributed group, what appropriate interventions need to be taken, and also provides the ability to conduct a follow-up network analysis to ensure that interventions are having the desired impact.

In this case, though formal aspects of the organization were aligned, we learned that there were no initiatives in place to help employees learn others' expertise. As a result, the organization took a number of steps to help build this awareness of "who knows what." First, they redesigned their approach to staffing both client projects and internal initiatives to help integrate people from the different locations. On a technical front, they implemented a skill-profiling system and a virtual environment to promote collaboration on consulting engagements. On a social

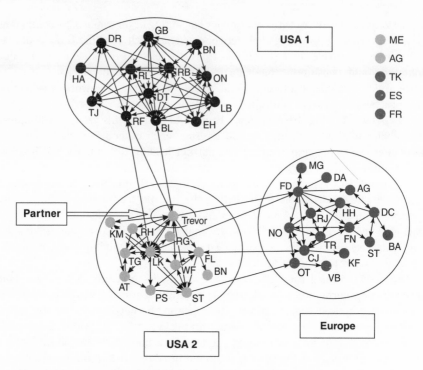

Figure 6.3 Information sharing in a global consulting practice.

front, a series of face-to-face meetings were conducted to help people meet and learn the projects that other people were working on and the expertise that they held. This was critical to the group's integration as it was not until people actually met face to face that the skill-profiling system began to be used. Finally, a shift in skills targeted in recruiting as well as performance measurement was made to encourage joint problem solving and de-emphasize individual expertise and task accomplishment.

The two groups in the U.S. represented another challenge for management. It turned out that the majority of people in these two groups not only had offices in the same building, but were interspersed along the same corridor. What we discovered in interviews was a political problem that had emerged and resulted in tensions between two sub-groups. While the partner leading the practice knew there were problems, the visual representation of the network diagram clearly showed the extent to which these issues were impeding the overall network. Various steps were taken to help resolve the problem, including: executive coaching, revised performance management practices, and an extensive off-site planning session with organizational development interventions to help the group integrate.

In addition to altering various aspects of organizational design, other more pointed interventions unfolded with various people in the network, depending on whether they were highly central or highly peripheral. For example, central people were interviewed to see if certain aspects of their job could be parceled out to others so that they were not over-burdened and in danger of becoming a bottle-neck. Alternatively, various approaches were taken with peripheral people to help get them integrated more effectively (depending on the specific issue that seemed to result in their being peripheral). A driving concern was to help develop relationships throughout the overall practice to improve knowledge sharing and the location of relevant expertise for both sales efforts and client engage-ments. Increasing connection within the network also reduced the extent to which the practice was exposed by the potential of central people leaving. In this and many other examples, we consistently find that a network view makes it clear that should certain central people in a network leave, they take more than just what they know, they also fundamentally affect the connectivity of the entire group.

Lessons from the Field

Throughout our research, we have consistently found SNA a powerful managerial tool largely because it makes visible the patterns of information sharing within and across strategically important networks. Simply reviewing these diagrams with managers usually results in myriad recommendations, as people immersed in the patterns of relationships define and resolve issues affecting group perfor-mance. In short, a picture really is worth a thousand words. Using social network diagrams as prompts in facilitated sessions can serve to identify issues that are currently hindering a group and the specific behaviors and organizational design elements requiring modification to improve group efficiency and effectiveness. Rich discussions will often evolve simply by showing network diagrams to the members of a group and asking them to diagnose the patterns they see, as well as the issues facilitating or impeding their effectiveness. Often this process simultaneously cre-ates common awareness of problems, helps define solutions, and gains agreement on actions—all critical steps to effecting organizational change.

We have consistently found it important for groups to identify and work with people who are highly central. Often these people are central for legitimate rea-sons, based on, for example, workflow demands or unique expertise that a person brings to bear. Alternatively, we also find people who are central and affecting an overall network's effectiveness by virtue of either becoming over-burdened by their job or having a tendency to hoard information. Network diagrams can help de-termine who these people are and what might be done to both allow other con-nections and work to occur around them as well as protect the organization should these people decide to go elsewhere.

It is just as important to use the network diagrams (or metrics) to identify peripheral people and find ways to improve their connection where appropriate. These people are often under-utilized by the group and are also frequently at the highest risk for turnover. Given the difficulty in attracting and retaining talented employees today, we have found it highly important to find ways to move people into the central part of the network more quickly. Unfortunately, it is rare to find practices where a new person has systematic opportunities to know what other people know in the organization and almost unheard of to find practices that teach the group what new individuals know. This is a critical shortcoming because as work becomes increasingly project-based, people are being drawn into the center of networks primarily as a result of what central people understand about their knowledge and skills when new opportunities arise.

We have also found social network diagrams to be a powerful tool for individuals to actively shape their personal networks. While certain managerial decisions and actions can be important to facilitate development of a network, an equally critical means of effecting change is for each person in the network to actively work on improving their own connectivity. Where possible, a key component of our debriefing sessions focuses on getting people to use the network diagrams to assess the effectiveness of their personal network along two dimensions. First, in terms of composition, we focus on the diversity within each person's network (e.g., "Do you rely too heavily on people from a specific functional area, a hierarchical level, or those that are simply closest to you?"). Second, in terms of content, we focus on the resources that people derive from these relationships (e.g., career advice, information, or other resources). Focusing on these two issues generally helps people recognize a need to invest in the development of specific kinds of relationships (and often times reduce an investment being made in existing relationships).

Of course, social network analysis is not a cure—all. In our experience, it is important to be cautious about over-correcting with groups. One organization we worked with believed that a group of research scientists would function more efficiently if there were greater interaction across geographical regions. As a result, they put in place several interventions to ensure that members of the department worked more closely with people in other locations within the organization. After we performed the network analysis, we noticed that as a whole the department had integrated very well across the various geographical locations but functional units within the department were not well connected with each other despite sometimes being in the same building. This over-correction had resulted in a series of effectiveness and efficiency problems for the group. Thus, as managers consider interventions, it is important to take a balanced approach and always realize that improving some connections likely takes time away from the development and maintenance of others. People have only so much relational energy to expend.

Conclusion

In today's fast-paced knowledge-intensive economy, work of importance is increasingly accomplished collaboratively through informal networks. As a result, assessing and supporting strategically important informal networks in organizations can yield substantial performance benefits. In addition, network relationships are critical anchoring points for employees, whose loyalty and commitment may be more to sets of individuals in their network than to a given organization. Our research (and that of others) has found that these informal networks are increasingly important contributors to employee job satisfaction and performance. Yet despite their importance, these networks are rarely well-supported or even understood by the organizations in which they are embedded. Social network analysis provides a means with which to identify and assess the health of strategically important networks within an organization. By making visible these otherwise "invisible" patterns of interaction, it becomes possible to work with important groups to facilitate effective collaboration.

Perhaps just as importantly, social network diagrams often serve to focus executive attention on informal networks that can be critical to organizational effectiveness. Scarce resources—ranging from funding and technology support on the one hand to executive recognition on the other—tend to go to those units that can be found on an organizational chart. Despite often not being reflective of how work is done, organizational charts and reporting relationships are the agreed on currency of executive decision makers and their trusted advisors. Network diagrams, such as the ones shown here, can be very compelling tools with which to re-focus executive attention on how organizational design decisions and leadership behaviors affect the relationships and information flows that are at the heart of how work is done. Our research has consistently shown that while social relationships cannot be mandated by management, they are strongly affected by elements under management control, such as hierarchical levels, horizontal departments, office location, project staffing, and so on. With social network analysis, managers have a means of assessing the effects of decisions on the social fabric of the organization.

APPENDIX

Table 6.2 Collecting Network Data: Some Questions to Ask

If Trying to Discover . . .	These Kinds of Questions Can Help . . .
Communication Network—The informal structure of an organization as represented in ongoing patterns of interaction, either in general or with respect to a given issue. *Rationale*—To understand the informal structure. It can be particularly helpful to identify sub-groups or cliques that might represent political problems or individual roles in these networks such as highly central parties, isolates, and bottlenecks.	• How often do you talk with the following people regarding (topic x)? • How much do you typically communicate with each person relative to others in the group?
Information Network—Who goes to whom for advice on work-related matters. *Rationale*—Just assessing who communicates with whom does not guarantee that the interactions reflect exchanges of information important to do one's work. Particularly in efforts that require a collective to effectively pool its knowledge (e.g., new product development), it is important to understand the effectiveness with which a group traffics in information.	• How frequently have you acquired information necessary to do your work from this person in the past month? • Information I receive from this person is useful in helping to get my work done. • Who do you typically seek work-related information from? • Who do you typically give work-related information to?
Problem-Solving Network—Who goes to whom to engage in dialogue that helps people solve problems at work. *Rationale*—Interactions with other people help us think about important dimensions of problems we are trying to solve or consequences of actions we are considering. Strong problem-solving networks often ensure that people are solving the right problem, thus improving both individual and network performance.	• Who do you typically turn to for help in thinking through a new or challenging problem at work? • How effective is each person listed below in helping you to think through new or challenging problems at work?
Know Network—Who is aware of whose knowledge and skills. *Rationale*—Awareness of what someone else knows dictates whether and for what problems you are likely to turn to them for help. Strong knowledge networks are an essential basis for strong information networks.	• How well do you understand this person's knowledge and skills?
Access Network—Who has access to whose knowledge and expertise. *Rationale*—Just knowing someone has relevant information or knowledge does not guarantee that they will share it with you in a way that is helpful. A strong access network is often critical to ensuring effective information sharing and problem solving in a sufficiently timely fashion.	• When I need information or advice, this person is generally accessible to me within a sufficient amount of time to help me solve my problem.

Notes

1 For example, research has shown that relationships are critical for obtaining information, learning how to do your work, and collectively solving cognitively complex tasks. For "obtaining information," see, for example, G. Simmel, *The Sociology of Georg Simmel,* translated by K. H. Wolff (New York, NY: Free Press, 1923, 1950); M. Granovetter, "The Strength of Weak Ties," *American Journal of Sociology.* 78 (1973): 1360–1380; T. Allen, *Managing the Flow of Technology* (Cambridge, MA: MIT Press, 1977); R. Burt, *Structural Holes* (Cambridge, MA: Harvard University Press, 1992); E. Rogers, *Diffusion of Innovations,* 4th edition (New York, NY: Free Press, 1995); G. Szulanski, "Exploring Internal Stickiness: Impediments to the Transfer of Best Practices within the Firm," *Strategic Management Journal,* 17 (Winter 1996, Special Issue): 27–43. For "learning how to do your work," see, for example, J. Lave and E. Wenger. *Situated Learning: Legitimate Peripheral Participation* (Cambridge: Cambridge University Press, 1991); J. S. Brown and P. Duguid, "Organizational Learning and Communities-of-Practice: Toward a Unified View of Working, Learning and Innovation," *Organization Science,* 2/1 (1991): 40–57; J. S. Brown and P. Duguid, *The Social Life of Information* (Cambridge, MA: Harvard Business School Press, 2000); J. E. Orr, *Talking about Machines* (Ithaca, NY: Cornell University Press, 1996); E. Wenger, *Communities of Practice* (Oxford: Oxford University Press, 1998); E. Wenger and W. Snyder, "Communities of Practice: The Organizational Frontier," *Harvard Business Review,* 78/1 (January/February 2000): 139–145. For "collectively solving cognitively complex tasks," see, for example, K. Weick and K. Roberts, "Collective Mind in Organizations: Heedful Interrelating on Flight Decks," *Administrative Science Quarterly,* 38/3 (September 1993): 357–381; E. Hutchins, "Organizing Work by Adaptation," *Organization Science,* 2/1 (January/February 1991): 14–29; R. Moreland, L. Argote, and R. Krishnan, "Socially Shared Cognition at Work: Transactive Memory and Group Performance," in J. Nye and A. Brower, eds., *What's Social about Social Cognition* (Thousand Oaks, CA: Sage, 1996); A. Hollingshead, "Retrieval Processes in Transactive Memory Systems," *Journal of Personality and Social Psychology,* 74/3 (1998): 659–671.

2 It is one problem to learn or act on knowledge with others who think like you (such as in a community of practice); however, it is an entirely different problem to do this in diverse social contexts, such as cross-functional teams, where people often do not share a common vision, language, metrics of performance, or even understanding of the problem itself. For example, sociologists have poignantly demonstrated how correct information can have little or no impact on critical decision processes. I. Janis, *Groupthink: Psychological Studies of Policy Decisions and Fiascoes* (Boston, MA: Houghton Mifflin, 1982); C. Perrow, *Complex Organizations: A Critical Essay* (New York, NY: McGraw-Hill, 1986); D. Vaughn, *The Challenger Launch Decision: Risky Technology, Culture and Deviance at NASA* (Chicago, IL: University of Chicago Press, 1996). Further, organizational theorists have shown that a person's knowledge can be role constrained (J. March and J. Olsen; "The Uncertainty of the Past: Organizational Learning under Ambiguity," *European Journal of Political Research,* 3 [1975]: 147–171; B. T. Pentland, "Organizing Moves in Software Support Hot Lines," *Administrative Science Quarterly,* 37/4 [1992]: 527–548) or not acted upon due to motivational or cognitive impediments resulting from introducing knowledge into diverse social contexts (D. Dougherty, "Interpretive Barriers to Successful Product Innovation in Large Firms," *Organization Science,* 3/2 [1992]: 179–202; C. M. Fiol, "Consensus, Diversity and Learning in Organizations," *Organization Science,* 5/3 [May/June 1994]; R. J. Boland, Jr., and V. T. Ramkirshnan, "Perspective Making and Perspective Taking in

Communities of Knowing," *Organization Science*, 6/4 (July/August 1995): 350–372; Szulanski, op. cit.).

3 See, for example, J. Coleman, "Social Capital in the Creation of Human Capital," *American Journal of Sociology*, 94 (1988): S95–S120; R. Burt (1992), op. cit; R. Burt, "The Contingent Value of Social Capital," *Administrative Science Quarterly*, 42/2 (June 1997): 339–365; M. Hansen, "The Search-Transfer Problem: The Role of Weak Ties in Sharing Knowledge across Organization Sub-Units," *Administrative Science Quarterly*, 44/1 (March 1999): 82–111; J. Podolny and J. Baron, "Resources and Relationships: Social Networks and Mobility in the Workplace," *American Sociological Review*, 62/5 (October 1997): 673–693; J. Nahapiet and S. Ghoshal, "Social Capital, Intellectual Capital, and the Creation of Value in Firms," *Academy of Management Review*, 23/2 (April 1998): 242–266; R. Leenders and S. Gabbay, *Corporate Social Capital and Liability* (Boston, MA: Kluwer, 1999); D. Cohen and L. Prusak, *In Good Company: How Social Capital Makes Organizations Work* (Boston: MA. Harvard Business School Press, 2000); N. Lin, *Social Capital: A Theory of Social Structure and Action* (Cambridge: Cambridge University Press, 2001).

4 W. Baker, *Networking Smart: How to Build Relationships for Personal and Organizational Success* (New York, NY: McGraw-Hill, 1994); W. Baker, *Achieving Success through Social Capital* (San Francisco, CA: Jossey-Bass, 2000).

5 See, for example, D. Krackhardt, "The Strength of Strong Ties: The Importance of *Philos* in Organizations," in N. Nohria and R. Eccles, eds., *Networks and Organizations: Structure, Form, and Action* (Boston, MA: Harvard Business School Press, 1992); D. Krackhardt, "Constraints on the Interactive Organization as an Ideal Type," in C. Heckscher and A. Donnellon, eds., *The Post-Bureaucratic Organization: New Perspectives on Organizational Change* (Thousand Oaks, CA: Sage Publications, 1994); D. Krackhardt and J. R. Hanson, "Informal Networks: The Company behind the Chart," *Harvard Business Review*, 71/4 (July/August 1993): 104–111.

6 To be sure, academics and practitioners have discussed shifts to network forms via mechanisms such as joint ventures, partnerships, strategic alliances, and R&D consortia for some time now. (R. Miles and C. Snow, "Network Organizations: New Concepts for New Forms," *California Management Review*, 28/3 [Spring 1986]: 62–73; R. Miles and C. Snow, *Fit, Failure, and the Hall of Fame* [New York, NY: Free Press, 1994]; R. Miles and C. Snow, "The New Network Firm: A Spherical Structure Built on a Human Investment Policy," *Organizational Dynamics*, 23/4 [Spring 1995]: 4–18; C. Handy, *The Age of Paradox* [Boston, MA: Harvard Business School Press, 1994]; C. Heckscher, "Defining the Post-Bureaucratic Type," in C. Heckscher and A. Donnellon, eds., *The Post-Bureaucratic Organization: New Perspectives on Organizational Change* [Thousand Oaks, CA: Sage, 1994]; J. Galbraith, *Designing Organizations: An Executive Briefing on Strategy, Structure, and Process* [San Francisco, CA: Jossey-Bass, 1995].) Such forms are presumed to allow for the effective integration of knowledge and capabilities across organizational entities. However, there has been much less practical attention paid to how informal networks of employees in either traditional or networked organizations facilitate or impede organizational effectiveness.

7 See, for example, D. Krackhardt, "Cognitive Social Structures," *Social Networks*, 9 (1987): 109–134; D. Krackhardt, "Assessing the Political Landscape: Structure, Cognition, and Power in Organizations," *Administrative Science Quarterly*, 35/2 (June 1990): 342–369; T. Casciaro, "Seeing Things Clearly: Social Structure, Personality, and Accuracy in Social Network Perception," *Social Networks*, 20 (1998): 331–351.

8 D. Krackhardt and J. R. Hanson, "Informal Networks: The Company behind the Chart," *Harvard Business Review*, 71/4 (July/August 1993): 104–111, at p. 104.

9 J. L. Moreno, *Who Shall Survive?* (Washington, DC: Nervous and Mental Disease Publishing Company, 1934).

10 S. F. Nadel, *The Theory of Social Structure* (New York, NY: Free Press, 1957); J. C. Mitchell, "The Concept and Use of Social Networks," in J. Clyde Mitchell, ed., *Social Networks in Urban Situations* (Manchester: Manchester University Press, 1969).

11 H. C. White, *An Anatomy of Kinship* (Englewood Cliffs, NJ: Prentice-Hall, 1963); J. P. Boyd, "The Algebra of Group Kinship," *Journal of Mathematical Psychology*, 6 (1969): 139–167.

12 F. Harary, *Graph Theory* (Reading, MA: Addison-Wesley, 1969).

13 E. Durkheim, *The Division of Labor in Society*, translated by G. Simpson (New York, NY: Free Press, 1893, 1933); G. Simmel, *Conflict and Web of Group Affiliations*, translated by K. H. Wolff and R. Bendix (New York, NY: Free Press, 1922, 1955).

14 See, for example, J. Lincoln, "Intra- and Interorganizational Networks," in Samuel B. Bacharach, ed., *Perspectives in Organizational Sociology* (Greenwich, CT: JAI Press, 1982), pp. 1–38; B. Wellman and S. D. Berkowitz, *Social Structures: A Network Approach* (Greenwich, CT: JAI Press, 1997); N. Nohria and R. G. Eccles, eds., *Networks in Organizations: Structure, Form, and Action* (Boston: MA: Harvard Business School Press, 1992); S. Andrews and D. Knoke, eds., *Networks in and around Organizations, Research in the Sociology of Organizations*, 16 (Stamford, CT: JAI Press, 1999).

15 P. R. Monge and E. M. Eisenberg, "Emergent Communication Networks," in F. Jablin, L. Putnam, K. Roberts, and L. Porter, eds., *Handbook of Organizational Communication* (Newbury Park, CA: Sage Publications, 1987); P. Monge and N. Contractor, "Dualisms in Leadership Research," in F. Jablin and L. Putnam, eds., *The New Handbook of Organizational Communication: Advances in Theory, Research, and Methods* (Thousand Oaks, CA: Sage, 2000).

16 Homophily refers to the extent to which communicating individuals are similar. P. Lazersfeld and R. Merton, "Friendship as a Social Process," in M. Berger, ed., *Freedom and Control in Modern Society* (New York, NY: Octagon, 1964).

17 See, for example, T. Zenger and B. Lawrence, "Organizational Demography: The Differential Effects of Age and Tenure Distributions on Technical Communication," *Academy of Management Journal*, 32/2 (June 1989): 353–376; H. Ibarra, "Homophily and Differential Returns: Sex Differences in Network Structure and Access in an Advertising Firm," *Administrative Science Quarterly*, 37/3 (September 1992): 422–447; H. Ibarra, "Race, Opportunity, and Diversity of Social Circles in Managerial Networks," *Academy of Management Journal*, 38/3 (June 1995): 673–703; M. McPherson, L. Smith-Lovin, and J. Cook, "Birds of a Feather: Homophily in Social Networks," *Annual Review of Sociology*, 27 (2001): 415–444.

18 See, for example, Lincoln, op. cit.; W. Stevenson. "Formal Structure and Networks of Interaction within Organizations," *Social Science Research*, 19 (1990): 113–131; W. B. Stevenson and M. Gilly, "Problem-Solving Networks in Organizations: Intentional Design and Emergent Structure," *Social Networks*, 22 (1993): 92–113; D. Brass, "Being in the Right Place: A Structural Analysis of Individual Influence in an Organization," *Administrative Science Quarterly*, 29/4 (December 1984): 518–539.

19 See, for example, Allen, op. cit.; P. Monge, L. Rothman, E. Eisenberg, K. Miller, and K. Kirste, "The Dynamics of Organizational Proximity," *Management Science*, 31/9 (September 1985): 1129–1141.

20 A. Bavelas, "Communication Patterns in Task-Oriented Groups," *Journal of Acoustical Society of America*, 22 (1950): 725–730; H. Leavitt, "Some Effects of Certain Communication Patterns on Group Performance," *Journal of Abnormal and Social Psychology*, 46 (1951): 38–50; M. Shaw, "Communication Networks," in L. Berko-

witz, ed., *Advances in Experimental Social Psychology* (New York, NY: Academic Press, 1964).

21 Social network researchers have also developed a wide range of quantitative analyses and tools for assessing networks. While beyond the scope of this chapter, readers interested in more depth on this front should turn to Scott or to Wasserman and Faust for an introductory treatment. J. Scott, *Social Network Analysis*, 2nd edition (Thousand Oaks, CA: Sage Publications, 2000); S. Wasserman and K. Faust, *Social Network Analysis: Methods and Applications* (Cambridge: Cambridge University Press, 1994).

22 G. Rummler and A. Brache, *Improving Performance: How to Manage the White Space on the Organization Chart* (San Francisco, CA: Jossey-Bass, 1990); M. Hammer and J. Champy, *Reengineering the Corporation: A Manifesto for Business Revolution* (New York, NY: HarperBusiness, 1993); M. Hammer and S. Stanton, *The Reengineering Revolution: A Handbook* (New York, NY: HarperBusiness, 1995).

23 A side benefit of our research program has been development of an extensive database that can be used for benchmarking purposes.

24 See, for example, P. Marsden, "Homogeneity in Confiding Relations," *Social Networks*, 10 (1988): 57–76; K. Carley, "A Theory of Group Stability," *American Sociological Review*, 56/3 (June 1991): 331–354; Ibarra (1992), op. cit.; Ibarra (1995), op. cit.; D. Brass, "A Social Network Perspective on Human Resources Management," *Research in Personnel and Human Resources Management*, 13 (1995): 39–79.

PART III
COMMUNITIES OF PRACTICE

Communities of practice are at the forefront of many organizations' knowledge management efforts. Spurred by the successes of companies such as Ford, British Petroleum, and Shell and government agencies such as the World Bank, many public and private entities have begun to recognize the importance of informal or semistructured groups of employees who regularly share knowledge with one another around a particular discipline or set of ideas. One of the early members of our Institute, Tom Boyle from British Telecom, once likened a successful community of practice to a small-town Irish pub—a central place where individuals with similar backgrounds (though potentially differing opinions) would come together to exchange information and build relationships. It is a place where "when you didn't show up—you were missed by others."

Like a good local watering hole, communities of practice require at least three critical resources: time for individuals to participate, space where people can engage one another, and passion around the various subjects of discussion. Without time, the community never has the opportunity to come together and build the social connections and develop a collective memory that members can draw from. Without a shared space, individuals spend more time and effort trying to locate other community members and their documents, thus wasting what precious free time they have available for interaction. Finally, without passion, individuals quickly lose the motivation necessary to go beyond their day-to-day tasks and extend themselves to a larger group of colleagues.

Our research on communities of practice has been an ongoing effort since the inception of our program in 1999. Our initial research has focused on five primary areas: the community's *development path, membership, activities, organizational support,* and *value.* One of our primary research thrusts was to understand how and why communities develop within organizations. Do they form as the result of formal intervention, or do they develop organically? Next we examined how communities gain critical mass through marketing and identifying potential individuals for membership. We explored why individuals choose to seek out others with similar interests and take valuable time and energy to learn from each other.

During our research, we have examined the activities that communities of practice engage in to ensure that knowledge is shared among the collective membership.

Another area of focus has been to understand how organizations can provide support and leverage for these informal communities. Organizations often find themselves in the precarious position of attempting to provide support for these communities of practice without trampling the independence that makes these informal groups ultimately successful. Finally, we have looked at the value that organizations can obtain from investing in communities. These benefits range from individual productivity gains to improvements in cost savings, revenue enhancements, and customer satisfaction.

From this research, we have selected two essays that reflect some of the lessons learned from working with communities of practice. In chapter 7, Eric Lesser and John Storck establish a link between the activities performed by communities of practice and the business outcomes that result from community interactions. Applying the underlying tenets of social capital theory, they posit that the activities undertaken by communities of practice help build connections, relationships, and common context between community members. For example, a community of software developers that we examined found that face-to-face meetings, supplemented by a Web site where they could post answers to questions and exchange documents, made it easier to share common programming modules and prevent re-creating existing software solutions. It is the development of social capital that, in turn, enables organizations to more effectively respond to customer issues, share relevant practices, develop ideas for new products and services, and decrease the learning curve of new employees. Using data from case studies developed from a variety of industries, the authors reinforce the importance of communities as an engine for producing social capital and highlight implications for managers who are looking to leverage these communities as a knowledge-sharing vehicle.

Whereas in chapter 7 Lesser and Storck focus primarily on the link between community activities and business value, chapter 8 addresses a particular type of support necessary to sustain the community. In chapter 8, Michael Fontaine examines the subject of community roles: what they are, how they work, and how they evolve over the life of the community. He also identifies the primary roles and responsibilities that enable communities, and the relative amount of time individuals spend performing these tasks. He suggests that community roles emerge depending upon the community's maturity level and the extent to which the community develops organically (what is referred to as a bottom-up approach) or is initiated by the formal organization (a top-down approach). Overall, this chapter highlights the importance of community roles as a key enabler to making communities run effectively.

While many organizations have focused attention on internal communities, others have extended their reach to support customer communities. Recognizing that customers often are interested in talking with others who have similar interests, several companies and public organizations have fostered communities by providing virtual spaces where customers can post messages for one another, direct questions to company experts, take online classes, and share similar experiences. In chapter 9, Eric Lesser and Michael Fontaine examine several of these customer communities, considering their different features, and the benefits they provide both to customers who participate in them and to the organizations that sponsor them. They find that customer communities can help organizations learn more about their customers' needs and preferences, reduce service costs, and provide a vehicle for improving brand loyalty.

Communities both inside and outside of organizations have one thing in common: passion around a specific topic or interest. Whether taking the time to share one's knowledge around a new chemical discovery during a brown-bag lunch or posting a recipe for a foolproof apple pie, communities require a level of commitment to a disciple and a willingness to help others. Our experience has shown repeatedly that organizations that can leverage this commitment, from either their employees or their customers, can improve their knowledge-sharing capabilities. By assembling the right ingredients, we believe that an organization can create the environment that allows communities to play an integral role in creating, sharing, and applying its knowledge resources.

7

Communities of Practice and Organizational Performance

ERIC L. LESSER
JOHN STORCK

Steve walked into the meeting room and quickly grabbed a seat. Having just recently joined the company, his boss had recommended that he attend this weekly lunchtime meeting of VisualBasic programmers. He felt it was a good way for Steve to get "plugged into" the company, and would give him an opportunity to see some of the projects that others, across the firm, were working on.

The meeting began with a series of short introductions around the table. Then, one of the senior designers, Cindy, plugged a laptop into the overhead projector and started demonstrating a new set of programming tools that had been developed by one of the company's strategic partners. Steve took notice of the extended functionality of some of the tools, and saw an opportunity to use it on one of the new projects he would be spending time on. At the end of the meeting, Steve walked up to Cindy and introduced himself. They spent another 20 minutes discussing the opportunity to use the tools on Steve's project and how Steve might be able to also use some existing code from one of Cindy's recent development efforts. After writing down Cindy's contact information on a napkin, he headed back to his office, thinking about this new course of action.

As organizations grow in size, geographical scope, and complexity, it is increasingly apparent that sponsorship and support of groups such as the one described above is a strategy to improve organizational performance. This kind of group has become known as a community of practice (CoP)—a group whose members regularly engage in sharing and learning, based on their common interests. One might think of a community of practice as a group of people playing in a field defined by the domain of skills and techniques over which the members of the group interact. Being on the field provides members with a sense of identity—both in the individual sense and in a contextual sense, that is, how the individual relates to the community as a whole.[1] A sense of identity is important because it determines how an individual directs his or her attention.[2] What one pays attention to is, in turn, a primary factor in learning. Therefore, identity shapes the learning process. The relationships within the community are enacted on the field, which provides an initial set of boundaries on the interactions among its members and on their goals. And, as with most field-based games, overall community welfare ultimately is more important than individual goals.

The playing field analogy is imperfect, however, for two reasons. First, in the "game" played on the field, the number of "players" is indeterminate. In fact, being able to maintain the community by bringing new members onto the field—

like the fictional programmer in the vignette above—is an important defining characteristic. New members build legitimacy through participating in learning interactions with other members of the community. The nature of participation must be engaging, although there is clearly room for what is called legitimate peripheral participation.[2] Indeed, peripheral members bringing new ideas can catalyze innovation. One usually thinks of face-to-face communication as the way that members of a community achieve the necessary level of engagement to develop their identities, relationships, and learn. In fact, most prior studies of the ways that people engage with each other have focused primarily on face-to-face communication. Nevertheless, there is nothing in the classical sociological definition of community of practice that rules out communication media such as e-mail, discussion groups, or chat rooms as support mechanisms for participating in distributed communities of practice.[3]

The second problem with the playing field analogy is that it can lead to thinking about communities as large, unstructured teams. The distinction between communities and teams sometimes leads to confusion. Storck and Hill[4] suggest that the differences between the two constructs can be characterized as follows:

1. Team relationships are established when the organization assigns people to be team members Community relationships are formed around practice.
2. Similarly, authority relationships within the team are organizationally determined. Authority relationships in a community of practice emerge through interaction around expertise.
3. Teams have goals, which are often established by people not on the team. Communities are only responsible to their members.
4. Teams rely on work and reporting processes that are organizationally defined. Communities develop their own processes.

Others tie the difference between teams and communities to the legitimizing process. In a team, legitimizing occurs principally through the assignment of formal roles and relationships (i.e., team membership and structure are defined external to the team). As indicated above, members of a community of practice establish their legitimacy through interaction about their practice.[3]

Communities of practice have previously been thought of as coming into existence when people interested in a common work-related area or in an avocation feel a need to share what they know and to learn from others. Professional associations, groups of software developers, and skilled craft guilds are examples of work-related communities of practice. Avocational examples range from communities of quilters to communities of rowers. In the past few years e-mail, electronic discussion groups, and electronic chat rooms have facilitated the development of communities of practice whose members are not all colocated. Regardless of the mode of interaction, the traditional notion of a community of practice is that it emerges from a work-related or interest-related field and that its members volunteer to join.[5]

In some organizations, the communities themselves are becoming recognized as valuable organizational assets. Whereas the value was previously seen as being relevant primarily to the individual members of a community, it is often now recognized that benefits can also accrue to the organization itself. Acknowledging that communities of practice affect performance is important in part because of their potential to overcome the inherent problems of a slow-moving traditional hierarchy in a fast-moving virtual economy. Communities also appear to be an effective way for organizations to handle unstructured problems and to share knowledge outside of the traditional structural boundaries. In addition; the community concept is acknowledged to be a means of developing and maintaining long-term organizational memory. These outcomes are an important, yet often unrecognized, supplement to the value that individual members of a community obtain in the form of enriched learning and higher motivation to apply what they learn.

Although we (and others, e.g., see notes 4, 6, and 7) assert that communities of practice create organizational value, there has been relatively little systematic study of the linkage between community outcomes and the underlying social mechanisms that are at work. The difficulty in assessing their contribution is that communities are often hidden assets, appearing neither on an organization chart nor on a balance sheet. To build understanding of how communities of practice create organizational value, we suggest thinking of a community as an engine for the development of social capital. We argue that the social capital resident in communities of practice leads to behavioral change—change that results in greater knowledge sharing, which in turn positively influences business performance.

The concept of social capital has been widely addressed in the sociology, political science, and economic development literatures.[8–13] More recently, a number of scholars have begun to apply social capital principles to a wide variety of business issues. These include understanding the development of intrafirm networks,[14] the formation of cross-organizational relationships in the biotechnologyindustry,[15] the success of firms within Silicon Valley,[16] the development of professional ethics in the legal profession,[17] and variations in managerial compensation.[18] In addition to scholarly journals, there have been a number of mainstream managerial books focused on the role of the individual[19] and the organization[20] in developing social capital. While there has been a plethora of definitions that describe this topic (see Note 21 for an extensive list), a useful framework for understanding social capital in a business context was developed by Janine Nahapiet at Oxford University and Sumantra Ghoshal at the London Business School. They define social capital as "the sum of the actual and potential resources embedded within, available through, and derived from the network of relationships possessed by an individual or social unit."[22] Further, they express social capital in terms of three primary dimensions:

- There must be a series of connections that individuals have to others. In other words, individuals must perceive themselves to be part of a network (the structural dimension).
- A sense of trust must be developed across these connections (one aspect of the relational dimension).

- The members of the network must have a common interest or share a common understanding of issues facing the organization (the cognitive dimension).

These conditions apply quite aptly to communities of practice. Thus, our hypothesis is that the vehicle through which communities are able to influence organizational performance is the development and maintenance of social capital among community members. By developing connections among practitioners who may or may not be colocated, fostering relationships that build a sense of trust and mutual obligation, and creating a common language and context that can be shared by community members, communities of practice serve as generators for social capital. This social capital, in turn, creates an environment in which business performance is positively impacted. Figure 7.1 illustrates this process. Our objective in this chapter is to demonstrate how the three dimensions of social capital provide a window into how communities create value.

The conclusions in this chapter are based on a study of seven companies in which communities of practice are acknowledged to be creating value. During the study, we focused on a number of critical questions, including, "What value do communities provide?" For each of the companies that participated in the study,

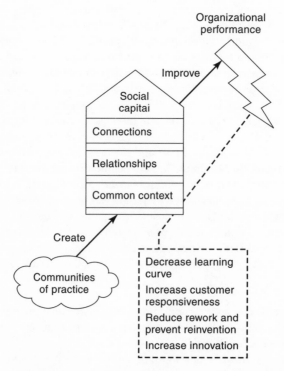

Figure 7.1 Communities of practice are linked to organizational performance through the dimensions of social capital.

we interviewed between five and ten members of existing communities of practice regarding their perceptions of value at both an individual and organizational level. The research team then developed a "mind map," which in turn led to the categorization scheme used to review the interview transcripts. From the categories, we abstracted the key sources of individual and organizational value.

The communities in this sample were identified jointly by the research team and the study participants, using our previously described definition of communities of practice as a guideline in selecting potential candidates. The CoPs we examined represent different stages of development, cross several industries, are both global and local in scope, and, most importantly, offer the opportunity to consider different kinds of contributions to organizational performance. Table 7.1 summarizes these characteristics.

We build on these examples to illustrate how each of the three dimensions of social capital relates to the creation of value by a community, with particular focus on outcomes that are a result of greater knowledge sharing and innovation. Finally, we conclude with a discussion of the linkage between the special kind of social capital represented by a community of practice and organizational performance.

Dimensions of Social Capital

Our sample of companies provides significant evidence that communities represent an important vehicle for developing social capital in organizations. Using Nahapiet and Ghoshal's framework, we can describe how the various activities that a community of practice undertakes influence the development of social capital's three key dimensions: structural, relational, and cognitive.

Structural Dimension

Fundamentally, the structural dimension of social capital refers to the ability of individuals to make connections to others within an organization. These connections, as Nahapiet and Ghoshal write, "constitute information channels that reduce the amount of time and investment required to gather information" (Note 22, p. 252). The communities of practice within our sample focused a significant amount of their resources and attention on making these connections between members using a number of different techniques.

One technique that was used to build ties between previously disconnected employees was the use of face-to-face meetings. In some situations, such as in the project manager and the software developer communities we examined, a kickoff meeting served as an initial venue to bring together similar individuals who were unfamiliar with one another. Other communities, such as that of the urban service specialists, sponsored a number of brown bag lunches to attract individuals who had a keen interest in the topic. Another technique that was also employed was the leveraging of information technology to make it easier for individuals to locate and contact fellow community members. For example, the repository used by the

Table 7.1 Communities studied

Organization	Community	Objectives	Community Activities	Key Value Outcomes
Multinational lending institution	Urban services specialists	Share experience and expertise across similar projects	• Held informal lunchtime seminars • Conducted formal training sessions • Facilitated Web site repository • Produced CD of relevant intellectual capital • Captured experiences of retiring practitioners in multimedia	• Faster project delivery • Greater reuse of intellectual capital developed by projects
Multinational lending institution	Land and real estate specialists	Share experience and expertise across similar projects	• Held informal lunchtime seminars • Conducted training sessions • Sponsored conferences with outside speakers • Facilitated Web site • Developed Web links to relevant outside content sources	• Faster project delivery • Greater reuse of intellectual capital developed by projects • Improved linkages to outside knowledge sources
Manufacturing company	Quality champions	Develop and exchange implementation and training techniques	• Held informal discussions among practitioners • Developed Web sites with relevant training material and advice	• Increased reuse of previously developed assets
Pharmaceutical firm	Research chemists	Share knowledge about a new industry development	• Held face-to-face discussions and meetings to share insights • Used video-conferencing to connect research labs • Maintained Web site, using one of the technologists as a webmaster	• Development of a new business capability based on advanced research techniques
Software development company	Programmers	Respond to needs for customization of a standard product	• Maintained internal listservs for individuals to post comments about modifications • Maintained Web site to support sharing of software components • Provided access to "spearhead" experts around the company	• Greater reuse of existing software assets • Increased innovation around new software products
Specialty chemical company	Researchers	Share and innovate new solutions to satisfy customer needs	• Maintained extensive discussion database where individuals can post and seek answers to customer problems	• Faster response time to customer problems • Greater linkage between customers

Organization	Community	Objectives	Community Activities	Key Value Outcomes
			• Employed knowledge brokers and editors to cull through discussion databases and identify frequently asked questions and other knowledge needs • Held informal "breakfast seminars" to share discoveries and engage other researchers in problem solving	and research staff in developing new solutions
Telecom company	Project managers	Transfer experience and techniques across industry groups	• Held initial face-to-face meeting with community members to outline community objectives and opportunities • Developed e-mail-based expert access/question-and-answer system to post and distribute inquiries	• Faster response to project bids and request for proposals • Greater reuse of existing knowledge assests

land and real estate specialists (see Table 7.1) identified experts, both inside and outside the organization, who could be valuable in addressing questions posed by community members. Also, both the e-mail system used by the telecommunications projects managers and the discussion database used by the researchers at the specialty chemical company gave community members the opportunity to "reveal" their expertise to others through answering posted questions.

Relational Dimension

Making connections through networking is one important component of building social capital. Another is the development of the interpersonal relationships that reinforce these initial connections between individuals. Nahapiet and Ghoshal suggest that there are four components to this relational dimension: obligations, norms, trust, and identification (note 22, p. 254). Obligations refer to a sense of mutual reciprocity, for example, the willingness to return a favor with a favor. Norms include the setting of common standards of behavior that individuals are willing to abide by. Trust involves the predictability of another person's actions in a given situation, whereas identification refers to the process whereby individuals see themselves as united with another person or set of individuals.

The data from the case studies suggest that communities of practice play an important role in influencing the relational dimension within an organization. Many of the face-to-face activities that were discussed earlier not only made it easier for individuals to identify others with similar interests, but also enabled individuals to develop a sense of empathy around common trials and tribulations. Face-to-face meetings not only built connections between community members, but also fostered access to more experienced practitioners that newer employees would be less likely to have. Given that the most knowledgeable practitioners often have the greatest demand on their time, community membership served as a selection mechanism for determining whom they were willing to spend time with.

Another mechanism that fostered a sense of mutual trust and obligation was the development of shared repositories and discussion databases that were actively managed by the community. In these shared spaces, individuals began to evaluate who was making contributions to the greater community knowledge pool, and they began to judge the willingness of others to share the documents, templates, and other similar knowledge artifacts.

Cognitive Dimension

In addition to connections and trust, the third important dimension of social capital is the development of shared context between two parties. As described by Nahapiet and Ghoshal, "To the extent that people share a common language, this facilitates their ability to gain access to people and their information. To the extent that their language and codes are different, this keeps people apart and restricts their access" (note 22, p. 253). This use of common language includes, but goes beyond languages, such as English, Spanish, Japanese, etc. It also addresses the acronyms, subtleties, and underlying assumptions that are the staples of day-to-day interactions. Further, this idea of a common context can also be extended to the use of shared narratives or stories that can enable individuals to make sense of their current work environment and their relative role within it.

Another activity that was useful in building shared context was the development of taxonomies within the common repositories managed by community members. Virtually all of the cases that we studied involved the development of some structured repository, where individual members could submit knowledge artifacts, such as research papers, presentations, and other forms of intellectual capital that could be reused by others. By classifying and organizing these documents within taxonomies where others could find materials, many of the communities helped establish a common mechanism for structuring and storing the collective memory of their members.

Linking Communities of Practice and Organizational Performance

As part of our research, the community members in our study suggested a number of different mechanisms in which communities of practice influenced business outcomes. Although many of these were tied to the specific business environment that each of the communities operated within, our analysis highlighted four areas of organizational performance that were impacted by the ongoing activities of communities of practice. These included:

- Decreasing the learning curve of new employees
- Responding more rapidly to customer needs and inquiries
- Reducing rework and preventing "reinvention of the wheel"
- Spawning new ideas for products and services

Decreasing the Learning Curve of New Employees

A common challenge faced by many companies is the need to rapidly increase the productivity of new employees. As employee mobility continues to increase across organizations, the ability to quickly assimilate individuals into the methods, tools, and activities of a new position represents an important capability. This task becomes especially important in dispersed organizations where an employee's direct supervisor may be located across town, or in a different country altogether. In the companies that we examined, communities of practice enabled new practitioners to "get wired" into the organizational memory and made it easier to learn both the technical and cultural aspects of their new roles and responsibilities.

In our sample, we found that communities of practice were quite valuable in helping newcomers identify subject matter experts who could answer questions and guide them to resources within the organization. Within a community of practice, new employees were able to make the connections that allowed them to identify a number of people with the same or similar work activities and answer questions about their new position. As one project manager in telecommunications explained,

> It's useful for the new graduates coming in to ask a question about something that they might be unsure about. . . . They will get a response to it that will help them out.

In addition to simply helping new people identify and locate experts, communities fostered relationships between newer, more junior employees and established practitioners within the organization. These relationships became important for a number of reasons. Community membership appeared to serve as a screening mechanism by senior employees who were limited in the amount of time they could assist new practitioners. As one new community member in the telecommunications company stated,

> I feel more comfortable calling on them [more senior practitioners]. They know me more because they have seen my face; they know who I am. They know me as part of the community so they identify me . . . Originally, they wouldn't necessarily pay me the same attention.

Further, the community helped foster the development of mentor-mentee relationships that could be valuable for both parties. Through community events and interactions, new employees were able to seek out more experienced practitioners that could provide them with insights and guide them in their career development. One of the senior community members within the multinational lending institution noted the importance of mentoring relationships within the community:

> It [the community] certainly has given me the opportunity to share some of what I have at this stage in my career. There are a lot of new entrants to the work force that are coming in and working on this, and being able to have a way of registering institutional memory on this particular topic is critical. . . . The community has been doing a lot of mentoring. We're trying to do that more and more.

Another challenge faced by new employees is to understand the larger context in which they perform their day-to-day tasks. Being new to an organization, it is often difficult to understand how individual activities impact other individuals and processes. According to several of the individuals we interviewed in the study, communities helped individuals gain a broader perspective on their specific roles. One of the researchers in the specialty chemical company provided a description of this phenomenon:

> [The community] . . . is dealing with a lot of people working on different parts of a large problem, so you come to understand and you have more perspective as a result. You can look at how individual tasks really fit in with everything else, and start to reinforce that whole way of thinking.

Finally, communities were seen as useful vehicles for creating shared narratives that could be used to transfer tacit knowledge. As Nahapiet and Ghoshal stated, ". . . myths, stories and metaphors also provide powerful means in communities for creating, exchanging and preserving rich sets of meanings—a view long held by some social anthropologists" (note 22, p. 253). Through the use of training courses, internal conferences, and mentoring relationships, new community members were able to hear and exchange useful tips and anecdotes that were not located in any community archive. As one of the specialists in the multinational lending institution indicated,

> The opportunity to have a point where you can go into depth in one thing and share that with your colleagues across regions is critical. In the days when we were just starting this [evaluation of urban services], those of us that are here now were a very small group working on similar projects. We had a chance to get together to talk and exchange every day, or at least every week. That's how we learned. The community is giving us that opportunity again.

Responding More Rapidly to Customer Needs and Inquiries

In an era where both prospective and existing customers are expecting rapid answers to inquiries, communities of practice can play an important role in quickly transferring the knowledge necessary to address customer issues. From a connection perspective, communities can help individuals rapidly identify an individual with the subject matter expertise necessary to provide the best answer to a client problem. This is especially true in organizations where the expertise needed to solve a particular client problem may be separated by time zones, distance, and/or organizational boundaries. For example, in the specialty chemical company that we examined, technical support personnel were able to tap into a community of researchers through the use of discussion boards to identify individuals who may have encountered similar problems in other customer locations. This ability to rapidly identify and locate individuals with particular knowledge was considered to be a significant source of competitive differentiation in the marketplace.

Also, as many communities maintained some form of centralized electronic repository, the reuse of intellectual capital located in a common location made it easier to find valuable explicit knowledge that could be used to respond to a customer need. The material in this type of repository included marketing presentations, proposals developed for previous prospects, and implementation plans that had been created from similar types of projects. An example of this is provided by one of the project managers within the telecommunications firm:

> Because we can find out what happened in the past much quicker, the community helps us to deliver solutions to the customer a lot better and give customers better information. Also, if there are issues or concerns coming up, we can let the customer know in advance and make arrangements to start work on different solutions.

Reducing Rework and Preventing "Reinvention of the Wheel"

Perhaps the most valuable contribution that communities of practice can make to a sponsoring organization is the ability for members to more easily reuse existing knowledge assets. Given the aging of the workforce population and the increased worker mobility that has been witnessed within the United States over the last several years, the need to retain "organizational memory" has become ever more important. For example, a recent survey conducted by the International Data Corporation suggests that the annual cost of this "knowledge deficit," which includes costs and inefficiencies that result from intellectual rework, substandard performance, and inability to find knowledge resources, will grow to over $5,500 per worker per year.[23]

Virtually all of the communities within the study cited the ability to locate, access, and apply existing intellectual capital to new situations as an important result of community participation. As several community members stated:

> For starters, the community means you get your work done more quickly. . . . If you've got to start from scratch to put that documentation together, it's going to take you longer. If you've got somewhere that you can go to where you've got a

template that says that this particular product fits, it helps you. (Project Manager at a telecommunications company)

It's the fact that we don't have to reinvent the wheel all the time. If we're sharing our information, then I can use what somebody else has learned and work on it somewhere else, instead of spending 80 hours doing it myself. It not just saves time, but it has improved the effectiveness of people's delivery material. (Quality Champion at a manufacturing company)

The repository systems that were used by many of the communities served a number of important functions. First, they provided a common virtual work space, where members could store, organize, and download presentations, tools, and other materials that community members could find valuable. What was of equal value, however, was the presence of meta-data that enabled the individual to identify and locate the author of the document. Given the difficulty in automatically reusing a piece of intellectual capital without knowledge of the situational context in which it was developed, the added ability to contact the developer was very important to community members. Further, the attachment of a community member's name to a particular piece of explicit knowledge in a repository served to reinforce the potential value of the content. As one of the project managers in the telecommunications company stated, "You are believing that someone who is answering [an inquiry] is answering it because they believe they know they have either that experience or they believe it is correct."

Also, we found that virtually all of the repositories incorporated some form of human moderation. Often, the community used content managers, or teams, to ensure that the content within the repository remained fresh and relevant to the users. Often these content managers also served to connect individuals not only to the original author of a particular document, but to other individuals who might be able to provide insight on a particular problem.

Repositories not only were used as storehouses for community knowledge, but also served as a mechanism for evaluating the trustworthiness and reciprocity of others within the community. Through the combination of posting documents and face-to-face interactions, communities of practice helped individuals build reputations both as subject matter experts and as individuals that were willing to help others. This reputation development was cited as an important benefit from participating in community activities by many of those who participated in the study. One member of the programming community in the software development company remarked,

If you've done some good work on a project, you can package it up and put it into the Tool Pool. That is well perceived by other developers around the world, and it's a good way of getting your name known and raising your profile in the organization.

Spawning New Ideas for Products and Services

In several of the companies that we examined, the communities of practice served as breeding grounds for innovation. These communities provided a forum in which individuals were able to share a variety of perspectives around a common topic. For example, software developers who worked with different customers often got together to exchange ideas about fixes for existing products and ideas for new software. One of these software developers commented on the community's role in bringing people together to come up with new solutions:

> [The community] . . . drives our software development from a real, in-the-field experience, and people exchange ideas about what the software would do, and about the situations they encounter with customers. It's very much appreciated by people in development so they see that what they develop is actually used, and how people are using it in the field. They find out what they are doing with it, what they like about it, and what they don't like about it.

Bringing in new or divergent points of view was also a technique used to spark innovation within the community. Several of the groups that we studied brought in outside speakers during community events to educate members on new developments in the field or provide alternative viewpoints. These outside influences were seen as valuable in ensuring that the community was exposed to a broad range of thinking from inside and outside the organization.

One of the primary reasons that communities were seen as an important vehicle for innovating was their ability to create a safe environment where people felt comfortable in sharing challenges. The development of these interpersonal relationships within the community was especially useful in asking sensitive questions or testing ideas that were not fully "baked." In many of the companies that we examined, the ability of individuals to use other community members as a sounding board was a highly valued feature of community life. In these situations, individuals were willing to share innovative thoughts with those whom they trusted, yet were also able to tap their expertise to refine and explore these new ideas. As one member of the lending institution remarked:

> In terms of support, I think that if I had any bottlenecks or any questions, I could always go to the community. There was a sense of belonging to a family of like-minded people who faced similar issues before. I feel very free to go to people who are part of it.

Summary

Table 7.2 summarizes the relationship between the dimensions of social capital and the business outcomes influenced by communities of practice. The table can be interpreted in two ways.

Looking at the columns of the table, we see that each dimension of social capital developed within these communities makes an important and unique contribution to the corresponding business outcomes. For example, communities help members locate individuals with expertise, discover others with similar experiences, locate tools and artifacts that have been previously developed, and identify outside influences that can help spark new ideas. Similarly, the table highlights the importance of the different dimensions of social capital and their relationship to business outcomes. When examining the drivers of reducing rework and preventing reinven-

Table 7.2 Linking business outcomes with the dimensions of social capital

	Connections	Relationships	Common Context
Decrease learning curve	Find experts	Mentor and coach new employees	Understand rules of the firm
Increase customer responsiveness	Find individuals with similar experiences	Develop willingness to respond to random questions	Understand the common language
Reduce rework and prevent reinvention	Find artifacts and the individuals who developed them	Establish positive reputation	Understand situational nature of knowledge
Increase innovation	Leverage weak ties that provide exposure to new ideas	Build safe environment for brainstorming and testing new ideas	Understand which problems are of common interest

tion, we believe that communities can help individuals find and reuse existing materials, form relationships that enhance the credibility of the developers of these materials, and build a common understanding that is necessary to apply these tools in new settings.

Future Directions

As we have seen across our cases, communities play a significant role in the development of social capital, which in turn influences organizational outcomes. These findings provide us with guidance to using communities as a vehicle for improving performance. However, the real challenge is to identify the management actions that will build the social capital necessary to achieve these goals. In addition, a second challenge is the development of measures that can guide and link the social capital building activities with actual business outcomes.

Management Actions

Although a full examination of the activities that can influence the development of social capital is beyond the scope of this chapter, our results suggest a number of potential interventions that can benefit communities of practice.

Provide opportunities for individuals to make new connections. There are a number of ways that firms can enable community members to make connections with one another. One method is to sponsor face-to-face events, such as knowledge fairs, training sessions, and other activities designed to introduce individuals with each other and the work they are currently involved in. Another method is to provide communities with technologies that can support both collaboration and expertise location. By giving people the opportunity to find one another using individual profiles, or through discussion databases and/or other forms of managed repositories, individuals can make connections to others with similar interests beyond in-person meetings. In addition, the use of human intermediaries can also be quite valuable in helping connect individuals to other community members.

Allow time and space for relationship building among individuals. While making connections is an important part of the community building process, the willingness of individuals to share knowledge requires additional time and effort. Employees need the opportunity to interact with each other so that they can evaluate the trustworthiness of others and gauge a sense of mutual obligation. However, we do not suggest that "trust building" activities such as experiential learning events are the key to building these important relationships. Rather, we believe that interactions that focus around work activities, such as repository management, play an important role in building the rapport and common sense of appreciation needed to effectively share knowledge.

Find ways to communicate the norms, culture, and language of the community and the organization. For communities to effectively share their knowledge, they need to develop a common set of norms, standards, and language that provide appropriate context for the community knowledge. Structured storytelling is one mechanism that firms have used to pass along the community "memory" and knowledge of the organization as a whole. Through the use of oral histories and multimedia technologies to capture the audio and visual context of specific situations, communities can capture and pass along the underlying "rules of the firm" in addition to providing the vocabulary necessary to pass along the community wisdom.

Measurement

Another future direction for community research would be to measure the effectiveness of various social capital activities with respect to organizational performance. For example, what is the impact of using expertise location technologies or holding face-to-face meetings on reducing the learning curve of new employees? Similarly, how can the use of stories enable individuals to better understand the context of best practices in other parts of the organization? These are additional issues that should be addressed as we continue to learn about the return on investment of organizational interventions.

Conclusion

It is widely recognized that communities of practice provide value to organizations. From our case studies, we have identified some of the specific business outcomes that are influenced by communities. Further, we have used the concept of social capital to highlight the mechanisms by which communities deliver this value. By understanding how communities deliver benefits to their larger organizations, we hope to be able to clarify and target potential management interventions that will be most likely to support community formation and development.

Acknowledgments This chapter is based on research conducted through the IBM Institute for Knowledge Management. We would like to thank Michael Fontaine from the IBM Institute for Knowledge Management and Jennifer Mikucki at Northeastern University for their early insights and work in this area. In addition, we would like to acknowledge the other members of the project team for their assistance in analyzing the data: Linda Carotenuto, Matthew Simpson, and Jason Slusher from IBM, and Etienne Wenger. We would also like to thank the Institute for Knowledge Management member companies who participated in this study.

Notes

1 E. Wenger, *Communities of Practice: Learning, Meaning and Identity*, Cambridge University Press, Cambridge, UK (1999).

2 J. Lave and E. Wenger, *Situated Learning: Legitimate Peripheral Participation*, Cambridge University Press, Cambridge, UK (1991).

3 P. Hildreth, C. Kimble, and P. Wright, "Communities of Practice in the Distributed International Environment," *Journal of Knowledge Management* 4, No. 1, 27–38 (2000).

4 J. Storck and P. Hill, "Knowledge Diffusion Through 'Strategic Communities'," *Sloan Management Review* 41, No. 2, 63–74 (2000).

5 J. S. Brown and P. Duguid, "Organizational Learning and Communities-of-Practice; Toward a Unified View of Working, Learning and Innovation," *Organization Science* 2, No. 1, 40–57 (1991).

6 E. Lesser and L. Prusak, "Communities of Practice, Social Capital and Organizational Knowledge," *Information Systems Review* 1, No. 1, 3–9 (1999).

7 E. Wenger and B. Snyder, "Communities of Practice: The Organizational Frontier," *Harvard Business Review* 78, No. 1, 139–145 (2000).

8 J. Jacobs, *The Decline and Rise of American Cities*, Random House, New York (1961).

9 M. S. Granovetter, "The Strength of Weak Ties," *American Journal of Sociology* 78, No. 6, 1360–1380 (1973).

10 J. S. Coleman, "Social Capital in the Creation of Human Capital," *American Journal of Sociology* 94, S95–121 (1988).

11 R. Putnam, "Bowling Alone: America's Declining Social Capital," *Journal of Democracy* 6, 65–78 (1995).

12 M. Woolcock, "Social Capital and Economic Development: Towards a Theoretical Synthesis and Policy Framework," *Theory and Society* 27, No. 2, 151–208 (1998).

13 A. Portes, "Social Capital: Its Origins and Applications in Modern Sociology," *Annual Review of Sociology* 24, 1–24 (1998).

14 R. Burt, "The Contingent Value of Social Capital," *Administrative Science Quarterly* 42, No. 2, 339–365 (1991).

15 G. Walker, B. Kogut, and W. Shan, "Social Capital, Structural Holes and the Formation of an Industry Network," *Organization Science* 8, No. 2, 109–125 (1997).

16 S. Cohen and G. Fields, "Social Capital and Capital Gains in Silicon Valley," *California Management Review* 41, No. 2, 108–130 (1998).

17 B. Arnold and F. Kay, "Social Capital, Violations of Trust and the Vulnerability

of Isolates: The Social Organization of Law Practice and Professional Self-Regulation," *International Journal of the Sociology of Law* 23, 321–346 (1995).

18 E. Meyerson, "Human Capital, Social Capital and Compensation: The Relative Contribution of Social Contacts to Managers' Income," *Acta Sociologica* 37, 383–399 (1994).

19 W. Baker, *Achieving Success through Social Capital: Tapping Hidden Resources in Your Personal and Business Networks,* John Wiley & Sons, Inc., New York (2000).

20 D. Cohen and L. Prusak, *In Good Company: How Social Capital Makes Organizations Work.* Harvard Business School Press, Boston, MA (2001).

21 P. Adler and S. Kwon, "Social Capital: The Good, the Bad, and the Ugly," *Knowledge and Social Capital,* E. Lesser, Editor, Butterworth Heinemann, Woburn, MA (2000).

22 J. Nahapiet and S. Ghoshal, "Social Capital, Intellectual Capital and the Organizational Advantage," *Academy of Management Review* 23, No. 2, 242–266 (1998).

23 G. Murray, *Knowledge Management Factbook,* International Data Corporation Report (1999).

8

Keeping Communities of Practice Afloat: Understanding and Fostering Roles in Communities

MICHAEL A. FONTAINE

"Communities of Practice house the valuable knowledge and practice of how things really get done in an organization and where people really learn."[1] Even though these informal groups typically emerge out of a common connection or practice, in many organizations they are fostered to address untapped collaborative opportunities. As this organizational transformation develops, communities such as those at the World Bank, IBM, and Bristol-Myers Squibb are lauded as models of success. This success has not happened because they have provided their communities with greater funding and technology than their counterparts. These organizations have seen success because they have supported their communities by defining the roles needed to keep them afloat.

For example, take a sailboat. Even small sailboats have a captain. However, as they get larger and their purpose and practice become more complex, additional roles are added to ensure that important responsibilities are met. Small boats often have one or two individuals who perform a number of roles: captain, helmsman, shipmate, cook, rigger, and repairman. Larger boats, such as America's Cup 12-meter racing yachts, are staffed with a person to fill each role.

Who Should Do What?

To better understand how roles function and evolve in communities of practice, the Institute for Knowledge Management (IKM) studied communities in 18 firms. Working with communities in several organizations, the IKM identified 11 formal and informal community roles:

1. subject matter expert (SME)
2. core team member
3. community member
4. leader
5. sponsor
6. facilitator
7. content coordinator
8. journalist
9. mentor
10. administrator/events coordinator
11. technologist

Through our research, we wanted to learn how roles can be used to help organizations better support communities. We conducted in-depth interviews with almost 100 community members, leaders, and KM professionals across the organizations studied. Looking at who played these roles and how organizations support them, we gained an insight into the roles that exist in communities and their development through the community's lifecycle. To discover roles that may be needed and yet remain unrecognized in organizations, we structured interviews to point to places where roles were missing and responsibilities were unmet. Responsibilities were further studied to distinguish which tasks fell to which role.

After collecting and analyzing the data, case studies were produced, compared, and then mapped against roles defined in community of practice literature. Additional time and salary analysis approximated how much time organizations were allocating for individuals who fill community roles and to benchmark associated annual compensation (see Table 8.1). The functions and attributes of community roles were drawn from IKM's research into knowledge intermediaries to deliver a comprehensive community/knowledge roles typology and toolkit (see Table 8.2).

We uncovered four categories of roles that exist in a community of practice: knowledge domain or practice roles, leadership roles, knowledge intermediary roles, and community support roles.

The Base for Success: Knowledge Domain Roles

Knowledge domain or practice roles are those that are specific to the community's subject matter expertise or knowledge base. These roles form around the community's practice and are filled by individuals who embody deep knowledge of the practice. Most importantly, in communities that form "bottom-up," these individuals are generally involved in early workings of the community. In fact, subject matter experts (SMEs) who spend years honing their craft and are commonly regarded as practice leaders within the organization are part of a network that meets regularly to share knowledge and expertise. Over time, their passion for the subject matter works to attract others who hold similar interests.

In many communities, SMEs become core team members. As they become empowered to influence the organization, they begin to meet as peers seeking

Table 8.1 Time allocated to community roles

Role	% Time/Week
Subject matter expert	21.4%
Core team	10.0%
Member	6.9%
Leader	20.0%
Sponsor	5.7%
Facilitator	53.4%
Content coordinator	25.0%
Journalist*	N/A
Mentor	5.0%
Admin/Events	26.0%
Technologist	25.0%

*The role of Journalists was discovered after the survey was completed.

Note: The percentage of time allocated to each role is an average reported by survey respondents in March 2001. The amount of time reported should serve only as a generalized benchmark and is not specific to industries or geographic regions.

unity and mutual understanding. As the community begins to take shape, they are responsible for its daily operations. After a community leader emerges or is selected, the core team serves as the leader's cabinet, helping to make important decisions on behalf of the general membership. Community members, on the other hand, take active ownership in the community by participating in its events and activities. As the community begins to coalesce around informal lunch meetings, e-mail lists, or newsgroups, community members join the ranks as their work requires them to become more involved in the community's practice. Moreover, members are the glue that holds the community together. Without their active participation and involvement, the community quickly folds.

Driving the Community: Leadership Roles

The two leadership roles—leaders and sponsors—are often considered the most important roles in a community's recognition, support and legitimization by the organization. These roles secure funding for the community and often help to fund additional community roles. Leaders provide the overall guidance and management to build and maintain the community, its relevance and strategic importance in the organization, and its level of visibility.

Sponsors, who're generally not part of the community, are senior managers who recognize the strategic importance of the community and its contribution to the overall business objectives of the organization. Sponsors help secure needed resources, nurture and protect the community, and ensure its exposure in the organization.

Table 8.2 Community roles, descriptions and responsibilities

Role	Description	Primary Responsibilities
1. Subject Matter Experts	Keepers of the community's knowledge domain or practice who serve as centers of specialized tacit knowledge for the community and its members	• Develop and communicate deep expertise and tacit knowledge of the community's knowledge domain or practice • Serve as the community's base of thought leadership and expertise • Contribute knowledge of subject matter to all community activities • Serve as the community's keeper of specialized tacit knowledge
2. Core Team Members	Looked upon for guidance and leadership before or after a Leader emerges or is selected; guidance includes developing the community's mission and purpose	• Serve as the initial body of decision makers in a community • Provide the momentum to sustain the community's evolution • Play a strong role in the early community by setting boundaries, norms, and values • Nominate, support and advise Community Leader • Work with Leader to develop the community's mission and purpose
3. Community Members	Take active ownership in the community by participating in its events and activities and driving the level of commitment and growth of the community	• Participate and engage in community events and activities • Share knowledge and expertise with peers • Contribute to community conversations and discussions • Help set community governance, norms, culture, and policies
4. Community Leaders	Provide the overall guidance and management needed to build and maintain the community, its relevance and strategic importance in the organization, and level of visibility	• Build and maintain relationships with key stakeholders to strengthen the community's recognition and support by the organization • Work with Core Team to set community mission, purpose, and goals • Manage community budget and finances and support, create, and finance additional community roles • Hold and lead community meetings, activities, events, and conferences
5. Sponsors	Nurture and provide top-level recognition for the community while ensuring its exposure, support, and strategic importance in the organization	• Serve as the community's link to senior level management • Tie the community and its benefits to the organization's strategic objectives • Measure and evaluate the community's contributions to business objectives • Allocate budget and resources for the community • Advocate acceptance and recognition for the community • Work with Community Leader to support additional community roles

(continued)

127

Table 8.2 *(continued)*

Role	Description	Primary Responsibilities
6. Facilitators	Network and connect community members by encouraging participation, facilitating and seeding discussions, and keeping events and community activities engaging and vibrant	• Energize the community and serve as chief motivator • Encourage participation in community events and activities • Work to keep online discussions engaging, flowing, and vibrant • Provide closure when necessary and give constructive feedback • Seed and feed discussion topics
7. Content Coordinators	Serve as the ultimate source of explicit knowledge by searching, retrieving, transferring, and responding to direct requests for the community's knowledge and content	• Facilitate and coordinate the digital or physical library or repository • Ensure that the community's intellectual capital is categorized • Archive outdated material • Help members find knowledge nuggets, content, and information
8. Journalists	Responsible for identifying, capturing, and editing relevant knowledge, best practices, new approaches, and lessons learned into documents, presentations, and reports	• Observe and interview community members to make the community's tacit knowledge more explicit • Respond to direct requests for assistance in turning tacit knowledge into explicit • Prepare community artifacts for distribution to other internal and external groups • Edit pieces to communicate what the community knows to the larger organization • Create content maps and provide research services
9. Mentors	Act as community elders, who take a personal stake in helping new members navigate the community, its norms and policies, and their place in the organization	• Welcome and invite new members to the community • Introduce and orient members to the community norms, and policies • Motivate and encourage participation in events, activities, and discussions • Engage in storytelling and community history stewardship
10. Admin/ Events Coordinators	Coordinate, organize, and plan community events or activities	• Coordinate and plan community events or activities • Create and maintain community PR within the organization • Promote community events • Set up meetings and send out invitations and marketing materials
11. Technologists	Oversee and maintain the community's collaborative technology and help members navigate its terrain	• Provide technical and logistical support for the community • Work with IT and Facilitator to design the homepage look and feel • Set up access privileges, passwords, usernames, and profiles • Coordinate with technical teams and IT staff to ensure quality, performance, and reliability

Funneling the Knowledge: Intermediary Roles

Facilitators, content coordinators, and journalists fill the three knowledge intermediary roles—knowledge steward, knowledge broker, and knowledge researcher—that are currently embraced in many organizations. (For more information see "Identifying the Key People in Your KM Effort," *KM Review* vol. 3, issue 5.)

Knowledge intermediaries are primarily responsible for capturing, codifying, retrieving, and transferring the explicit and tacit knowledge of the community and then facilitating its exchange. To fulfill their part in these tasks, facilitators are responsible for brokering, networking, and connecting community members who require or need to share tacit knowledge. They encourage and energize participation by interacting with the community, by endorsing ideas, and by directing knowledge to the appropriate experts. Content coordinators perform a library science function and act as the ultimate sources of explicit knowledge. They are generally responsible for searching, retrieving, transferring, and responding to direct requests for the community's explicit knowledge and content. Finally, journalists interview or observe community members to identify and capture knowledge nuggets, best practices, new approaches, and lessons learned. Acting as the primary coordinator of transferring tacit knowledge into documents, reports, and presentations, they help the community share its knowledge with other internal or external groups.

Stabilizing Forces: Support Roles

The community support roles help administer events and technology and navigate norms and policies. Mentors often emerge from SMEs or from more experienced community members and work to help new members understand the community's culture and practices. Admin/events coordinators plan online or face-to-face community events or activities and help create marketing and PR for the community. Finally, technologists oversee and maintain the community's technology and communication infrastructure. Working with the organization's IT staff to ensure quality, performance, and reliability, the technologist ensures smooth operation of the community's collaborative technology and helps members to navigate its interface.

Cyclical Nature of Roles

Additional learning surfaced from our research: roles, like the communities, form along two paths: sometimes they emerge "bottom-up" and other times are deliberately created "top-down." In fact, in some of the communities studied, members automatically filled roles as the community began to coalesce. Others were deliberately created or assigned by sponsors, leaders, and KM professionals. Additionally, while community participation was primarily voluntary in most communities—with individuals opting to play different roles with varying levels of intensity and time commitment—some roles were assigned as a means to steer the community's course or to direct resource allocation.[2] Along either path, however, it was clear that as the community grew in size and importance, roles provided it with the necessary structure and support for future activity and success.

"Bottom-Up" Communities

In communities that emerged bottom-up (see Figure 8.1), such as those at the World Bank and Bristol-Myers Squibb, the community evolved from a core group of SMEs who met informally to explore their common passion. As SMEs actively shared their experience and expertise with others of similar interest, the community began to coalesce as additional community members joined the group. Next, a leader and core team emerged that took responsibility for day-to-day operations. Senior-level sponsorship was also secured. Later, mentors emerged from the ranks of benevolent, experienced members and helped new recruits to learn the group's norms and practices. As the community matured and became well-

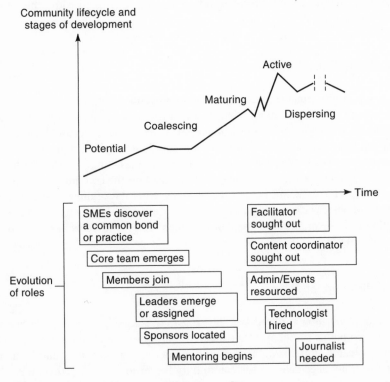

Figure 8.1 Communities emerged "bottom-up."[3,4]

established, the organizations supplied it with an admin/events coordinator, a content coordinator, and a technologist.

In such cases, members generally take on roles because they care deeply about the practice and the community's success. Leaders are not chosen, nominated, or selected, but emerge from the ranks of the impassioned. Often they are the community's most vocal evangelists. Likewise, core team members fulfill most or all 11 roles when the community is in its infancy, collectively ensuring that all community responsibilities are met. As a community grows, though, roles tend to become more formal, especially when the organization staffs or supports them directly.

Communities that evolve in this manner present a challenge. The time from the initial meeting of SMEs to a full-blown functioning community can span years. Without resources and established roles in the early part of a community's development, it can, and often may, flounder. In fact, some community leaders and KM professionals who participated in our study admitted that a lack of formal roles and limited resources contributed to the failure of some of their communities.

"Top-Down" Communities

When communities are deliberately created (see Figure 8.2), roles are often established and staffed at the outset. In communities such as those at IBM and British Telecom, the following roles were assigned in succession: sponsors, community leader(s), and then a core team helped to ramp up the community and plan its launch. Subject matter experts were enlisted and an admin/events coordinator put in place to plan and invite members to the community at an official launch. A technologist, content coordinator, facilitator, and mentors filled out the group by providing the support needed to sustain the community and help it mature.

Communities created "top-down" can have a much more difficult time breeding trust and active participation than ones that grew "bottom-up," where a shared passion has brought members together. Members may view created communities as yet another corporate initiative to reorganize the existing hierarchy. Unfortunately, this may be true in many cases. "Top-down" communities often have low levels of active participation because transparency and reciprocity are not evident. For example, the attitude is often, "If I put something in to the community, I better see that I'll get something out of it!" Further, created communities often lack the much-needed member ingredient of common context and purpose.

Not surprisingly, members may neglect the newly mandated community and retreat to their existing informal networks. To counter these natural responses, created communities should be designed with roles, such as core teams, facilitators, mentors, and admin/events coordinators, to develop as much member involvement as possible and to build an early sense of ownership.

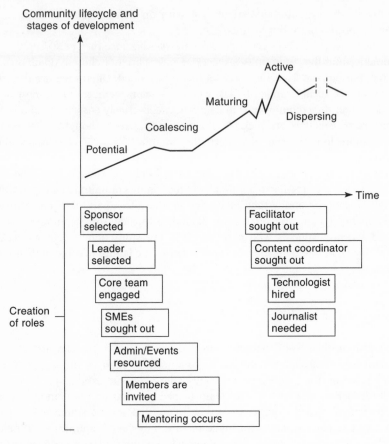

Figure 8.2 Communities created "top-down."

Benefitting from Structure

Supporting communities of practice has already proven beneficial to many organizations. Understanding and supporting community roles provides further benefits to the community as well as the organization. Not only do roles provide the community with the momentum that keeps it on course, but they also may keep it from running aground. To navigate these obstacles, roles supply communities with three significant benefits: reassurance, continuity and structure.

1. *Reassurance.* Roles provide reassurance that the community is being taken seriously. This not only reinforces and spurs participation, but also provides the community with needed recognition and legitimacy throughout the organization. Roles, such as leaders and sponsors, hammer home this point by securing funding or providing the community with strategic di-

rection. Further, this reassurance may breed other communities and assist in their formation by communicating that the organization has embarked on a new direction.

2. *Continuity.* Roles provide continuity. When the membership changes due to new opportunities or attrition, roles help the community maintain a steady course. Over time, community members may come and go, but roles such as subject matter experts, content coordinators, journalists, and mentors provide grounding for the community's purpose and practice. This connection to the community's past—through documents, stories, and history—helps span corporate reorganizations, mergers, or new business ventures.

3. *Structure.* Roles provide structure. Understanding the formal and informal roles that exist in a community and those that should be supported at different stages in a community's lifecycle provides the community with a sense of balance. Facilitators, core teams, admin/events coordinators, and technologists help the larger membership share knowledge and expertise that is critical to the community's practice and the organization's business objectives. Without well-coordinated roles, communities—like the America's Cup 12-meter racing yachts—would be forced to navigate open oceans without a map or sense of direction.

Notes

1 Cohen, Don and Prusak, Lawrence, *In Good Company: How Social Capital Makes Organizations Work,* HBS Press (2001).

2 Lesser, Eric L., Fontaine, Michael A. and Slusher, Jason, A. *Knowledge and Communities,* Butterworth-Heinemann (2000).

3 APQC, "Building and Sustaining Communities of Practice" (August 2000).

4 Wenger, Etienne, *Communities of Practice: Learning as a Social System,* Systems Thinker (June, 1998).

Further Reading

Horvath, J., Sasson, L. Sharon, J. and Parker, A., "Intermediaries: A Study of Knowledge Roles in Connected Organizations," IKM White Paper Series (June, 2000).

Sharon, J., Sasson, L. Parker, A., Horvath, J. and Mosbrooker, E., "Identifying the Key People in Your KM Effort: The Role of Human Knowledge Intermediaries." *KM Review,* vol. 3, issue 5, pp. 27–29 (Nov/Dec 2000).

9

Learning from the Connected Customer: Enhancing Customer Web Sites with Community

ERIC L. LESSER
MICHAEL A. FONTAINE

How does a small, employee-owned business with a commodity product survive in an era of mega brands and price-sensitive customers? For the last 212 years, King Arthur Flour (KAF), a leading seller of flour and baking supplies, has continuously focused on, and learned from, a base of loyal and enthusiastic customers. To further tap into its customers' energy and devotion, King Arthur Flour recently launched its Baking Circle, an online community for professional and home bakers. An integral part of the company's commitment to e-business and understanding its customers' needs, the site provides an opportunity for KAF to interact directly with tens of thousands of its customers. This Web site is designed to help members become better bakers and at the same time provide KAF with valuable insights about its customers and how they use the company's products and services.

Organizations have always looked for new and innovative ways to learn from customers about their preferences, wants, and needs and educate customers about their products and services. Over the last few years, we have seen organizations adding community functions to their traditional e-commerce sites to allow customers to make connections and build relationships with one another. Through our research within the IBM Institute for Knowledge-Based Organizations, we have found that online customer communities can provide a number of valuable learning opportunities for both customers and the organizations that sponsor them (see Table 9.1 for a listing of customer sites referenced as part of this study).

Table 9.1 Referenced Community Websites

Organization	Target Audience	URL
Agilent	Users of testing and measurement devices	http://www.measurement.tm.agilent.com/appcentral.html
Cabela's	Users of camping and outdoors equipment	http://www.cabelas.com/
Compaq	Owners of Compaq computer equipment	http://7.compaq.com/forum?choice@@!top=1&lang=English
Hallmark	Selected individuals willing to discuss life events	private community—not open to the public
King Arthur Flour	Professional and home bakers	http://www.bakingcircle.com/msgboard/
Mercury Interactive	Software developers and users	private community—open to customers only
Palm	Palm personal digital assistant users	http://www.palm.com/community/
SAP	Software developers and users	http://www.sap.com/community/
Sony	Video game (Playstation) enthusiasts	http://scea.com/underground/
Sun	Software developers and users	http://www.sun.com/forums/

Customer Communities: The Right Space at the Right Time

Recent interest in fostering customer communities in an online environment has been fueled by a number of forces:

- *The need to attract repeat visitors by creating additional value during the Web experience.* As the number of individuals who are connected online continues to the rise, many of them are using the Internet to reach out to others with similar needs and interests. A recent study by the Pew Internet & American Life Project found that approximately 23 million Americans participate in at least one online group several times per week. When asked what types of online groups they participated in, more than 50% said they were involved in trade and professional organizations, or groups that shared a hobby or interest.[1] Many firms, recognizing this as an opportunity to attract and learn from their customers, have begun to provide this virtual "space" where individuals can connect and engage with others around shared topics and concerns. By providing an additional source of value for visitors to their Web sites, many organizations have been able to increase both the number of repeat visitors and the average amount of time spent per visitor during any single visit. In addition, McKinsey and Co. recently found that users of community features represented about one-third of all visitors to leading e-tailing sites but generated two-thirds of the sites' overall sales.[2]
- *The need to create effective customer learning and communication channels.* While the advent of customer relationship management systems has produced a

glut of data about customer transactions, many organizations are still wrestling with the challenge of actually learning about their customers. Customer communities can provide a forum in which organizations can engage with their customers and extract learnings from those interactions. By conducting extended dialogues with individuals within the community, observing conversations between participants in the community, and reviewing frequently asked questions and discussion postings, firms are finding new windows into customer preferences and behaviors.

One company that has been using customer communities as a vehicle for learning is Hallmark, which has been observing the online conversations of 200 consumers on its "Idea Exchange" Web site. Hallmark researchers are reviewing and participating in these conversations to identify different types of events and audiences that reflect potential greeting card subjects and trends. Based on these dialogues, Hallmark has developed new ideas for cards, such as mother-in-law cards and sympathy cards for the anniversary of a death.[3] On a larger scale, Compaq Computers has set up an online community that has attracted more than 92,000 registered users in its first year. Compaq has leveraged the questions and answers posted in the community space to identify software glitches, alter product designs, and adjust promotional campaigns.[4]

• *The need to provide effective customer service in a cost-effective manner.* In customer communities, customers have an opportunity to pose questions to one another, share documents, post photographs, and discuss topics of mutual interest. When faced with a particular problem, an individual can engage the collective wisdom of hundreds, if not thousands of others, rather than a few employees within a company's customer support organization. Enabling customers to answer other customers' questions can significantly reduce an organization's overall support costs. For example, Mercury Interactive, a provider of enterprise testing and performance management software, launched a community that provided customer support assistance in 2000. In the first quarter of 2001, it found that it was 95% cheaper for a question to be answered from postings to a support forum than from a call or e-mail to the customer support center.[5] Further, communities can allow customers to get their answers more quickly, and enable the company to discover solutions to problems that the organization had not previously encountered or even considered.

Components of a Customer Community Space

In the community sites that we examined, we saw multiple opportunities for gathering data and insights that can support learning about customers. For example, during the registration process, we found that companies can obtain a great deal of information about new members, ranging from valuable demographic data to understanding an individual's specific areas of interest. Also, discussion boards provide the opportunity for customers to learn from other customers, while at the same time allowing companies to observe these conversations and glean important insights. In addition, interactive events, such as synchronous chats and Web seminars, enable customers to connect directly with the corporation, simultaneously learning about and sharing experiences about purchasing and using the company's products and services. Each of these different learning opportunities can be leveraged to create value for both the participating customer and the sponsoring organization.

Registration

Nearly all the sites we examined require individuals to go through a registration process to participate in community activities. The first part of the process is to create a unique "identity" that includes a registration name and a password. This allows individuals to be recognized by other participants on the community site. Second, many of the sites ask individuals to provide demographic information and select areas of interest related to a particular product or service. This information serves several purposes. It enables the organization to develop rich profiles of its online users that can be used for customer segmentation. Also, this registration information is used by several of the sites to tailor specific content views to their members, adjusting the community experience to individual needs. By allowing members to specify their interests, these sites attempt to reduce the amount of time individuals spend searching for relevant information.

Community Discussion Boards

At the heart of many customer communities are discussion boards, where members post questions, comments, and suggestions for others. These forums allow users to conduct organized discussions where multiple people can comment on a single topic. Discussion boards are useful tools for maintaining the "community memory" while providing a forum for members to express their viewpoints and ask for assistance. For example, Palm, the developer of handheld personal digital assistants, provides a community discussion board (which is now operated and moderated by Brighthand.com, a larger community site for handheld enthusiasts) that offers an extensive set of areas focused on general product issues, specific handheld models, and ideas for new features. Similarly, Cabela's, an outdoor equipment retailer, provides a discussion space that engages individuals interested in hunting, fishing, and advice on the latest camping gear. On this board is a section that solicits feedback on Cabela's own products and services. The company actively monitors this board and provides answers to questions and concerns about its products. Overall, virtual spaces such as those provided by Palm and Cabela's play an important role as they help build connections that encourage repeat visits, engage customers in dialogues that can be used to spot early trends in the market, and support customers looking for additional information.

Company-Sponsored Events and Activities

In addition to using discussion boards, community members often take advantage of interactions with, and content provided by, the company itself. While these features do not directly foster discussion between individual members, they can add significant value by providing interesting and relevant content to community members. These activities, in turn, can further encourage community members to return to the site.

- *Synchronous chats with experts.* Many customer community sites offer opportunities to engage members in online dialogues with internal experts. For example, SAP holds a number of "Ask-the-Expert" discussions on a regular basis about technical and business-related topics for its community members. These sessions allow participants to ask questions on topics such as industry trends, planned enhancements, and future product directions. These chats can then be captured and stored for individuals who are not able to participate in the online discussion. These types of interactions often give members a sense of having access to company "insiders" and at the same time enable the company to establish a real-time dialogue with its customers.
- *Web seminars.* Several of the community sites provide online training courses that members can take to learn about the company's products and services. These range from very basic courses where individuals can follow simple instructions augmented by pictures to well-orchestrated multimedia productions that were augmented by voice discussions and synchronous chat. Sun Microsystems is an example of an organization that frequently runs Web seminars conducted by its technical staff to educate interested software developers about Sun's product lines and technologies. Organizations that conduct Web seminars can help customers use their products and services more effectively, and encourage complementary or follow-on purchases.
- *Online polling.* Many community sites use online polling as a mechanism to both generate content for members and learn about customer ideas and preferences. Members are asked to answer short questionnaires and the results are posted and archived for members to view when they return to the site. Sony, in its "Playstation Pulse" section, recently asked its members which characters they would like to see matched up in its video games. The results of the survey were quickly posted on the site. Polling can be a valuable tool for engaging members and learning valuable lessons without a significant time commitment or effort.
- *E-mail newsletters.* E-mail newsletters are often used to send out regular updates to community members without requiring them to go to the Web site. Agilent Technologies, for example, provides e-mail updates to members of its Test and Measurement community on a range of topics such as product support information and new developments in the world of testing and measurement equipment. Members can customize their e-mail and only re-

ceive information on topics that they select as part of their profile. While e-mail newsletters themselves do not support the interaction that helps build a successful online community, they provide members with a periodic reminder that there is new and interesting content to check out on the community site.

Building an Online Customer Community: King Arthur Flour

At King Arthur Flour, the creation of its online customer community, the Baking Circle, came about as the result of some of the company's initial forays into the world of electronic commerce. Starting in 1997, one of the firm's first Web-based activities was to give individuals the opportunity to order its catalog online. When individuals requested the catalog, they were asked to complete a short online questionnaire about themselves. The firm was amazed to find that 88% of people who requested the catalog filled out the survey, and more than 40% provided additional comments about the firm's Web site and the company in general. Recognizing that King Arthur Flour had a devoted clientele in cyberspace, the company's Director of MIS and Internet Operations, Tom Sweet, began to envision ways the Web could be used to help KAF get closer to its customers. In previous years, King Arthur Flour had conducted in-person focus groups and mail surveys, but found it could never develop a true representation of its customers and their needs.

In the years before the launch of the Baking Circle, KAF had begun to establish the components of its community strategy. In November 1999 KAF created the Round Table, an electronic newsletter that initially reached more than 5,000 people, but quickly grew to a distribution of 20,000 people. At the same time, it began to produce online baking classes via its Web site, using a combination of step-by-step directions and photographs to enable site visitors to bake their own goods.

Based on the initial success of these components, KAF decided to launch a community site in September 2001. The company created a broader community site that, in addition to the online classes, consisted of a bulletin board that could store discussion threads and an area where individuals could view recipes and store them in a personal section. Initially, KAF gave the community site only a limited amount of structure. As Tom Sweet described, he wanted to have the community members decide what the site would look like and how it would evolve, "like a group of settlers coming together to decide what their town would look like." During the site's first weekend of operation, more than 750 people sent in questions and suggestions about the site. Tom and his team addressed each of them personally during the initial launch. Within the first three months of operation, more than 10,000 people had registered on the site.

Members of the firm's operating team frequently monitor and occasionally contribute to the community site. As a result of the Baking Circle, KAF has already learned a great deal about its customers. For example, KAF found that over 20% of their inquiries were regarding sourdough bread—a development that was quickly shared with members of the firm's new product development group. Further, through the community, the firm was able to evaluate the types of stores where KAF products were available—insights that were particularly valuable to the firm's sales and marketing teams. The firm is also beginning to look at community members' purchasing behavior on the Web site, and is rewarding frequent purchasers with Baker's Points that are tracked online.

Moving forward, KAF is continually looking to upgrade its community site. Some ideas for future enhancement to the community include: the ability for members to create profiles that others can view online, enabling members to post photos of themselves using King Arthur Flour and displaying their creations, and facilitating online chats with the company's Master Bakers. Each of these modifications is designed to create additional content for members, allow them to interact with one another on a regular basis, and build a greater sense of loyalty and affiliation to the site, and ultimately, to King Arthur Flour and its products.

Community-Enhanced Customer Sites: Connecting and Learning

As the King Arthur example illustrates, adding community functionality to a Web site can provide real benefits for both customers and organizations. Customers use these communities as a method for connecting with individuals with similar ideas and interests, finding out answers to difficult questions, and learning more about an organization's products and services. At the same time, companies can leverage these communities to increase repeat site visits, reduce support costs, engage customers in dialogue about current and future products and services, and learn from community members' extended discussions with each other. The insights from these customer interactions can yield important learnings that can be shared and leveraged by many parts of the enterprise, ranging from customer support to new product development.

Notes

1 Horrigan, John B. *Online Communities: Networks That Nurture Long-Distance Relationships and Local Ties,* Pew Internet & American Life Project, October 31, 2001.

2 Brown, Shona L., Andrew Tilton and Dennis Woodside, "The Case for On-line Communities," *The McKinsey Quarterly,* Number 1, 2002 (Web exclusive).

3 Keenan, Faith, "Friendly Spies on the Net," *Business Week,* July 9, 2001.

4 Tedeschi, Bob, "E-Commerce Report," *The New York Times,* February 11, 2002, p. C8.

5 Cothrel, Joe and Patrick Saeger, "Increasing Customer Satisfaction and Reducing Costs through an Online Technical Support Community," presentation made at the *Horizons 2002 World Conference,* October 2, 2001, Savannah, GA.

PART IV
KNOWLEDGE AND STRATEGIC ALLIANCES

Many of the knowledge management efforts that we have seen in organizations have focused primarily on the exchange and application of knowledge *within* the firm. There has been, however, a growing recognition that much of the knowledge that is valuable to firms and government agencies lies beyond their boundaries. A number of trends begin to reinforce this point. The number of joint ventures and alliances in today's corporate environment has increased many times over the last several years, as firms recognize the value of partnering in research efforts, standards development, and component sourcing. Recent world events have required government intelligence and defense organizations to focus on the importance of collaboration and knowledge sharing across their agencies and with international partners to address threats to national security. In short, it is not only about what your organization knows—but how it can make the best use of the knowledge of its key partners and customers.

While the importance of knowledge sharing beyond one's borders continues to grow, the problems associated with accomplishing this are not easily overcome. For example, locating relevant knowledge can become increasingly difficult when the knowledge resides with employees who work for outside entities. Just finding someone who is knowledgeable about a particular topic in a large firm or government agency can be difficult enough; locating knowledge beyond organizational boundaries can be an especially daunting task. In addition, identifying what knowledge can, and should, be shared among organizations can be quite challenging. Issues associated with the ownership of intellectual property, the perception of collusion between competing firms, and the potential leakage of firm-specific knowledge to potential competitors can hinder the speed and effectiveness of knowledge transfer between organizations. Given the risks involved, it is logical for individuals to err on the side of caution and limit their knowledge disclosure to the outside world. Further, the ability to motivate individuals to share may be complicated by conflicting reward schemes, geographic and contractual constraints, and a lack of positive relationships between the involved parties. For example, sales targets that are based on selling a certain level of one company's products might limit the time and effort a salesperson spends on learning about a partner's solution. Given these potential knowledge pitfalls, it is not surprising that managing knowledge beyond one's borders is fraught with difficulty.

In our research, we have focused our attention on understanding the relationship between knowledge and strategic alliances. The chapters in this part use two different perspectives to address the primary challenges associated with managing knowledge across alliances. Chapter 10 examines the relationship between business strategy, alliance strategy, and the exchange of knowledge between alliance partners. Salvatore Parise from the KOPF and John Henderson from Boston University have developed a model that addresses three dimensions of knowledge that is shared within a strategic alliance. The first dimension looks at the *tacitness* of the knowledge. While some alliances simply exchange tangible resources such as equipment, licenses, and other materials that are easily codified, others involve the investment of time by individuals who have knowledge that is not easily transferred or duplicated in the marketplace. The second dimension involves knowledge *specificity*. This dimension looks at the extent to which the knowledge is pertinent to a specific arrangement and cannot be applied for other uses. For example, a partnership that involves the development of a software program that works with the hardware of only one particular vendor represents a high degree of specificity. Finally, the third dimension highlights the *complexity* of the knowledge that is involved in the alliance. If the alliance involves the cocreation of new knowledge by members of both parties of the effort, the knowledge is considered to have a high degree of complexity. The joint exploration of an offshore oil field involving specialized resources over a long period of time is a good example of a highly complex alliance. From these three dimensions, the authors create a resource exchange model and argue that different combinations of resource exchange between partners create different forms of value. They also suggest that firms entering into an alliance potentially realize higher value creation and competitive advantage when the knowledge both parties exchange is more tacit, has a higher specificity to the arrangement, and is more complex in its development.

The knowledge resource exchange model addresses the interaction between two partners. However, many organizations have a number of ongoing alliances, each with its own particular set of knowledge exchange characteristics. These alliances can be formed with customers, suppliers, complementary firms, and even competitors. By applying the resource model to each of these alliance partners, Parise and Henderson believe that organizations can develop a clearer understanding of the relationship between their overall business strategies and their alliance efforts. Using two examples from the computer hardware industry, the authors apply the resource exchange model to demonstrate how different firms leverage their alliances to execute their overall business strategy.

Chapter 11 moves from a strategic viewpoint on knowledge and alliances to a tactical perspective on how firms can actually manage the knowledge used within a specific alliance. Leveraging research examples from a number of member companies, Salvatore Parise and Lisa Sasson highlight the rationale and opportunities for firms to apply knowledge management techniques to their strategic alliance efforts. In this chapter, they examine three parts of the alliance process and the critical knowledge used within each. The first phase, *Find*, involves making strategic decisions about the types of alliances a firm should enter into, and identifying and choosing potential partners. Key knowledge associated with this phase includes highlighting the need for developing an alliance based on an understanding of the organization's strategy, identifying and screening potential alliance candidates, and determining whether other alliances within the organization will impact, or be impacted by, a new partnership. In the second phase, *Design*, sharing knowledge about firm objectives and joint capabilities can help successfully negotiate an arrangement between the two firms and lay the groundwork for successful execution. In this stage, knowledge of potential individuals who could manage or work on the alliance can play an important role in building effective working relationships between the two entities. In the last phase, *Manage*, ensuring that there are mechanisms in place to effectively find and apply alliance-specific knowledge becomes an important priority. Further, upon completion of the partnership, organizations should have processes in place to learn from their experiences and apply those insights to further alliance efforts. For example, conducting after-action learning sessions and developing a shared repository of key alliance documents can help managers learn from an alliance and prepare for future efforts.

Within each of these phases, the authors identify a number of knowledge management techniques that can be used to improve the firm's alliance management capability. These include the use of defined alliance management roles, dedicated repositories for managing content, fostering communities of practice to facilitate sharing among alliance practitioners, and the use of expertise location technologies to identify relevant subject matter experts. Each of these techniques, when appropriately applied to the stages of the alliance process, can help both parties in an alliance improve their odds for creating a successful partnership.

10

Knowledge Resource Exchange in Strategic Alliances

SALVATORE PARISE
JOHN C. HENDERSON

Alliances between organizations have become an increasingly important aspect of strategic management and are playing a major role in the transfer and management of knowledge resources. Whereas most of the literature on knowledge management has focused on the creation, acquisition, transfer, and value creation associated with knowledge *within* an organization, comparatively little work has been done to understand the management of knowledge *across* organizations.

The alliance, in its various forms, continues to be a popular means of conducting business. The number of U.S. alliances has grown by more than 25 percent annually for the past five years.[1] While alliance use is appearing across many industries, the spread of alliances seems especially prevalent in the high-technology industries, where both the number of alliances and the average value per alliance have been increasing steadily.[2] These alliances tend to focus on the transfer of knowledge and technology in industries characterized by rapid change in both structure and competitive dynamics. Indeed, an emerging management view is that firms no longer can develop, manufacture, and market products on their own, and alliances are a means to gain access to complementary resources and capabilities they lack. Hagedoorn[3] found that technology complementarity, innovation time-span reduction, market access, and market structure influence are the most mentioned motives behind technology alliances. Other motives behind alliance formation in volatile, high-tech industries include: the immense costs of developing the technology, uncertainty in terms of emerging technologies, the convergence of several industry segments, and a "follow the herd" mentality. Although there seems to be an increase in the number of alliances formed, at the same time, there is also evidence that strategic alliances are underperforming. Success rates of less than 50 percent have often been cited in the literature.[4,5]

Recent research has indicated that alliances can be viewed as mechanisms to acquire know-how and to learn from other firms.[6-8] Henderson and Subramani,[9] for example, propose a topology of alliance types that emphasizes differences in the role of knowledge. The types of knowledge resources exchanged in alliances can range from intangible, tacit resources such as employee expertise or company brand name, to tangible, physical resources such as equipment, components, or products. The management and implications for value creation, we argue, are dependent on the nature of the knowledge resource exchange between alliance partners.

One critical aspect of the knowledge exchange between partners is the position or *role* of the partner relative to a firm (which we refer to as *focal firm* throughout the chapter) within an industry. Alliance partners can be suppliers, customers, complementors, competitors, or others (i.e., a partner outside the industry). Brandenburger and Nalebuff[10] use the term *co-opetition* to describe the multiple roles of a partner, and how a partner may simultaneously be both a competitor and complementor to a firm. In fact, this seems to be occurring with respect to alliance formations in practice: over 50 percent of organizations surveyed today admit they are partnering with competitors.[1] If we extend the notion of partner role to alliance formations, we can investigate why firms form alliances with their competitors, complementors, suppliers, and customers. In particular, we seek to understand the implications of these alternative roles on the knowledge exchange between partners.

Therefore, both the nature of the knowledge resource exchange and the role of the partner raise strategic and management questions such as:

- Is there the potential for more value creation in alliances characterized by the exchange of tacit, specialized resources versus explicit, nonspecialized resources?
- How do firms with differences in business strategy differ with respect to their alliance strategy?
- What are the implications for alliance management based on the role of the partner in an industry value network (e.g., alliances with competitors versus alliances with complementors)?

In this chapter, we provide a conceptual model, the Partner Resource Exchange Model, to help the manager answer the above questions. The model addresses the nature of the knowledge resource exchange based on three critical dimensions of knowledge (tacitness, specificity, and complexity), as well as the role of the partner in an industry context (complementor, competitor, supplier, customer, and other). To illustrate the use of the model, we analyze alliance announcements from two major computer hardware firms, Sun Microsystems, Inc. and Dell Computer Corporation, from 1990 to 1998. We also seek to understand the alignment between the announced business strategy and the alliance strategy for each firm. The alliance examples included in the chapter are for example purposes only and may not represent the companies' current business strategies—since these companies may have moved away from the alliances used in the examples.

The Partner Resource Exchange Model

The issue of value creation through alliance structures has received significant attention over the years. One perspective that addresses this value question is called the relational view of the firm.[11,12] The relational view of the firm argues that a firm's critical resources may extend *beyond* its boundaries, and that firms that combine resources in unique ways with alliance partners may realize a competitive advantage over competing firms. The firm's network of alliance partners is the important unit of analysis, and network positioning is the key performance issue. A strong network position provides the firm with competitive advantage. The relational view differs from the more traditional perspectives of the firm, such as the resource-based view of the firm[13–15] and capabilities view of the firm,[16,17] which describe competitive advantage as an outcome of resources and capabilities residing *within* the firm.

Dyer and Singh[11] also argue that the exchange of knowledge resources provides value to the alliance partners. Substantial knowledge exchange results in joint learning, and the integration of complementary resources results in the joint creation of new products, technologies, and services.

If the resources exchanged in an alliance are the source of value and competitive advantage, then what aspects of these resources are critical? We identify three dimensions of knowledge resources that are critical to the knowledge exchange between alliance partners: *tacitness, specificity,* and *complexity.* These three dimensions make it difficult to imitate a resource, and thus provide a source of both value creation and competitive advantage.[11,18] They are represented in the Partner Resource Exchange Model (PREM) shown in Figure 10.1.

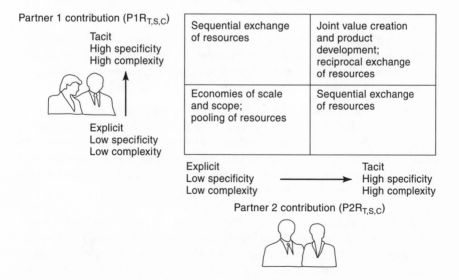

Figure 10.1 Partner Resource Exchange Model (PREM): Four quadrants of value creation.

The Model

Figure 10.1 describes a two-partner resource exchange in which the resources each partner contributes can be measured against the dimensions of tacitness, specificity, and complexity. We define a variable that reflects the degree to which a given partner contributes tacit, specific, and complex knowledge resources to the alliance. Thus, a high value of $P1R_{T,S,C}$ would indicate Partner 1 contributed highly tacit, highly specific, and highly complex knowledge resources to the alliance. This could be accomplished, for example, by Partner 1 providing on-site, experienced engineers to the alliance. Alliance value creation, Y, is a function of both the main effects of each partner's resource contribution, $P1R_{T,S,C}$, and $P2R_{T,S,C}$, as well as the interaction between the two, $P1R * P2R$.

$$Y = f(P1R_{T,S,C}, P2R_{T,S,C}, P1R * P2R)$$

As shown in Figure 10.1, the nature of knowledge resource exchange and the anticipated value vary significantly as one moves from alliances characterized by the lower-left quadrant to ones reflecting exchanges in the upper-right quadrant.

Resource dimension 1: Explicit → tacit. Explicit resources are resources that are codified and transferable in a formal, systemic language. It is knowledge that can be found in contracts, manuals, databases, licenses, or embedded in products. Tacit resources are those resources made up of knowledge that has a personal quality, making it difficult to formalize and communicate.[19] Tacit resources can reside in individuals, such as employees with expertise and know-how resulting from years of on-the-job experience, as well as in organizations, such as those with an established brand name and company culture. Tacit resources therefore by definition are more strategic than explicit resources, because they are more difficult to transfer and imitate.

On 9/18/97, Compaq Computer Corp. and Intel Corp. entered into a strategic alliance to develop 100-megabit ethernet equipment. Under the terms of the agreement, Compaq and Intel shared engineers and marketing resources in the development of the ethernet network equipment. [SDC database,[20] 9/18/97]

In the above example, both partners provide employees—highly tacit resources—to develop ethernet equipment. Most likely, these engineers will draw on their past experiences in product development projects to assist them in this alliance. Since this alliance involves tacit resources (engineering know-how), it will be difficult to imitate and therefore provides both Compaq Computer Corporation and Intel Corporation with a distinct advantage.

Resource dimension 2: Low specificity → high specificity. Resource specificity involves investments in durable, specialized resources that cannot be redeployed from existing uses and users except at a significant loss of productive value. Therefore, specificity refers to the condition that a resource is specialized to the needs of a specific transaction, either within a firm or between the firm and its external partners.[21] There has been evidence that resource specificity in an alliance leads to higher performance.[22]

Gold Disk Inc. granted Compaq Computer Corp. a non-exclusive license to market its Astound CSE software. Under the terms of the agreement, Compaq would market the multimedia presentation software called Astound CSE with Compaq's newest line of Presario multimedia. [SDC database, 4/3/95]

Accounting software developer State Of The Art Inc. Wednesday announced that it has finalized a distribution agreement with Apple Computer Inc., making the StarCore division of Apple the exclusive distributor of Expense It!, the business expense reporting software developed specifically for the Newton by State Of The Art. Under the agreement, Apple and its subsidiaries will license, market and resell the Expense It! software worldwide. [Business Wire, 9/29/93]

In the first alliance, there is low specificity since it involves a nonexclusive license. Therefore, another computer maker could market and bundle Gold Disk, Inc.'s software with its computers, as Compaq is doing now. This may result in low competitive advantage for Compaq if it fails to distinguish its product from the competition. The second alliance implies high specificity since the business software is being designed specifically for the Apple Newton platform. Therefore, this alliance has the greater potential for competitive advantage.

Resource dimension 3: Low complexity → high complexity. In the context of alliances, complexity refers to the degree of partner interdependence associated with alliance activities. Thompson[23] distinguishes between pooled, sequential, and reciprocal interdependence. Pooled interdependence exists in alliances when partners pool their resources to achieve a shared strategic goal. Usually, these alliances achieve economies of scale and scope by sharing high, fixed costs, or substituting existing resources with more efficient partner resources. Sequential interdependence indicates that the activities of each partner are distinct and linear so that the activities of one partner precede those of another. The objective in these alliances is to *gain access* to certain knowledge resources, such as market knowledge through a marketing agreement or technology knowledge through a licensing agreement. However, with both pooled and sequential alliances, the emphasis is on resource access/substitution and not on internalization or learning.

The highest degree of interdependence, or complexity, occurs with reciprocal interdependence when partners come together to exchange resources with each other simultaneously. These alliances involve a high degree of integration and coordination of each other's knowledge resources (e.g., research and development agreement), and offer the greatest opportunity to learn. From a relational-view perspective, complexity adds value in an alliance, because increased interdependence results in a unique combination of resources that is difficult to imitate.

Citrix Systems, Inc. (Nasdaq: CTXS) today announced a definitive licensing agreement with Hewlett-Packard for Citrix's Independent Computing Architecture (ICA), an emerging industry standard for thin-client/server computing. [Business Wire, 11/4/97]

Hitachi and Hewlett-Packard will jointly develop and manufacture an advanced model of HP's Precision Architecture RISC MPU. (SDC database, 6/13/90)

The first alliance involves a basic exchange agreement in which Hewlett-Packard Company receives licensed technology from Citrix Systems, Inc. There is most likely low interdependence and thus low complexity, because it involves a sequential exchange of resources. The second alliance has higher complexity, because both partners are involved in *joint* development and manufacturing, or reciprocal interdependence. This alliance will be difficult for other firms to imitate.

PREM: Four Quadrants of Value Creation

So far, we have defined three dimensions of knowledge exchange and have provided an example from the alliance literature. What is perhaps most significant is the interaction of each partner's resource contributions. In general, we argue that the potential for highest value creation and competitive advantage is achieved when both partners contribute strategic resources (i.e., those high on tacitness, specificity, and complexity dimensions) to the alliance, corresponding to the upper-right quadrant. Although all quadrants provide value, it is for different purposes. Therefore, relationships can be designed to deliver different levels of value based on strategic intent.

In the lower-left quadrant, where both partners contribute resources that are low on the tacitness, specificity, and complexity dimensions, emphasis is on improving operations, resulting in efficiency, risk reduction, and cost reduction. The purpose of these "operations-based" alliances is to interlink the two partners for better integration (e.g., firms align with their suppliers to achieve just-in-time deliveries, to improve the quality of materials and components and to reduce costs). An example of an operations-based alliance may be a manufacturing agreement. Since no one company may have enough market demand to build a plant of large capacity, it may make more sense to have a joint manufacturing alliance to improve scale costs. For example, in the semiconductor industry, with fabrication plants costing more than $1 billion, we are seeing more and more "fabless" (without fabrication facility) semiconductor firms forming manufacturing alliances with companies with excess capacity.

In the upper-left and lower-right quadrants of the diagram, one partner of the alliance provides a strategic resource while the other partner provides a low-level resource. An example includes a marketing agreement in which one partner provides customer knowledge, market access, or a brand name (each scoring high on the tacitness dimension), while the other partner provides the product to market (low on the tacitness dimension). Another common occurrence is a technology licensing agreement, with one partner paying royalties to gain access to the other partner's technology. Often, low complexity and specificity characterize these alliances. No new products or technologies are developed between partners, and there is very little joint effort or integration. The technology that is exchanged is usually in codified form. The tacit knowledge that is provided by one partner is often not shared, and very little learning takes place between partners.

In the upper-right quadrant, both partners provide strategic resources that are high on the tacitness, specificity, and complexity dimensions. As a result, the value created often results in strategic or highly differentiated capabilities. These alliances often involve partners that integrate their tacit knowledge to jointly develop new products or technologies. The resources that are exchanged are often customized to the relationship, and both partners usually have exclusive use of the technologies and products resulting from the alliance. The knowledge shared between partners is often tacit and integrated across several functions, and partner learning may be a major objective of each partner. Often, the partners may be from two different industries, and they combine resources in order to develop an emerging product market. In the next section, we use the PREM to explore alliance patterns in an industry setting.

PREM and the Industry Value Network

Another critical aspect of the relational view of the firm is the positioning of the alliance partners within a network structure. We use Brandenburger and Nalebuff's[10] model of an industry value network, which describes a firm's network position as its *role* relative to a focal firm in the industry. The role of the partner can take several forms, such as supplier, customer, complementor, competitor, and other (i.e., outside the industry). Brandenburger and Nalebuff[10] use the term *co-opetition* to describe the multiple roles of a partner, and how a partner may simultaneously be both a competitor and complementor to the focal firm. They define a competitor and complementor from both the customer and the supplier perspectives:

- A firm is your *complementor/competitor* if customers value your product *more/less* when they have the firm's product, than when they have your product alone.
- A firm is your *complementor/competitor* if it is *more/less* attractive for a supplier to supply resources to you when it is also supplying the firm, than when it is supplying you alone.

The motivations behind supplier, customer, complementor, and competitor alliances vary, which has implications on alliance management and performance.

We can now apply the PREM, shown previously, within this industry value network (Figure 10.2). A focal firm within an industry exchanges resources with its partner, who can be a complementor, competitor, supplier, or customer. We believe this integration is important since the resource exchange, and thus the value created, may be affected by the network positions of the alliance partners. For example, issues with misappropriation of critical knowledge may be more relevant in alliances with competitors than alliances with complementors. Also, by applying the PREM in an industry value network, we can analyze how a company's alliance strategy is affected by industry characteristics, such as time, concentration, and degree of technological change.

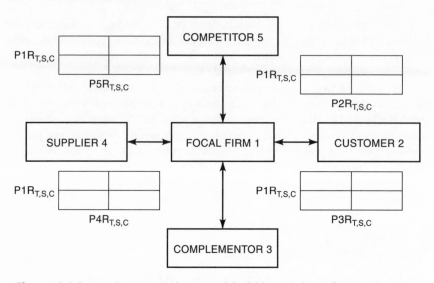

Figure 10.2 Partner Resource Exchange Model within an industry framework.

Complementor alliances. The underlying motivation behind alliances with complementors is to increase the customer base of a firm's product. If we designate a computer hardware firm as our focal firm, then alliances with complementors (e.g., software companies, network companies) are beneficial to both alliance partners, because the computer industry is dependent on network externalities and the benefits associated with an increased base of complementary products. These alliances often take the form of research and development (R&D) agreements, in which a product is developed that will help sell the focal firm's products, or joint marketing alliances, in which the focal firm will "bundle" the complementor's product with its own.

> The ASK Group Inc., a strategic business software developer and one of the largest independent software companies worldwide, expanded its partnership with Sun Microsystems to provide world-class enterprise computing solutions. (Business Wire, 11/10/93)

In this example, the ASK Group's software products are a complement to Sun, because it increases the installed base of software for Sun's computers, and this adds value for both existing and future Sun users.

Supplier alliances. Alliances with suppliers achieve tighter integration resulting in reduced costs, improved efficiencies, and improved quality for the focal firm. The supplier may also benefit from the legitimacy that comes with partnering or aligning oneself with a focal firm, especially if that focal firm is a market leader. Also, since the supplier understands the technology and components associated with the firm's products, supplier alliances may also involve product development. In the following example, Compaq and Storage Technology Corp., a supplier to Compaq, form an alliance to develop storage solutions.

> Storage Technology Corp. and Compaq Computer formed a strategic alliance to conduct advanced research and development projects to enhance the capabilities of emerging storage networks for Windows NT Enterprise Computing. (SDC database, 4/21/98)

Customer alliances. Customer alliances benefit both parties (the focal firm and its partner), because customers are an important source of innovation for enhancing existing products or developing new products, customizing design, improving customer service, and reducing costs through tighter integration of the distribution channel. Customer alliances, often referred to as "relationship marketing," tend to focus on customer retention, again through a deep involvement of the customer in the design and development of the firm's product or service offerings.[24]

> On 1/28/98, Compaq Computer Corp. and Radio Shack, a unit of Tandy Corp., signed a letter of intent to enter into a strategic alliance to market a line of specially exhibited Compaq Presario Computers and accessories. Compaq also granted Radio Shack a license to provide services for the entire line of Compaq Computers. (SDC database, 1/28/98)

In this example, the retail customer Radio Shack Co. is deepening its relationship with Compaq by providing specialized service and marketing for Compaq's computers.

Competitor alliances. Alliances with competitors may take the form of licensing arrangements, joint ventures, and consortia.[25] Joint ventures with competitors may occur for the following reasons: lower costs of high-risk, technology-intensive development projects; gain economies of scale and scope; learn from the partner through access to a partner's technology and accumulated knowledge; and shape a basis for future competition in the industry. Licensing with a competitor may be due to: an inability to capitalize on the technology by itself, the desire to set industry standards early in a product's life cycle, or the need for a defensive mechanism to protect against future litigation.

> Hitachi and Hewlett-Packard will jointly develop and manufacture an advanced model of HP's Precision Architecture RISC MPU. (SDC database, 6/13/90)

Hitachi and Hewlett-Packard are competitors, because they both compete in the workstation and server markets. In this example, Hewlett-Packard may want to make its core RISC (reduced instruction set computing) chip an industry standard so it is teaming up with a competitor to increase acceptance of its technology.

"Other" alliances. Alliances with partners outside the computer industry may allow for a new revenue stream for both firms in the alliance. Usually, each firm in the alliance brings a different capability or knowledge base, which is then integrated to produce a new product or service offering. In the following example, both Sun

Microsystems and Eastman Kodak Company generate a new revenue stream by developing photography solutions for the computer. Sun provides computer technology expertise, while Kodak provides photography expertise. Most likely, it would be very difficult or inefficient for either firm to try to provide computer photography on its own.

> Sun and Kodak Announce Initiative to Provide Digital Photo Management and Internet Distribution. (Business Wire, 3/12/97)

Using this industry value network approach, we can now examine how firms with different business strategies pursue different alliance strategy portfolios. In the next section, we empirically examine the alliance strategy portfolio for two firms in the computer sector. We use the PREM to illustrate how firms can effectively link their business strategy to their alliance strategy.

Applying the Model: Two Case Studies

We applied the overall resource exchange model (Figure 10.2) within the computer hardware industry. We analyzed two-partner alliance announcements for both Dell Computer and Sun Microsystems in the period 1990–1998. We used two sources: (1) Securities Data Company's (SDC) commercially available database of alliance announcements, and (2) the Lexis-Nexis on-line database. SDC contains alliance announcements from press wires (e.g., Dow Jones, Reuters), major newspapers (e.g., the *Wall Street Journal*, the *New York Times*), and leading trade magazines. The keywords used to perform the Lexis-Nexis search were *agreement* or *alliance* or *partnership* and the name of the focal firm in the announcement title (i.e., Dell Computer or Sun Microsystems). For Lexis-Nexis, only alliance announcements obtained from either PR Newswire or Business Wire were used. We included all types of alliance announcements: licensing, equity investment, joint venture, OEM (other equipment manufacturers), marketing, R&D, technology transfer, and service agreements.

A coding scheme was developed to measure what each partner in the alliance provides in terms of *tacitness, specificity,* and *complexity* resources.[26] Scores for each resource variable ranged from "0" (low tacitness, low specificity, low complexity) to "1" (high tacitness, high specificity, high complexity).

Tacitness—the tacitness variable measures a firm's tacit resource contribution to the alliance. Resources that are more tangible or contractual in form (e.g., products, licenses) score low in tacitness, while resources that are more intangible in form (e.g., brand, employee expertise) score high in tacitness. Each of the two firms in the alliance receives a separate score for tacitness, depending on what each firm contributes.

Specificity—The specificity variable measures the specificity of a firm's resource contribution to the alliance. For alliances that involve exclusive and specialized resources, the specificity score is high. Alliances that involve nonspecific resource exchange score low with respect to specificity.

Complexity—The complexity variable measures the complexity of the alliance activities between the two partners. We define two separate measures of complexity: *number of alliance activities* (complexity#, for short) and *interdependency of alliance activities* (complexity-coordination, for short). The number of alliance activities variable is calculated by summing the number of activities in the alliance. An alliance can have more than one activity (e.g., an R&D and marketing alliance), and complexity# increases as there are more activities. The interdependency of alliance activities variable measures the degree of activity coordination between the two partners. Alliances with high coordination between partners (e.g., joint ventures, joint R&D projects) score high in complexity-coordination, while alliances with low coordination between partners score low.

Technology—We also included a resource measure called *technology*. Actually, we consider the technology variable to be closely related and correlated with the tacitness variable, but there is enough distinction to warrant measuring these variables separately. The technology variable measures a firm's technology resource contribution to the alliance. We define technology as input resources that are used in the development of products or services. Whereas the tacitness variable measures the types of resource (i.e., tangible versus intangible), the technology variable measures the resource as a factor of development. Therefore, there can be some empirical differences between the two variables. For example, a technology license scores low with respect to tacitness since it involves a contractual form with explicit information, but scores high with respect to technology since the technical information will be used to develop new products.

We followed Weber's[27] content analysis methodology when developing the coding scheme. The coding scheme is a process by which each variable is assigned a score between "0" and "1" based on the appearance of certain keywords in the alliance announcement. Special attention is paid to developing a list of synonyms for critical keywords and providing examples for the more ambiguous interpretations. Three M.B.A. (Master of Business Administration) students were the coders for this research. The coders were trained and given test sample alliance announcements. In total, the coders went through three iterations of test samples, and interrater reliability numbers using Cohen's Kappa went from .7, .75, to .8. The reliability of the coders was also assessed during and after the final coding was completed. The reliability numbers remained in the .7 to .8 range.

We also measured *partner role* in each alliance as "complementor," "competitor," "supplier," "customer," or "other" (Table 10.1). The main product classification of the partner was used to determine the role of the partner. The partner main product codes were obtained from the SDC database and 10-K SEC (Securities and Exchange Commission) filings. Since Dell Computer and Sun Microsystems, makers of computer hardware, are the focal firms in our study, complementors include software companies and network/telecommunications/information technology (IT) solution providers, since these partners "complement" or aid the computer hardware makers in selling more of their products. Competitors are other computer hardware makers. Suppliers include companies involved with peripherals (e.g., printers), electronics (e.g., semiconductors, motherboards), and storage

Table 10.1 Partner roles in the Dell Computer, Sun Microsystems study

Partner Role Assigned	Partner Main Product
Complementor	Software, networking, telecommunications, IT service
Competitor Supplier	Computer hardware Peripherals, semiconductors, storage, electronics
Customer	Computer reseller, distributor, retailer, end customer
Other	Outside the technology industry (e.g., media, publishing, entertainment)

(e.g., disk drives). Customers include IT distributors, retailers, and end customers. Finally, "others" include firms not involved in the above computer technology sectors, such as entertainment, pharmaceutical, news content, and publishing companies.

Dell Computer and Sun Microsystems Alliance Portfolios (1990–1998)

Based on our research methodology, Figure 10.3 shows the alliance portfolios for Dell Computer and Sun Microsystems based on the number of alliances each has had with each partner type. Table 10.2 lists the knowledge resource measures of contributions by Dell, Sun, and their partners. The five resource variables—tacitness, technology, specificity, complexity#, and complexity-coordination—are measured on a scale between "0" and "1." The overall statistics column contains entries of the form A(S), where A is the average and S is the standard deviation. The specificity and complexity variables are alliance-level variables and therefore have the same value for the focal firm and its partners.

These portfolios illustrate within the PREM the alliance strategy for both Sun and Dell. Figure 10.3 shows that Dell relies heavily on alliances with its suppliers (41.7 percent of total). Also, we see in Table 10.2 that Dell relies on its partners both for technology (.38 overall score) and tacit resources (.31 overall score). Both are higher levels than what Dell provides to its partners for technology (.22) and tacit resources (.21).

Meanwhile, as we see in Table 10.2, Sun relies heavily on licensing its technology to develop industry standards, and so Sun shows high levels of technology resource contributions (.52 overall), especially to competitors (.65). When comparing Sun versus Dell directly, Sun provides its partners with much higher overall tacit resources (.38 vs .21) and technology resources (.52 vs .22) than Dell provides its partners.

We also tried to understand the alignment of announced business strategy with alliance strategy and to understand the different approaches of Dell and Sun with regard to alliance strategy (Table 10.3). We used press releases, analyst reports, and company reports to understand each firm's business strategy, and we used the alliance data from this research to understand each firm's alliance strategy.

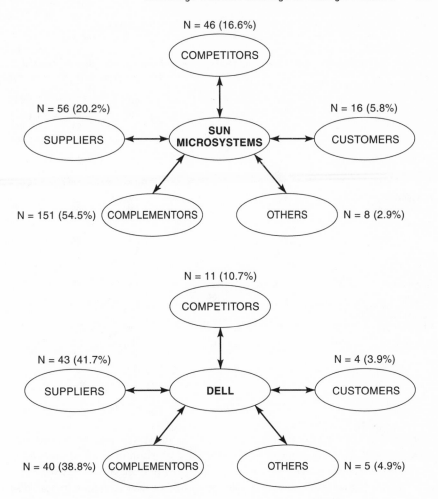

Figure 10.3 Sun Microsystems and Dell Computer alliance portfolios.

Sun Microsystems Business and Alliance Strategy

Sun Microsystems is vertically integrated, since it owns or controls the major components of its computer systems. It develops its own operating system, designs its own microprocessor and other hardware components, and provides services to its platform customers. Sun develops much of its technology in-house, and its alliance strategy (based on our research results) focuses on technology licensing agreements to develop industry standards.

Sun Microsystems is a market leader in computer servers and workstations, but unlike many of its peers, does not compete in the personal computer market. Sun's business strategy has been to pioneer the use of shared software and hardware components among competing computer makers in order to promote indus-

Table 10.2 Knowledge resource measures of partners' contributions

	Suppliers	Customers	Complementors	Competitors	Others	Overall Statistics
Tactiness						
Sun	.34	.08	.42	.40	.33	.38 (.32)
Dell	.23	.09	.16	.38	.23	.21 (.28)
Sun partners	.34	.31	.44	.37	.52	.40 (.34)
Dell partners	.25	.22	.39	.26	.30	.31 (.29)
Technology						
Sun	.53	.18	.53	.65	.41	.52 (.40)
Dell	.24	.09	.21	.23	.13	.22 (.27)
Sun partners	.39	.23	.50	.46	.45	.45 (.40)
Dell partners	.38	.09	.44	.41	.05	.38 (.33)
Specificity						
Sun/partners	.27	.22	.37	.28	.25	.32 (.30)
Dell/partners	.28	.25	.44	.41	1.0	.39 (.37)
Complexity #						
Sun/partners	.22	.31	.25	.17	.13	.23 (.31)
Dell/partners	.22	.13	.29	.32	.10	.25 (.31)
Complexity-Coordination						
Sun/partners	.35	.16	.39	.34	.28	.36 (.37)
Dell/partners	.20	.13	.26	.32	.35	.24 (.26)

try standards. In the late 1980s, Sun introduced its SPARC microprocessor, one of several RISC-based microprocessors in the industry running the UNIX operating system. Realizing the fragmented state of the UNIX market, Sun licensed SPARC to stimulate high-volume, low-cost sales of its SPARC-based computers and also to increase the application software support for its systems.[28]

In the early 1990s, Sun essentially became a hybrid hardware-software company by developing the Solaris operating system, which not only ran on its SPARC systems, but also on Intel-based microprocessors. This, again, increased application software support for its systems. In 1995, Sun introduced Java, a programming language and platform that allows users to run programs on any computer system. With the advent of the Internet in the mid-1990s, Sun has been very successful promoting its servers as the building block of the Internet.[28]

Based on our research results, Sun's alliance strategy in the 1990–1998 period has been to license its technology to develop industry standards. From our study sample, a large percentage of its alliances involve licensing, and the number of licenses it provides is twice the number of licenses it receives. A majority of Sun's licenses involve its Java and Solaris software. In fact, from our study sample, over 40 percent of Sun's total alliances involve software, and over half of Sun's alliances involve complementors (e.g., software, networking, IT service

Table 10.3 Sun Microsystems and Dell Computer announced business and alliance strategy

Focal Firm	Business Strategy	Alliance Strategy
Sun Microsystems	Highly vertical ownership of technology (operating system plus CPU), provide services	Align with partners to provide services (e.g., IBM, EDS, Andersen Consulting)
	Use of shared software and hardware components among different vendors to create industry standards	Licensing of technology (e.g., Java, Solaris, SPARC) to develop industry standards
		Align with resellers to sell into indirect channels
	Belief in open systems to allow computers to talk to one another	Outsource manufacturing of SPARC chips to Texas Instruments
	Internet/e-commerce specialist	Internet alliances (e.g., Netscape/AOL) to deliver applications and services
Dell Computer	Virtual integration control flow of information from suppliers to customers	OEM alliances with key component suppliers such as Intel
	Assembler versus owner of technology	Service alliances with Decision One, IBM, EDS, Andersen Consulting
	Direct model (with both suppliers and customers) offers competitive advantage (low cost, first-to-market with latest technology)	Generate revenue "outside the box" by aligning with Internet service providers (e.g., AOL)
		Streamline logistics with suppliers by implementing valuechain.com
	Desire to move into the enterprise computer market	Distribution alliances with value added resellers and retailers to gain international presence
		Technology transfer agreements (e.g., IBM) to move into enterprise market

firms). Sun will license its technology not only to its complementors, such as software companies, but also to its competitors or other computer hardware makers.

Sun does outsource the manufacturing of several of its hardware components, namely the manufacturing of its SPARC chips to Texas Instruments, Inc. Sun does rely on indirect channels to sell its systems, with alliances with resellers such as Ingram Micro, Inc., and Merisel, Inc. Sun contracted service alliances for its SPARC systems with consultant companies and system integrators such as Andersen Consulting and EDS, as well as with competitor IBM. More recently, Sun has formed Internet alliances with Netscape Communications Corporation and AOL in order to deliver applications and services that allow enterprise customers to get launched on the Internet. Future alliances, we predict, will involve the licensing and promotion of Sun's new software technology (called Jini) to connect a vast array of electronic devices and appliances to the Internet.

Dell Computer Business and Alliance Strategy

Dell Computer has a much different business and alliance strategy than Sun Microsystems. Dell designs, customizes, and assembles PC (personal computer) products and services to end-user requirements using industry standard components. Dell has never vertically integrated PC component production into its manufacturing model, instead leveraging supplier alliances to obtain parts on a build-to-order basis.[29] This direct model approach has given Dell a competitive advantage, and today Dell ranks as one of the leading PC vendors in the world.

Based on our research results, Dell's alliance strategy fully complements its business strategy of being the leading direct marketer of personal computers. From our study, 33 percent of Dell's alliance activities are OEM arrangements, and 42 percent of Dell's alliances are with suppliers, such as semiconductors and peripheral companies. These include agreements with key component suppliers such as Intel and 3Com Corporation. Also, Dell has streamlined logistics with suppliers by implementing valuechain.com, an electronic market of 50 of its suppliers.

From our study sample, Dell also has a relatively high percentage of service alliances. Customer service is a critical aspect of Dell's business model, and Dell may need to rely on alliances to perform this capability. Recent service partners include Decision One, IBM, Wang Laboratories, Unisys, EDS, and Andersen Consulting. Even though they have relied on the direct model of selling PCs in the United States, Dell has formed alliances with value-added resellers (VARs), distributors, and retailers in international markets where they have not yet established a presence, and in certain corporate accounts where selling direct is not possible. Dell has formed alliances with Ingram Micro, Inc., Tech Data Corporation, and Merisel in foreign markets. Dell may continue to align itself with foreign distributors or retailers until it has established a presence and achieved enough critical mass to set up a direct sales operation.

Our study shows that Dell has a relatively low percentage of R&D alliances, and relatively low tacitness and technology contribution scores among its peers. Dell has considered itself as much a marketing company as a hardware company, and has focused its R&D resources on selecting and evaluating appropriate technology and architectures, as opposed to new product development.[29,30]

However, Dell's announced future business model is to move into more complex enterprise computing and services, such as e-commerce service, and this will require more technology and service capabilities. We predict alliances will be a critical enabler of this strategy. Most likely, Dell will form joint R&D technology transfer, and service alliances with established companies that have these capabilities, as opposed to developing all these capabilities internally. In fact, we are starting to witness this trend with the recent announcements of joint technology and service agreements with IBM, Microsoft Corporation, Intel, and Redhat. Finally, like all PC makers, Dell is looking to generate revenue "outside the box" and their recent alliance with AOL is one such example.

Alignment between Business Strategy and Alliance Strategy Is Key

Based on our analysis, we do find an alignment between the announced business strategy and the alliance strategy for both Dell and Sun. In other words, Dell and Sun may have designed their alliances with their business strategy in mind. We also find significant differences between the firms in terms of strategy. Sun's strategy seems to be ownership of technology to create industry standards, whereas Dell positions itself as an assembler versus an owner of technology. Our point here is not that one particular strategy is more successful, but it is the alignment between business strategy and alliance strategy that is important. The implication is critical since most managers are focused on the allocation and management of *internal* resources to achieve business strategy. With more and more firms relying on *external* knowledge resources from its alliance partners, managers must now ensure the proper alignment between business and alliance strategy. Another implication is that we have to expand our thinking on alliance "success." Traditional alliance success measures such as duration and financial-based metrics may be insufficient if the business strategy is to reduce exposure to risk or to develop industry standards. Alliance success measurement, therefore, should include a linkage to business strategy.

Changes in Alliance Portfolio over Time

So far, we have shown that our Partner Resource Exchange Model is a useful lens to analyze the knowledge resources that a firm provides and receives in an alliance, as well as the different types of partners with which it conducts business. We believe our model is also useful in a *dynamic* environment, because it can represent changes in a firm's alliance portfolio over time. A firm's alliance portfolio changes over time, because the firm is either constantly adding or removing partners from its portfolio, or the firm is changing its behavior toward its partners in terms of resource contribution and management, or the firm's position in the industry network is constantly in flux. For example, a partner, who has been a supplier for many years, has now become a competitor. Most likely, this will change how the firm behaves toward this partner, in terms of resource exchange.

To illustrate how the resource exchange model can represent a dynamic environment, we use changes in Sun Microsystem's alliance portfolio over time. We divided our sample in half, from 1990 to mid-1994, and from mid-1994 to 1998 (Figure 10.4, Table 10.4). From 1990 to mid-1994, Sun has alliances with many competitors, in which Sun contributes computer technology in the form of licensing arrangements. From mid-1994 to 1998, we notice a drop-off in alliances with competitors and a large increase in alliances with complementors. Also, these alliances with complementors involve technology licensing, a large percentage of which involve Java licensing to software firms in order to establish Java as an industry standard. The emergence of the Internet in the latter half of the 1990s most likely had an effect on Sun's alliance strategy, and this is reflected in Sun's attempt to develop "open" software standards, such as Java.

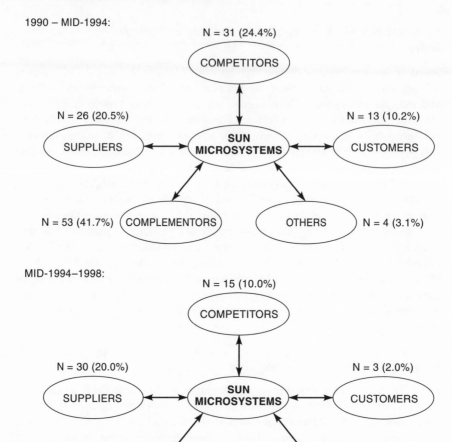

Figure 10.4 Change in Sun's alliance portfolio over time.

This example is at an aggregate level, since it takes into account all of Sun's alliance partners. However, we can use our model to analyze changes with a particular partner, or group of partners, over time. For example, Sun Microsystems may have had ten separate alliances with a particular partner. Over time, the role of the partner may have changed (e.g., from supplier to competitor to complementor), and the resource exchange may have changed. Therefore, what is critical to understand is not simply the number of previous ties with this partner (in this case ten), but the change in network positioning and resource exchange with the partner over time. Therefore, the resource exchange model is useful in analyzing changes in a firm's alliance portfolio over time.

Table 10.4. Knowledge resource measures of partners' contributions—pre- and post-Internet

	Suppliers	Customers	Complementors	Competitors	Others	Overall Statistics
Tacitness						
Sun pre-94	.40	.08	.40	.40	.25	.36 (.33)
Sun post-94	.28	.08	.44	.42	.41	.39 (.32)
Partner pre-94	.45	.32	.46	.37	.56	.43 (.33)
Partner post-94	.24	.25	.43	.38	.47	.39 (.34)
Technology						
Sun pre-94	.51	.20	.38	.62	.28	.44 (.37)
Sun post-94	.55	.11	.61	.69	.53	.59 (.41)
Partner pre-94	.48	.23	.54	.44	.56	.47 (.38)
Partner post-94	.32	.19	.48	.50	.34	.44 (.41)
Specificity						
Sun/partners pre-94	.27	.23	.42	.26	.25	.33 (.29)
Sun/partners post-94	.27	.17	.34	.33	.25	.32 (.30)
Complexity#						
Sun/partners pre-94	.25	.31	.35	.19	.13	.28 (.31)
Sun/partners post-94	.20	.33	.19	.13	.13	.19 (.30)
Complexity-Coordination						
Sun/partners pre-94	.39	.17	.44	.32	.25	.37 (.38)
Sun/partners post-94	.31	.08	.36	.37	.31	.35 (.36)

Alliance Learning Capability

So far, we have discussed knowledge resource exchange and the potential for value creation based on the type and nature of the resource exchange. We have also presented an overall model that looks at this resource exchange within an industry value network, and have used the model in a study of the alliances of Dell and Sun. However, we have not yet discussed the process of learning from, and managing, the knowledge obtained through alliances. Next, we discuss the implications of knowledge resource exchange on alliance management.

The partner resource exchange may be part of the initial structure to the alliance. For example, we have argued that alliances that involve an exchange of tacit, specialized knowledge resources have the *potential* to have high value creation. Our study analyzed the initial resource exchange at the time of the alliance announcement. However, as the alliance evolves, an important construct related to *realized* performance is *alliance learning capability* (Figure 10.5). In other words, alliances involving a significant exchange of tacit, specialized, and complex resources may be successful if there is an alliance learning capability. The literature has identified three types of learning associated with alliances,[31] which we refer to as *alliance learning capability.*

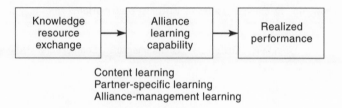

Figure 10.5 Alliance learning capability.

Content Learning

The first type of learning, and the most commonly studied, is content learning, and it is often referred to as private benefits. Content learning represents the ability of the focal firm leader to internalize the knowledge it receives from the alliance partner, and is dependent on such factors as learning intent and absorptive capacity. Intent to learn refers to the firm's propensity to view alliances as an opportunity to learn. As described earlier, alliances can be used as resource access or substitution mechanisms, with the intent on cost reduction or compensation for lack of knowledge, as opposed to opportunities to learn from the partner. In U.S.-Japanese alliances, for example, Japanese firms have often viewed collaboration as a way to learn, while U.S. firms have used alliances as a way to substitute for more competitive skills, resulting in an erosion of internal skills and ultimately competitive disadvantage.[32] Therefore, even if there is an exchange of tacit resources in an alliance, the partner must have learning as an objective in order to capture long-term benefits.

Absorptive capacity refers to the firm's ability to internalize the knowledge it receives from its partner. This involves the firm's ability to recognize the value of new, external information, assimilate it, and apply it to commercial ends.[33] Absorptive capacity is a function of the firm's level of prior related knowledge. For example, if a firm collaborates with a partner outside its industry, absorptive capacity might be an issue since the firm might not have the level of understanding needed to internalize a new knowledge domain. Alliances with competitors, meanwhile, often present an ideal situation to learn, because the knowledge bases of the partners are similar.

Partner-Specific Learning

Partner-specific learning involves the process of learning from, and learning about, an individual alliance partner. A key component of this process is called *transparency*, which is the firm's opportunity to learn from its partner.[32] The easier it is to transfer the knowledge and skills from a partner, the easier it is to learn. Often, compatible language and culture between the alliance partners enable transparency. Social aspects of the relationship, such as trust, reputation, and previous ties, are also very important to partner specific learning, because they allow for greater transparency. For example, previous ties or interactions with a partner enable a firm to understand where the critical partner's expertise resides and whom to contact in order to gain access to this knowledge. Trust and reputation allow for the establishment of knowledgesharing routines between partners without fear of opportunism or the free-rider problem. Trust and reputation also reduce transaction costs (e.g., costs of writing and enforcing contracts), while simultaneously allowing the alliance partner to invest in specialized resources or share tacit resources without fear of misappropriation.[11] Also, not everything has to be written in contracts. Emergent or changing goals, redefined joint activities, and management of decision rights and residual claims can be handled effectively through an informal structure due to the close working relationship with a partner. In summary, partner-specific learning is very critical when there is an exchange of tacit, specialized, and complex knowledge resources. The existence of partner-specific knowledge routines, coupled with an effective working environment, will enable learning to take place. If there is low trust, a cautious alliance environment will exist, resulting in a low likelihood of finding, transferring, and sharing knowledge.

Alliance Management Learning

The third type of learning is often referred to as *alliance-management learning* and is often built over time with alliance experience. This type of learning involves the management of a *portfolio of alliances*. Whereas partner-specific learning focuses on an individual alliance, alliance-management learning focuses on the firm's ability to manage multiple alliances simultaneously. The critical success factor, we believe, is the ability to manage the interdependencies between alliances to produce a complementary portfolio. The role of the partner plays an important part in understanding the interdependencies. For example, a portfolio of alliances that consists of competitors promoting competing standards might result in a "negative" portfolio, even if the objective of the focal firm is to learn from its competitors. Partners might be protective and reluctant to share any important knowledge with the focal firm when they realize the focal firm is also partnering with their competitor. However, a portfolio consisting of partners promoting similar standards or technology innovations might be considered a complementary portfolio, because partners are more likely to share their knowledge resources. The manager could perhaps think of a complementary portfolio as a balanced number of competitor partners for learning, developing standards, and sharing costs; complementor partners to increase the user base of its products; supplier and customer partners to improve logistics; and "other" partners to diversify from the core product line. Similarly, a complementary portfolio could mean a balance between receiving knowledge resources and providing knowledge resources. Finally, the manager must ensure that the capabilities and resources the firm receives from its alliance partners complement the capabilities and resources it already has internally. The important point we want to convey is that the manager must manage alliances holistically as well as individually, since the firm has multiple alliances, with each alliance having an effect on the other alliances.

Concluding Remarks

Strategic alliances are no longer a strategic option but a necessity in many markets and industries. Dynamic markets for both end products and technologies, coupled with the increasing costs of doing business, have resulted in a significant increase in the use of alliances. Yet, practitioners are finding it increasingly difficult to capture value from alliances. In this chapter, we have presented a model (PREM) that illustrates the knowledge resource exchange between alliance partners. This model focuses on the different dimensions of the resources and their associated value implications. We applied this model in an industry value network, where we studied the different roles of the partner. We have also argued that in order to capture and internalize knowledge obtained through alliances, a firm must have an alliance learning capability. We illustrated this model in the computer industry by analyzing the publicly announced alliances of Dell Computer and Sun Microsystems. By applying our Partner Resource Exchange Model, we were able to analyze the alliance strategy for each firm, and to understand the alignment between their announced business strategy and alliance strategy. We hope this chapter stimulates further thinking and research in the area of learning and knowledge transfer in alliance relationships and networks.

Notes

SPARC, UNIX, Solaris, Java, and Jini are the trademarks or registered trademarks of Sun Microsystems, Inc., or The Open Group.

1 J. R. Harbison and P. Pekar, *Smart Alliances: A Practical Guide to Repeatable Success,* Jossey-Bass Publishers, San Francisco, CA (1998).

2 Alliance Analyst, "Computer Collaboration," May 15, 1995, pp. 14–18.

3 J. Hagedoorn, "Understanding the Rationale of Strategic Technology Partnering: Interorganizational Modes of Cooperation and Sectoral Differences," *Strategic Management Journal,* 14, 371–385 (1993).

4 K. R. Harrigan, "Strategic Alliances and Partner Asymmetries," in *Cooperative Strategies in International Business,* Lexington Books, Lexington, MA (1998), pp. 205–226.

5 J. Bleeke and D. Ernst, "Is Your Strategic Alliance Really a Sale?" *Harvard Business Review* 73, 97–105 (1995).

6 G. Hamel, "Competition for Competence and Interpartner Learning within International Strategic Alliances," *Strategic Management Journal* 12, 83–104 (1991).

7 J. Hagedoorn and J. Schakenraad, "The Effects of Strategic Technology Alliances on Company Performance," *Strategic Management Journal* 15, 291–309 (1994).

8 X. Stuart, "Interorganizational Alliances and the Performance of Firms: A Study of Growth and Innovation Rates in a High-Technology Industry," *Strategic Management Journal* 21, 791–811 (2000).

9 J. C. Henderson and M. R. Subramani, "The Shifting Ground between Markets and Hierarchy: Managing a Portfolio of Relationships," *Renewing Administration,* Anker Publishing Company, Inc., Bolton, MA (1999), pp. 99–125.

10 A. M. Brandenburger and B. J. Nalebuff, *Co-opetition,* Doubleday, New York (1996).

11 J. H. Dyer and H. Singh, "The Relational View: Cooperative Strategy and Sources of Interorganizational Competitive Advantage," *Academy of Management Review* 23, No. 4, 660–679 (1998).

12 R. Gulati, N. Nohria, and A. Zaheer, "Strategic Networks," *Strategic Management Journal* 21, 203–215 (2000).

13 B. Wernerfelt, "A Resource-Based View of the Firm," *Strategic Management Journal* 5, 171–180 (1984).

14 J. Barney, "Strategic Factor Markets: Expectations, Luck, and Business Strategy," *Management Science* 32, No. 10, 1231–1241 (1986).

15 J. Barney, "Firm Resources and Sustained Competitive Advantage," *Journal of Management* 17, 99–120 (1991).

16 G. Hamel and C. K. Prahalad, *Competing for the Future*, Harvard Business School Press, Boston, MA (1994).

17 D. J. Teece, G. Pisano, and A. Shuen, "Dynamic Capabilities and Strategic Management," *Strategic Management Journal* 18, 509–533 (1997).

18 R. Reed and R. J. DeFillippi, "Causal Ambiguity, Barriers to Imitation, and Sustainable Competitive Advantage," *Academy of Management Review* 15, 88–102 (1990).

19 M. Polanyi, *Personal Knowledge: Towards a Post-critical Philosophy*, University of Chicago Press, Chicago, IL (1962).

20 Securities Data Company's commercially available database.

21 O. E. Williamson, *The Economic Institutions of Capitalism*, Free Press, New York (1985).

22 J. H. Dyer, "Specialized Supplier Networks as a Source of Competitive Advantage: Evidence from the Auto Industry," *Strategic Management Journal* 17, 271–291 (1996).

23 J. D. Thompson, *Organizations in Action: Social Science Bases of Administration*, McGraw-Hill, Inc., New York (1967).

24 A. Magrath and K. Hardy, "Building Customer Partnerships," *Business Horizons* 37, No. 1, 24–29 (1994).

25 D. Lei and J. W. Slocum, Jr., "Global Strategic Alliances: Payoffs and Pitfalls," *Organizational Dynamics* 19, No. 3, 44–62 (1991).

26 A coding scheme was developed and tested for reliability by the first author.

27 R. P. Weber, *Basic Content Analysis*, Sage Publications, Newbury Park, CA (1990).

28 *International Directory of Company Histories*, Vol. 30, St. James Press, Detroit, MI (2000).

29 R. Cihra, ING Baring Furman Selz LLC Report, Dell Computer Corporation, October 13, 1998.

30 *International Directory of Company Histories*, Vol. 9, St. James Press, Detroit, MI (1994).

31 P. Kale, H. Singh, and H. Perlmutter, "Learning and Protection of Proprietary Assets in Strategic Alliances: Building Relational Capital," *Strategic Management Journal* 21, 217–237 (2000).

32 Y. L. Doz and G. Hamel, *Alliance Advantage*, Harvard Business School Press, Boston, MA (1998).

33 W. M. Cohen and D. A. Levinthal, "Absorptive Capacity: A New Perspective on Learning and Innovation," *Administrative Science Quarterly* 35, 128–152 (1990).

11

Leveraging Knowledge Management across Strategic Alliances

SALVATORE PARISE
LISA SASSON

With an annual growth rate of 25 per cent and a projected value of $40 trillion by the year 2004, there is little doubt that alliances will have a major impact on management in the 21st century. The "make versus buy" decision that once confronted decision makers has expanded and is now a more complex "make versus buy versus partner" decision. Alliance managers must make difficult decisions about when to partner and with whom, as well as how to structure and manage the partnership. Managers who can leverage information and knowledge across each stage of the alliance process will find that a knowledge-based approach is critical to the success of any partnership. In this chapter, we discuss the importance and effectiveness of sound knowledge management practices in the context of an alliance.

Any discussion of a knowledge-based approach to alliance management must be based on several truths.

- If managed correctly, alliances can significantly increase a company's financial returns. As a recent study pointed out, companies expect that by 2003, 35 per cent of their revenues will come from alliances, up from 21 per cent in 1998 and 15 per cent in 1995. (Harbison J. R., and Pekar P., *A Practical Guide to Repeatable Success,* Jossey-Bass Publishers, San Francisco, 1998; "Alliance Management," December 1999/January 2000, *CMA Management,* 73(10); 14–15.) But alliances do more than contribute to a firm's bottom line. Firms can no longer develop all the resources, technologies and products to compete in today's dynamic marketplace, and so many of those firms use alliances to acquire the critical skills, knowledge and capabilities that they lack.

- Companies form R&D alliances, not simply to reach short-term financial milestones, but to observe, learn and internalize the know-how of their partners. In U.S.-Japanese alliances in the past, for example, Japanese companies saw these partnerships as a way to learn from their partner, while their U.S. counterparts used these alliances as a substitute for more competitive skills, ultimately resulting in an erosion of their own internal skills. (Doz, Y. L., and Hamel, G., *Alliance Advantage*, Harvard Business School Press, Boston, 1998.) Therefore, with companies that look on alliances as a way of learning from their partners, practices that enable knowledge sharing, creation, dissemination and internalization become critical.
- An alliance knowledge management capability is both an important component of alliance success and a differentiating factor. Managing knowledge resources in an alliance is extremely challenging, and it is a primary reason for high failure rates in knowledge-based partnerships. Alliance success rates of less than 50 per cent have been cited in the management literature.

However, recent evidence shows that using a knowledge-based approach to alliances is effective. Companies that have greater alliance experience seem to enjoy higher success rates. This implies that companies should learn from their past and institutionalize their knowledge rather than take an ad-hoc approach to alliances. In a recent study, those companies that learned from their alliance experience, and then shared and disseminated the knowledge throughout their organization, had greater success. (Kale, P., and Singh, H., *Alliance Capability and Success: A Knowledge Based Approach*, Wharton School of Business White Paper, 1999.) Based on interviews we conducted with alliance managers in several companies, we noticed a wide variance in an alliance group's knowledge management capabilities. Those companies who employed standard, effective alliance processes or systematically captured alliance and partner information were more successful than those companies that did not have a knowledge management capability.

- Having an alliance knowledge management capability allows companies to deal with the increasing complexity that managing a portfolio of alliance partners entails. Most companies are involved with managing many partners simultaneously and are often working on several alliance projects with the same partner. It is critical that individual alliance managers share information with other managers, since the alliances are often interdependent. For example, alliance managers often indicated that, if they had known that their company was already involved in an existing alliance with Partner A, they would have structured the partnership with Partner B differently, given that Partner A and Partner B were competitors in certain market segments. Also, having knowledge about other partners in the portfolio creates new opportunities by combining the capabilities of multiple partners. Therefore, mechanisms that allow alliance managers to access information about the other alliance projects and partners in their company are important for alliance success.
- Finally, research has revealed that different types of learning occur in a partnership. It is important to distinguish among the different types since

each one may require a different knowledge management practice. Content learning is perhaps the most common type of learning and involves acquiring the partner's skills and know-how. Partner learning involves building social capital with the partner. The intent is to understand the partner's culture and work routines, and use this knowledge to continuously build an effective relationship with that partner. The intent with alliance process learning is to understand what went right and what went wrong with the alliance project, and to build an organizational memory of this knowledge. These alliance lessons can then be documented and shared with the entire alliance team.

The Strategic Alliance Defined

Despite the variety of partnership arrangements, academics and industry practitioners agree on those characteristics that differentiate strategic alliances from mergers and other forms of inter-organizational collaboration. Strategic alliances are co-operative relationships between two or more independent organizations, designed to achieve mutually beneficial business goals for as long as is economically viable. They carry uncertainties that are not manageable in a contractual arrangement.

The recent partnership between Nortel Networks and Accenture is one example of a strategic alliance. These two independent organizations are co-operating to offer service providers networking solutions, software, equipment and necessary skills for building emerging internet protocol networks and service and business strategies. Nortel Networks brings a rich portfolio of networking products and services to the alliance, while Accenture offers business and systems integration consulting services. Using complementary skills and capabilities, both companies benefit by improving their ability to respond to clients' needs.

The multi-year alliance between Intel and Hewlett-Packard to develop a next-generation computer chip, which began in the mid-1990s, is an example of a very complex alliance. The two companies had to learn to integrate and coordinate not only their respective technologies, but also teams of chip designers working together to develop and validate a very complex product.

We want to emphasize that the strategic alliance is usually a long-term endeavour that consists of multi-projects, is mutually dependent and beneficial, and integrates people, process, technologies or products. Unlike shorter-term partnerships or arrangements between companies that are highly contractual, the strategic alliance provides the companies involved with the opportunity to learn and acquire know-how.

Phases of an Alliance

Creating a typical strategic alliance is a process that occurs in three major phases, Find, Design and Manage. Each phase requires different types of relevant knowl-

Table 11.1 Information requirements for the alliance process

Alliance Phases	Find Phase	Design Phase	Manage Phase
	Alliance strategy development and proactive partner screening process	Structuring of alliance activities	Relational components of an alliance including trust, collaboration and learning
Critical Information Requirements	Identify internal gaps with respect to capabilities, resources and skills	Evaluate and align partners' strategic objectives	Develop an effective working environment
	Develop, evaluate and communicate internal alliance objectives	Identify and align required alliance skills with partners' skills	Manage relationships and maintain trust
	Understand legal ramifications of partnering	Make staffing decisions using best personnel with long-term commitment to the alliance	Evaluate alliance performance and implement feedback mechanism
	Access partner-specific and industry-specific information		Capture and disseminate alliance lessons learned

edge and information for success. Table 11.1 summarizes the phases along with their critical information requirements.

1. Find Phase

The first phase involves making alliance strategy decisions as well as screening and selecting potential partners. Having information and knowledge about your own organization's objectives in the alliance, and its capability resources and gaps, is critical before beginning the partner screening process. Without first understanding and articulating the alliance strategy issues internally, decisions about whom to partner with are uninformed.

At this stage, a record of past and current alliance projects is important for senior leadership to understand the resource capabilities or gaps. Corporate strategy documents and vision statements are also useful for developing alliance goals. As these internal objectives are developed and evaluated, it is equally important that they are communicated to the appropriate people in the organization, such as alliance managers and team members.

Successful companies have a proactive screening process, as opposed to an ad-hoc approach, for selecting partners. Ideal partners have compatible objectives, complementary resources and skills, organizational fit in terms of culture and processes and a willingness to ally with each other. When alliance managers in our study were asked what critical information for alliance success was currently not available, nearly all responded that they needed more partner-specific information. Thus, to facilitate a proactive screening process, decision makers must have information and knowledge about a potential partner's objectives, financials, resources and skills, processes and culture.

During the Find phase, legal knowledge is needed to understand the ramifications of aligning with a particular organization. This knowledge is particularly useful when forming an alliance with one organization that may affect a relationship with an existing partner. For instance, in the pharmaceutical arena, where competition is fierce and R&D costs are high, joining forces with one company may leave another partner feeling uneasy; it may also breach existing contracts with that partner.

In the Find phase, industry knowledge is also important when selecting partners. For instance, one financial services organization always examines various industries such as telecommunications and retail to identify key e-commerce strategies in those areas. By identifying the key players and strategies in these spaces, the organization is better able to target compatible and complementary partners.

2. Design Phase

The Design phase includes structuring and negotiating an agreement with the partner. During negotiations, successful partners evaluate and align the strategic objectives for the alliance. Knowledge about a partner's strategic objectives, products and services is important at this point in the alliance process. In our study, we found that one large software company used information about a potential software partner's strategic objectives to entice that partner into joining a strategic alliance. By accessing information about the targeted partner's strategic objectives, the large software company was able to identify one of the targeted company's key strategic partners. The large software company used this information and built a relationship with the targeted company's strategic partner. As a result, the large software company developed a partnership with the originally targeted software company.

Staffing decisions are usually made during the Design phase. In successful alliances, partners strive for a reasonable share of control that encourages equal involvement from both sides. Another key success factor in the Design phase is to commit the best personnel to the alliance and to strive for long-term resource placement rather than high turnover. When alliance personnel change too often, it is difficult to establish a commitment to an alliance partner. Relationships take time to build, and frequently changing alliance personnel disrupts this trust-building process.

Knowledge about your own company's skills is particularly important for defining work roles and support requirements with your partner. One alliance manager in our study explained why it was important to have the right people in the alliance: "Since a lot of folks that I'm dealing with are entrepreneurs and CEOs of start-up companies, I've got to be able to work with them and convince them that I carry a little bit of weight in my organization. Otherwise they don't have time for me. They want to work with people who can really help them do something."

3. Manage Phase

In the last, of Manage phase, organizations develop an effective working environment with the partner to facilitate the completion of the actual work. The types of information and knowledge that are critical at this stage include performance measures as well as feedback from both partners on how they think the alliance is progressing.

At this point in the alliance, the social aspects of the partnership become important, since team members from both partners are communicating and interacting with each other. Managing relationships and maintaining trust are critical during this phase. Often associated with alliance success, trust between partners reduces the need for the strict monitoring of the alliance and time-consuming contract renegotiations. Many companies involved in alliances organize non-work-related activities for alliance teams on both sides. Providing an outlet for developing personal relationships among alliance team members is important for increasing trust between partners. For instance, one leading pharmaceutical company offered tickets to a local sporting event. Another technology company organized a golf event, while other companies provided after-work social gatherings. These examples offer team members from both organizations an opportunity to get to know one another outside their daily work environment.

During the Manage phase, it is extremely important to promote and maintain open communication about both organizations' performance in the alliance and to incorporate this feedback formally. Successful alliances often have feedback and learning mechanisms. For example, one leading pharmaceutical company known for its reputation as a preferred alliance partner, asks all partners a set of specific questions concerning its alliance performance. Using this survey mechanism is a useful way of improving alliance performance in the Manage phase.

Successful alliance partners also learn to manage the termination of the partnership. Maintaining a positive bond with the partner even after the project is complete is useful, since new opportunities will ultimately arise. Also critical is a company's willingness to capture and disseminate lessons learned after a project is complete. This enables the company to build an organizational memory and competency around alliance management.

Applying Knowledge Management Solutions

Knowledge management principles and techniques play an important part in the success of an alliance. Some basic principles include: a systematic approach for capturing, codifying and sharing information and knowledge, a focus on building social capital to enable collaboration among people and communities, an emphasis on learning and training, and a priority on leveraging knowledge and expertise in work practices. Our study indicates that easy access to information and knowledge is a recurring theme in successful alliances. While our understanding of the exact nature of these knowledge-management techniques is still limited, companies need to recognize the importance of building these techniques into their alliance processes.

The Building Blocks of Alliance Management

Repository

An alliance repository is an important component, particularly during the Find phase. A record of past and current alliances, relevant strategy documents, existing legal contracts and industry-specific information are all critical when developing an alliance strategy and when screening and selecting alliance partners. While some companies may invest in sophisticated alliance portal technologies that offer relationship management and collaboration tools, as well as search and retrieval capabilities, other organizations have succeeded by using their organization's existing IT infrastructure. For example, alliance managers in one leading software company developed a Lotus Notes database to store information on internal alliance history, meeting minutes, strategy documents, vision statements, lessons learned, existing contracts and partner-specific and industry-specific information. Alliance managers and senior leadership use the database when developing internal alliance objectives.

Knowledge Management Intermediaries

However, lessons from first-generation knowledge management initiatives have shown that technology alone will not ensure the success of a knowledge management program. Human support is needed to ensure that the information in a repository remains current and is of high quality. Hiring a "knowledge steward" is a useful step to achieve this goal. Knowledge stewards typically capture, codify and disseminate relevant knowledge for a given project. For strategic alliances, stewards capture detailed information on existing alliance contracts, which is critical when deciding whether or not to partner with a particular organization. Stewards should also capture, codify and disseminate industry-specific information so that strategy developers are equipped with the knowledge to identify key players and strategies in a given industry. Due to the nature of their work and the type of knowledge being captured (i.e., contracts and industry-specific information), alliance knowledge stewards should have strong writing and communication skills as well as a good understanding of both the legal terminology and the industry.

Profiler

One knowledge management technology that is particularly useful in the Design phase is an alliance expertise location system. A profiler is typically an expertise location system that finds people with the relevant skill sets in your organization. Descriptions of previous partner work experience as well as work title, job area and contact information should be included in employee profiles. Knowledge stewards share an important role in updating and maintaining employee profiles for expertise location systems.

Director

As discussed earlier, companies often manage a portfolio of partners at any given time. Understanding the interdependencies, synergies and constraints between partners is a very challenging task. Whereas alliance managers might understand the individual partnerships they manage very well, they often cannot see the bigger picture that includes all the partners in the portfolio. An alliance director's role should be created to oversee and manage the complexity a portfolio implies. Ideally, this person should also be closely linked with the company's business strategy development team so the company's business strategy and its alliance strategy are aligned

Social Capital

Knowledge creation and sharing in an alliance is very much a social activity. To appreciate how knowledge is created effectively in an alliance requires an understanding of the social relationships among the individuals in the partnership. As discussed previously, building trust and effective communication with the partner are necessary ingredients for an effective relationship. First impressions are critical, and the way companies interact during the Design phase of an alliance goes a long way to building a trusting relationship. Negotiations in which both partners act in good faith and strive for a "win-win" outcome will result in trust being established quickly. Also, both partners should be clear about the process and norms of interaction (e.g., frequency of review meetings). Informal, non-alliance-related events are another way of building social capital with the partner.

Communities

Communities of practice allow for the sharing of personal experiences and tacit knowledge based on a common interest or practice. Alliance communities should be established to allow managers and team members to share their personal experiences and to help each other with challenging problems. Communities of practice can also serve as a mechanism for developing tools and intellectual capital that alliance managers can leverage. These communities can take several forms, such as electronic meeting rooms and forums or more formal alliance committees.

Training

Companies that rely heavily on strategic alliances should have formal training for managers and team members. Formal training not only enables learning, but also ensures that practices in the alliances are consistent and that they use standard processes. Mentoring is an effective learning mechanism that allows personnel to provide guidance to inexperienced alliance team members. Also, rotating experienced alliance managers across different alliance teams or alliance groups within the company allows for alliance know-how to be shared.

Formal Processes and Programs

Finally, companies should institutionalize their alliance know-how by creating formal alliance processes and programs. While some companies may opt for a more grass roots, community-based approach, others may choose to implement dedicated alliance organizations. Such decisions depend on an organization's context and culture. Companies who have reached this level of maturity are often viewed as preferred partners, and enjoy the benefits of a preferred partner. IBM, for example, has established their PartnerWorld program for software partners, which includes co-marketing, education and certification, technical support, incentives and relationship management. IBM has also documented an alliance process by outlining the 40 steps or criteria that precede reaching an agreement with a partner. Eli Lilly, a leading pharmaceutical firm, has created a dedicated organization, called the Office of Alliance Management, responsible for alliance management.

Given the importance of alliances, it is unfortunate that companies still approach forming them as "closing the deal" or a series of "one-offs." There is also the perception that managing alliances is more an art form than a skill that can be learned. Also, alliance management is often treated as a support function, and as a result, is not assigned the necessary or most effective resources. As we have discussed, alliance management can become a capability created by employing a knowledge-based approach. Most importantly, leveraging knowledge management across your company's strategic alliances is both a critical success factor and a differentiator among partnering companies.

PART V
STORYTELLING

Our Member Forums have always been special events. Two or three times per year, we bring our membership together for two and a half days to disseminate the results of our research, bring in outside experts, and, perhaps most important, enable our members to share their experiences and issues. At these forums, one of our most popular segments is our "Member Spotlight" session, where we invite representatives from our member companies to present to the larger group about a particular project or challenge they are facing. During these sessions, we hear about real dilemmas that practitioners face, whether introducing a new collaborative platform to a group of skeptical users, or justifying knowledge management expenditures to a steering committee. While many of the learnings and examples are well documented as part of our research reports and toolkits, a great deal of the actual lessons from our Institute are disseminated to, and internalized by, our members in the form of "tales from the front lines."

In addition to the "formal" stories that are told during our sessions, our members and staff also exchange accounts of memorable events that have occurred during the life of our program. We reminisce about the hurricanes and snowstorms that have tested our creative mettle in getting to various events, members who regaled us with Gilbert and Sullivan songs after dinner, and the scavenger hunt that challenged our map-reading skills. Rather than simple reminiscing, these stories help maintain a bond among our members and staff and provide newcomers with a sense of common history. Although some of the details may get altered over time, the retelling of these stories helps reinforce the sense of community that we have tried to engender across our membership over the last several years.

Thus, within our own consortium, we have seen the power of narratives as a vehicle for passing on knowledge from one person to the next. Many organizations have also begun to place value on this technique. They recognize that traditional communication vehicles, such as memos and management reports, are not particularly effective in conveying important messages or motivating audiences to action, and are often lost among the myriad of information sources that compete for our attention. As Stephen Denning, the former program director of knowledge management at the World Bank (and one of our early and influential members), said in his book *The Springboard*, "Time after time, when faced with the task of persuading a group of managers or front-line staff in a large organization to get enthusiastic about a major change, I found that storytelling was the only thing that worked" (p. xiii).

The two chapters in this part address critical issues in the use of storytelling in organizations. In chapter 12, Walter Swap, Dorothy Leonard, Mimi Shields, and Lisa Abrams describe the importance of two techniques, storytelling and mentoring, as effective mechanisms for sharing tacit knowledge in organizations. Drawing upon research in the areas of learning and cognitive psychology, they highlight the difficulties of transferring knowledge between experts and novices. They distinguish experts from the rest of the population by two primary characteristics: the length of time they have been accumulating insights on a given topic (typically thought to be greater than ten years) and their ability to solve problems through the use of pattern recognition, which is honed from their large experience base. Using lessons learned from the interactions between venture capitalists and less experienced entrepreneurs, they argue that both mentoring and storytelling are valuable techniques to transfer experiential knowledge from experts to novices. They believe that stories from experienced personnel add context to situations that might be unfamiliar to individuals just starting their own companies and allow the neophytes to more effectively apply lessons to new situations. The authors also believe that executives need to be cognizant of the existing stories within their organizations, as they are easily spread and not easily disabused once out in the public domain.

In chapter 13, David Snowden provides a cautionary note regarding the use of stories within organizations. While stories are indeed a powerful technique for sharing tacit knowledge, simply developing and spreading stories throughout an organization can sometimes result in negative, rather than positive, results. First, stories need to be well constructed; traditional components such as protagonists, a plot, a conflict that needs to be addressed, and a resolution must be integrated in such a way that individuals can ultimately identify the message or moral of the story. Further, stories need to be realistic—reflecting actions that correspond to the actual activities occurring within the organizations. Nothing can destroy a story faster than having one person discredit the facts that the story is built upon. When narratives are developed that are poorly constructed, or are not reflective of organizational life, they can easily result in what Snowden describes as antistory—a counterreaction that negates the intended benefits of the original story.

Despite these challenges, the author identifies a number of areas where stories can play a valuable role. One is in the construction of knowledge maps to increase the visibility of knowledge within organizations. Rather than simply asking people about what knowledge resources they use, allowing employees to share stories can enable organizations to more realistically determine what knowledge sources are important and under what situations the knowledge is used. Another potential use is to redirect or amplify parts of an organization's culture. Stories that spread important norms, values, signs, symbols, and language can be particularly useful when trying to integrate divisions as part of a merger, or when undertaking a change in corporate strategy. Finally, stories can play an integral role in preserving institutional memory, a topic that has been receiving a considerable amount of attention given changes in today's workforce demographics and employee mobility. Many government agencies, ranging from Sandia Laboratories to the World Bank, have allocated significant resources to capturing stories from retiring employees to retain critical subject matter expertise.

Much like knowledge management itself, the use of narrative techniques is not new. Stories have been used for many years to pass down knowledge from generation from generation. Indeed, storytelling's staying power can be attributed to both the simplicity of the concept and its effectiveness over the years. However, as long as companies continue to focus on knowledge as a critical resource, continued attention will be paid to the use of narratives as a vehicle for both conveying and retaining organizational wisdom.

12

Using Mentoring and Storytelling to Transfer Knowledge in the Workplace

WALTER SWAP
DOROTHY LEONARD
MIMI SHIELDS
LISA C. ABRAMS

Knowledge assets, or core capabilities (Leonard-Barton 1995), are the means through which organizations compete in the marketplace. As numerous scholars and practitioners have noted, a large proportion—perhaps the most critical parts—of such capabilities are intangible knowledge assets (Cohen and Prusak 2000; Itami 1987). That is, the intangible assets exist in the tacit dimensions of knowledge, built up over time in peoples' heads, hands, and relationships. Knowledge management is challenging because these intangible assets accumulate in the organization through dynamic, unstructured, and often subtle processes that are not easily codified into formal training programs or captured in information systems. Attempts to transfer knowledge assets within and across organizations (e.g., embedded in best practices) have met with incomplete success (Skulanski 1996) in part because of their tacit dimensions. Insight into why such transfers are difficult is provided by Nonaka and Takeuchi's (1995) characterization of the transfer of tacit knowledge from one set of individuals to another as "socialization" and the transfer of explicit to tacit knowledge as "internalization." We argue in this chapter that managerial influence over these essentially cognitive processes depends upon understanding how individuals within and across organizations informally teach and learn. Although such informal learning occurs in many settings and in multiple ways, we selected two interrelated mechanisms for study and reflection: mentoring and storytelling. Our criteria for selecting these two were: (1) these mechanisms, more than others, promote the transfer of the tacit dimensions of knowledge; (2) mentoring and storytelling are clearly understood representations of internalization and socialization and relatively easily implemented in organizations; and (3) existing management and cognitive psychology literature can be mined to inform managerial action.

Research Background

The primary observations in this chapter are derived from literature in management and cognitive psychology. From an initial literature search on mentoring that yielded hundreds of citations, 68 from journals or books were selected for review and narrowed to 27 that either reported specific empirical studies or reviewed such research. The most rigorously conducted of these tended to focus on specific, such as gender-related, mentoring situations. The literature on storytelling was similarly winnowed from 115 citations to 44 empirical studies (including case studies) or research reviews. Intersections with the cognitive psychology literature were sought by reviewing research on informal learning, including aspects of implicit learning, memory, and development of expertise. Moreover, the two senior authors are currently conducting an extensive field study on mentoring upon which we draw for managerially relevant illustrations. Since January 2000, we have been interviewing mentors of start-up companies and the teams being mentored in Silicon Valley, Boston, Washington, DC, India, Singapore, and Hong Kong. Our broad concern has been to track the flows of knowledge between experienced entrepreneurs serving as "mentor capitalists," as well as venture capitalists and incubators, and those aspiring entrepreneurs whom they are coaching.[1] As of this writing, over 100 interviews have been completed, about evenly divided between coaches and coached. These rich data are currently being coded and formally analyzed. Findings will be reported in future publications.

The Nature of Expertise and Knowledge Transfer

Scholars studying knowledge management often point out that knowledge accrues through experience. Leonard and Sensiper (1998) define knowledge in the business context as "information that is relevant, actionable and at least partially based on experience" (p. 113), and Davenport and Prusak (1998) speak of knowledge as "a fluid mix of framed experience, values, contextual information and expert insight" (p. 5).[2] But how does one become an expert? True expertise, as contrasted with competence, takes at least 10 years to develop (Simon and Chase 1973) and there is little evidence that the process can be significantly accelerated. Whereas history provides some examples of true inborn genius, even chess prodigy Bobby Fischer required nine years of intense preparation to attain international stature. Expertise is developed through learning-by-doing. Even the most gifted must practice, practice, practice, almost always under the guidance of a more knowledgeable teacher. This is not to say that anyone can develop expertise through sufficient diligence. Rather, between 2 people of equal natural ability, the one who becomes more expert is the one who engages in the activity more, be it music composition or law or entrepreneuring.

The way that experts exercise their knowledge is by calling on their long years and countless experiences in a great variety of contexts to recognize *patterns.* They then can selectively retrieve relevant information and extrapolate from a given pattern to fluidly chart an appropriate response (Ericsson 1996). It is always possible, of course, that experts will extrapolate incorrectly, misguided by a few familiar cues into believing they have identified a well-known pattern. However, assuming that they are correct, it is often difficult for them to describe the pattern precisely or to articulate how the recognition of a given pattern should lead to some specific behavior. In short, this pattern recognition process draws upon the tacit dimensions of the expert's knowledge, underlying the more explicit (and explicable) rule-based reasoning they also excel at. Experts can express rules of thumb, but these shorthand statements are deeply contextualized (Simon 1980). The expert knows when the rule applies and when an unusual pattern of experiences requires an exception. In general, the rule of thumb, "focus, focus, focus," will be appropriate to an entrepreneur attempting to develop a new business, and it is a rule that can be easily learned—if not easily put into practice. An experienced mentor, however, knows that there are times to broaden the range of activities. In our research, for example, a mentor working with an entrepreneur in a very early-stage start-up company first urged focus, then realized that the market for the company's product was not clear. He therefore urged temporarily pursuing three potential markets and allowing the outcome of the experiment to dictate the final market. Whereas the rules are easily transferred, the pattern recognition that allows a decision about when to apply the rule is not so easily taught.

Another mentor described his own ability to work with start-up businesses by recognizing patterns:

> You have these models you carry around. . . . You have hired, promoted and fired hundreds of people in your life, you have seen the way it looks; during the interview, you have seen the way people do and don't tell you certain things in the referencing process; you have seen how people are either political or nonpolitical . . . After awhile, you say about a given situation: That's going to be one of these, . . . you can project what's going to happen.[3]

These 2 characteristics of expertise, the 10-year rule and pattern recognition based on experience, both constrain the ability to transfer knowledge from experts to novices—especially its tacit dimensions. However, in their seminal work on knowledge creation, Nonaka and Takeuchi (1995) suggest 2 processes by which the tacit dimensions of knowledge can be created and transferred. The first, internalization, "is a process of embodying explicit knowledge into tacit knowledge. It is closely related to 'learning by doing' " (p. 69). The second is socialization, which they define as "a process of sharing experiences and thereby creating tacit knowledge such as shared mental models and technical skills" (p. 62). While formal instruction may be involved, internalization and socialization generally occur through informal processes.

People drink in knowledge informally and, at times, unconsciously. That is, they learn much incidentally, while eating in the cafeteria, chatting in the halls, observing their colleagues' and supervisors' behavior—and through the vicarious experience of others. Therefore knowledge transfer can occur even in the absence of deliberate intention to teach or learn. However, experienced individuals in an organization can help newcomers or novices interpret events, understand technology and business processes, and identify the values and norms of an organization. The processes of internalization and socialization can be aided or hindered by such organizational experts—and this informal learning can be encouraged or discouraged by management practices. Two potential avenues for informal teaching are mentoring and storytelling, and we turn now to a discussion of each.

Mentoring as Informal Teaching

The word *mentor* can be traced back to Homer's myth of Odysseus. The king of Ithaca left his son Telemachus in the care of Mentor, who guided and taught the youth for the 10 years his father was away fighting the Trojans. A mentor, therefore, has always been considered one who draws upon a deep knowledge base to teach and guide. The recognition of mentoring as an important transfer mechanism for knowledge within organizations has grown significantly in the past couple of decades. However, the mentoring literature focuses primarily on how to structure the mentor/protégé[4] relationship (Noe 1988), on the desired behavior of mentors (Benabou and Benabou 1999) and on identifying mentoring functions (Kram 1985; Kram and Isabella 1985). The benefits of mentoring are measured in enhanced job satisfaction and retention (Mullen 1994) but, in the 68 articles reviewed, none tested the relationship between mentoring and an increase in organizational knowledge. However, a number of studies have found that individuals who are mentored perform better and are promoted more rapidly (Lunding, Clements, and Perkins 1978; Scandura 1992), presumably because they have learned and absorbed knowledge from their mentors. Clearly, whether officially appointed or not[5] mentors are serving as informal teachers, and knowledge is being transferred[6] In recent years, the concept of mentoring has been extended to include peer-to-peer help (Dahle 1998; Kram and Isabelle 1985) and "reverse mentoring," or protégé-to-mentor learning (Mullen and Noe 1999).

What Are Mentors Teaching?

Most discussions of core competencies (Prahad and Hamel 1990) or dynamic capabilities (Teece, Pisano, and Shuen 1997) focus on two dimensions of the knowledge assets: critical skills and managerial systems. But Leonard-Barton (1995) suggests that norms and values are equally important in building knowledge assets, as they govern how and whether individual employees create, access, absorb, and diffuse different kinds of knowledge. Therefore we might expect to see all three types of knowledge as the content of mentors' teachings.

Looking first for evidence that mentors transfer *skills*, we find surprisingly little in the mentorship literature about the informal learning of *technical* skills. One can infer that technical expertise is built up, in part through the mentor feedback mentioned by numerous researchers (Benabou and Benabou 1999; Covaleski et al. 1998; Pfleeger and Mertz 1995) or in the coaching mentioned by Noe (1988). Kram (1983) describes coaching as part of the career function filled by mentors. Benabou and Benabou (1999) include training the protégé in "technical and managerial skills" in their category of "professional function" performed by mentors.

One study (Morrison 1993) that investigates the sources of information sought by newcomers in organizations found that newcomers sought technical information, defined as "how to perform specific aspects of your job" primarily by asking others—mostly supervisors.[8] This kind of information was more often sought through direct inquiry than through what Morrison calls monitoring (observation). Morrison speculates that "because technical information is highly valuable, yet difficult to obtain through monitoring, newcomers may be willing to ask for it directly" (p. 582). In our research on the mentoring of start-ups, we found some support for this notion, as we observed mentors responding to top management's requests for explicit technical knowledge, such as advice on valuation of the fledgling company or explanations of legal processes. Similarly, Covaleski et al. (1998) report that some mentors in the accounting firms they studied provided "guidance and advice [that] could be highly specific and 'gritty,' covering the protégé's relationship with clients and key partners, the commercial aspects of the firm, the protégé's appearance and behavior and the politics of practice" (p. 314).

The literature provides much more evidence of mentors conveying knowledge about organizational routines and *managerial systems.* "Through career functions including sponsorship, coaching, protection, exposure and visibility, and challenging work assignments, a young manager is assisted in learning the ropes of organizational life and in preparing for advancement opportunities" (Kram 1983, p. 614). Mentors also identify opportunities for training (Geiger 1992; Van Collie 1998). Perhaps even more important is the knowledge of informal managerial systems conveyed through what some researchers call the "political function" of the mentor (Benabou and Benabou 1999) or refer to as the "power perspective" (Ragins 1997). These terms cover a wide variety of information about who does what and how in the organization. Benabou and Benabou (1999) find that mentors provided "access to privileged information" and familiarized the protégé "with nonformal aspects of the organization." Wilson and Elman (1990) suggest that mentors teach their protégés "how to navigate the subtleties of the organization's political system." Particularly useful is "know-who," that is, introductions to influential "decision-making networks" (Benabou and Benabou 1999) and contacts developed by the mentor (Geiger 1992; Pfleeger and Mertz 1995; Simonetti, Ariss, and Martinez 1999; Walsh and Borowski 1999). Our research amply demonstrates the important role mentors play in introducing start-up teams to sources of management talent (including search firms), financing (e.g., venture capitalists and angel investors), and potential partnerships (Leonard and Swap 2000).

Mentors also teach *norms* of behavior and convey knowledge about the *values* of an organization—what Morrison (1993) calls "normative information."[9] Norms imply guidance for behavior. Covaleski et al. (1998) report: "Mentoring requires that the mentor display himself or herself to the protégé as an embodied symbol. According to one [mentor], 'Being a good mentor means making myself visible to my protégé in order for him to more fully understand what it means to behave, look like, and be a partner' " (p. 314). However, many mentoring studies tend to lump norms and values together[10] under the rubric of organizational culture. "[M]entoring succeeds in efficiently transmitting the enterprise culture, as measured by the acquisition of language (casual and technical) specific to the enterprise, and the adoption of company values and traditions. Official channels of communication are too slow and cumbersome, but high-level mentors close to strategic decisions can quickly communicate the meaning of those decisions to their protégés, facilitating the adoption of the company values" (Benabou and Benabou 1999 p. 9). Our research reveals that setting the values for a start-up company occurs very early in the mentor-protégé relationship—often at the first meeting. We repeatedly were told by mentors and their teams that they consciously chose one another on the basis of shared values, for example, the desire to grow a business of enduring worth rather than just to make a quick sale and profit ("build to flip").

We conclude from the literature review that there is little evidence of a direct positive relationship between mentoring and organizational performance. However, mentoring does play a role in building up the core capabilities of an organization, as the literature offers evidence for the transfer of skills, managerial systems, and values—including their tacit dimensions. The mentoring process fits the descriptions of both socialization ("sharing experiences") and internalization ("embodying explicit knowledge into tacit" and "learning by doing").

Next we consider what prior research can tell us about *how* the informal learning via mentoring takes place.

Cognitive Mechanisms in Learning via Mentoring

Novices cannot be expected to leap directly to becoming experts. All experts pass through levels of knowledge acquisition. In trades, one thinks of first apprenticing, then becoming a journeyman, before attaining the status of a master violin maker or plumber. Future concert pianists start as beginners, then reach intermediate and advanced levels before becoming virtuosi. For mentors working with novices, the wide gap in knowledge presents problems. Experts may lack patience to guide a novice, and, from the novice's viewpoint, someone more proximate in experience may be a better teacher than the expert because the knowledge gap is not as great. The literature on cognition suggests both why wider gaps are harder to bridge and how informal learning occurs.

Preparedness for Learning. Lacking the necessary knowledge and experience foundations, the novice has no "hook" or receptor to truly assimilate the mentor's instructions. Cognitive psychology tells us that "[e]xperiences are encoded by brain networks whose connections have already been shaped by previous encounters with the world. This preexisting knowledge powerfully influences how we encode and store new memories (or vicariously experienced events conveyed through stories)" Schacter 1996, p. 6). In order for information to become knowledge, the learner must share some context, some meaning, with the one imparting the knowledge. Lacking that shared contextual base, messages will be assimilated to people's own idiosyncratic experiences and memories (Schacter 1996). To extrapolate from Vygotsky's (1978) insights into childhood intellectual development, the information lies outside the protégé's "zone of proximal development." As experiences accrue, perhaps under the guidance of a mentor, the learner becomes increasingly prepared for more advanced instruction—his or her zone of proximal development widens.

Active Learning. Theorists and practitioners are unanimous in claiming the importance of active learning in building up exposure to patterns that are at the heart of developing expertise (Simon 1980). Research in cognitive psychology confirms that when people actively participate in learning new material they are much more likely to remember it. For example, a word is more likely to be recalled later when it is "filled in" by the learner ("What word starting with the letter *F* is a synonym for *rapid?*") than when *fast* is simply provided as a synonym (the "Generation Effect" [Soraci et al. 1994]). In our study of "mentor capitalists," we find mentors suggesting experiments through which the green entrepreneurs can learn: One mentor urged presenting a prototype to a different customer set than was currently being courted. Another required her protégé to personally conduct informal market research on the meaning of his brand. Noe (1988) cites a study revealing that mentors for women executives had "created opportunities for them to operate outside of the organizational norms . . . and provided an environment that was conducive to experimenting with new behaviors and ideas" (p. 66). The management literature identifies such actions as increasing the protégé's responsibility for projects and leadership (Ibarra 2000; Kram 1983; Pfleeger and Mertz 1995) or allowing the protégé to make his or her own discoveries (Starcevich and Friend 1999). Providing actual (or, as with case studies, virtual) learning experiences is crucial to the development of expertise, and the resulting enhanced ability to recognize patterns.

Metacognition and Self-Monitoring. The term "metacognition" (self-aware thinking about one's own mental processes) has entered the lexicon to describe how people monitor their understanding of a problem, recognize what additional information they need for more complete understanding, and seek out that information. Experts typically self-monitor their understanding in this way and they can teach by asking questions to elicit the protégé's degree of comprehension, then reflecting the answers back in ways that encourage deeper exploration of the issues. This type of Socratic dialogue is a variant of active learning and internalization, but one concerned more with learning by thinking than learning by doing. One of the protégés we interviewed said that he learned a great deal about the business strategy of his company through self-reflecting on the answers he was forced to give to the questions asked by his mentor. Several protégés interviewed in our study acknowledged the value of "hammering" by mentors to think deeply about their company's mission, their strategies, and the "elevator speech" describing their companies. Feedback by the mentor is an important part of this process—feedback about whether the mentor believes the protégé has actually absorbed the lesson. Current research indicates an important point for mentors and managers: Feedback that focuses the learner on the task is particularly helpful in learning and feedback that focuses attention on the self (e.g., how competent or incompetent a person one is) is generally harmful to learning (Kluger and DeNisi 1996).

Learning by Observing. American behaviorists long assumed that people learned solely as a result of reinforcement or punishment. However, research revealed that children and adults also learn through simply observing others—particularly models who are trusted, powerful, or otherwise valued, even in the absence of any reinforcements and whether or not the mimics intended to learn (Bandura 1977). "What is critical to memory is how one processes material and not whether one intends to learn the material" (Anderson 1995, p. 192). Thus, when novices are immersed in an organization or culture they value, and are being mentored by an expert they admire, a great deal of learning can occur through observing the expert's behavior. Brown, Collins, and Duguid (1989) emphasize the importance for learning of becoming part of a culture in which activities are "authentic," that is, "coherent, meaningful, and purposeful. . . . What people pick up is a product of the ambient culture rather than of explicit teaching" (p. 34). In our research, some of the mentors assumed the role of "virtual CEO," taking on many of the top-level executive functions of the new company while the protégé observes—and learns. One of the protégés noted that his mentor, who came into the company as acting president, demonstrated how to effectively build the team, establish priorities and budgets, and manage disputes. An expert's modeling of behavior for a protégé clearly reflects Nonaka and Takeuchi's "socialization," in which learning takes place informally and often unconsciously.

In addition to encouraging hands-on experiences, providing feedback skillfully, and serving as models, mentors have the ability to draw on their extensive experiences to relate stories to protégés. Ibarra (2000) notes, "The most successful junior professionals repeatedly mentioned how much they were helped by a partner who took the time to tell them stories about the business and how to succeed as a partner"(p. 153). We turn now to consider in depth the role of stories in conveying knowledge—whether or not the stories are related by people considered to be mentors.

Stories as Informal Teaching

We define an organizational story as *a detailed narrative of past management actions, employee interactions, or other intra-or extra-organizational events that are communicated informally within the organization.* Such narratives will ordinarily include a plot, major characters, and outcome. A moral, or implication of the story for action, is usually implied if not explicitly stated. Normally, these stories will originate from within the organization and will therefore reflect organizational norms, values, and culture. However, mentors from outside the company may use stories from their past experiences to dramatize critical skills, managerial systems, and norms and values common to many organizations. Organizational stories tend to cluster within familiar archetypes. For example, Martin and her colleagues (1983) have identified seven types of common stories that occur regularly across a variety of organizations:

- The rule-breaking story
- Is the big boss human?

- Can the little person rise to the top?
- Will I get fired?
- Will the organization help me when I have to move?
- How will the boss react to mistakes?
- How will the organization deal with obstacles?

Cognitive science research tells us that *memorable* information is more likely to be acted upon than is information that remains unconscious and not retrieved from memory. Therefore, anything that tends to make information more memorable will have a greater likelihood of assuming significance. Because stories are more vivid, engaging, entertaining, and easily related to personal experience than rules or directives, the research would predict they would be more memorable, be given more weight, and be more likely to guide behavior. In addition, because of the rich contextual details encoded in stories, they are ideal carriers of tacit dimensions of knowledge (although what is ultimately encoded by the listener may not correspond closely to the intentions of the storyteller [Schank 1990]).

What Are Stories Teaching?

Stories do not lend themselves equally well to transferring different kinds of knowledge. As a *strategy* for building core capabilities within an organization, an indiscriminate use of stories to transfer critical skills, managerial systems, and norms and values would probably be misguided. Critical skills, including deep knowledge of a content domain, would be very difficult to transfer via stories. For such concrete forms of knowledge, people rely on formal education, apprenticeships or mentoring, training programs, and self-study for mastery. Indeed, we know of no studies where critical skills have been transferred by stories. Martin (1982) has noted, "Organizational representatives prefer to use explicit, unambiguous means of communication, whenever this is possible, so that misunderstandings and differences in interpretation will not occur" (p. 257).[11]

The use of stories to communicate managerial systems does occur. An incident from our research on mentoring start-ups illustrates:

A green CFO reports to his board that he intends to invest the company's free cash to produce some additional income. One board member, an experienced entrepreneur, relates the story of another CFO who proposed to invest his company's cash in a high-yield instrument. The sage on his board responded, "No one will remember the extra 1½% you earned. They will remember the $10 million you lost."

Or consider another story, related by Wilkins (1984), typifying Martin's "Will I get fired?" archetype:

Hit by hard times, a company chose not to fire 10% of its people, but instead required everyone, including top management, to take a 10% pay cut in exchange for working nine days out of ten. (p. 46)

In this story, the more explicit knowledge being transferred is about how things get done in the company (managerial systems). However, the implicit message is that all employees are important, and that in times of crisis, everyone works together as a team (values).

One of the bitter truths about successful management systems in start-ups is that founders are often moved aside as the company grows and requires different skills. In our research, mentors sometimes communicated the likelihood of a CEO succession through stories. One founding team of a young company told their mentor that they wanted the current president to be given the title of CEO. The mentor dissuaded them by relating the story of a similar situation:

> A founder/CEO was well liked by his team, who wanted him to be named permanent CEO. But the mentor realized he lacked the full skill-set to take the company to the next level and said no, much to the displeasure of the team. Several months later, the correctness of the decision was clear when the founder admitted that the mentor had been right, that he had learned a great deal that would eventually make him CEO material.

The mentor had recognized a familiar pattern, communicated this through a story, and persuaded the team of the wisdom of his decision.

Organizational values are more clearly and unambiguously illustrated in the following story—a good example of Martin's "How will the boss react to mistakes?" archetype:

> A mill superintendent at Chaparral Steel championed a very expensive magnetic arc saw for brimming finished steel beams. The resulting magnetic fields attracted bits of metal and persistent engineering attempts failed to correct the problem. The saw was ultimately replaced but the superintendent was promoted to vice president of operations. (Leonard-Barton 1995, p. 119)

Here, the value placed on intelligent risk-taking at Chaparral Steel is highlighted. Employees know that if they have a creative idea that is supported by the company, they will not be punished if that idea fails to work out. It is assumed, instead, that the person will learn from the mistake and will be a more valuable member of the company.

Several important points about the transfer of knowledge are illustrated by these stories. First, managerial systems, norms, and values can be readily communicated through the narrative and its (often implied) moral. Stories, particularly those that are concrete and readily identified with, are particularly powerful for transferring knowledge rich in tacit dimensions. As earlier noted, knowledge about skills and domain content relies on more explicit, codified means of communication rather than on stories.

Second, a single story, richly contextualized, may communicate knowledge, often tacit, about more than one component of a company's core capabilities. For example, a variant of the "dealing with obstacles" story tells how employees making presentations to top management can expect to be savaged—yelled at, demeaned, their papers hurled on the floor. While at the explicit level this story might not speak flatteringly of these particular organizational values or managerial systems, the tacit moral transferred to many employees is that management cares about quality, and survival of this initiation will launch you on your career (Wilkins 1984, p. 46).

Third, when the story supports the explicit statements of the company (as these all do), they provide powerful reinforcement and buy-in by members (Martin 1983). But stories do not always support more explicit forms of communication. And when the story conflicts with explicit statements, the tacitly conveyed moral from the story may well overpower the explicit message. Moreover, for each of Martin's seven story types, there are negative as well as positive exemplars. For every positive "the big boss is human" story, there is probably at least one depicting the boss as a jerk. Neuhauser (1993) surveyed 100 people across many organizations and found that 90 percent told *negative* stories about their companies.

In the following example, management failed to recognize the power and persistence of negative stories, and therefore missed an opportunity for progress.

A consultant hired to work with top management to promote innovation in a large manufacturing company asked about the climate for risk-taking. The managers shook their heads. "Our new CEO," they told her, "has talked a good game ever since he came in four years ago; he says he wants us to take risks—but you really can't." Pressed for evidence, the managers recounted several stories about specific employees whose careers had derailed after they took risks. However, every single story was at least eight years old, predating the current CEO's tenure. The sad tales about the dangers of risk-taking had not been replaced in the corporate lore with any positive stories. The CEO was unaware of the powerful myths still lurking in the organizational culture—and influencing current behavior.[12]

In this particular "How will the boss react to mistakes?" story, the boss did, in fact, genuinely wish to encourage intelligent risk-taking. But the continued circulation of vivid, powerful, but out-of-date stories undermined his stated value.

If stories are powerful, then we need to understand *why* they are in order to benefit from their potential for knowledge transfer and to alleviate their negative effects.

Cognitive Mechanisms in Learning via Stories

The Availability Heuristic. When an event is made more available from memory, there is a strong tendency to believe it is more likely to occur or to be true (Tversky and Kahneman 1973). For example, it is far more likely that a hiker will be killed by a moose than by a grizzly bear. However, because of the stories most of us have heard about gruesome bear-maulings, and the scarcity of tales of moose-tramplings, we have vivid images of the former and tend to exaggerate their likelihood. Therefore, if aspects of corporate culture or systems are made more vivid, such as through a story, the availability heuristic predicts they will become more memorable, more thoroughly processed, and judged to be more true than those supported only by probabilities or abstract data.

An experiment by Joanne Martin and Melanie Powers (e.g., Martin 1982) provides an empirical example. Stanford MBA students were presented with an advertisement for a new white wine from a California winery. All students read advertising copy consisting of a policy statement arguing that the winery would be consistently using special procedures from the Chablis region of France. Some students read only this paragraph, while others also read a supportive story about how the founder of the winery would be making his wine with the new procedures. A third group read just the policy statement and numerical data supporting the statement (i.e., how frequently the new procedures would be used). A final group read both the story and the data. Even though these quantitatively oriented MBA students indicated that they thought the data condition would prove to be a more persuasive advertisement, those who had read the story were more convinced of the truthfulness of the policy statement than were those in the other conditions. According to the availability heuristic, or the "vividness effect," the story made the new procedure more easily imaginable and, hence, judged more likely to be true.

Elaboration. To the extent that people reflect upon and integrate information with what they already know, they will remember it better. "What we already know shapes what we select and encode; things that are meaningful to us spontaneously elicit the kind of elaborations that promote later recall" (Schacter 1996), pp. 45–46). For example, we remember information better when we can elaborate it by constructing vivid images drawn from our own experience to organize it. Indeed, a common mnemonic for memorizing lists of words is to conjure up visual images or construct a narrative that includes each item (Schacter 1996). When verbal or numerical data are presented, we have only one obvious means of encoding them. If, however, the same information is presented and encoded with associated vivid images, there are two different ways of retrieving the information, making it more accessible (Paivio 1989). Stories provide a simple way of combining verbal and visual information. If the story is sufficiently clear or dramatic, it will almost certainly stimulate visual images complementing the story line, providing a vicarious experience that results in a greater likelihood of being remembered.

Episodic Memory. If you were asked to recall the capitals of the countries in the European Union (EU), you might have difficulty. How many countries are there in the EU? What are they? Is Bonn or Berlin the capital of Germany? If, however, you have just taken a grand tour of the European capitals, you would probably be able to recall them and, with a little thought, even recite them in the order visited. Furthermore, you would be able to reconstruct highlights in each city— castles explored, special meals eaten, and so on. The recall of events directly experienced is called *episodic memory*, while general knowledge about the world (including the names of those capitals) is called *semantic memory* (Tulving 1972). This is not to say that errors in episodic memory will not occur—was that cathedral in Madrid or Lisbon?—but those memories grounded in personal experience tend to be readily retrieved, perhaps with a bit of priming ("Wasn't that a glass of port we drank in that little restaurant outside that cathedral?"). Recent evidence suggests that for episodic memory, information is stored immediately in the hippocampal region of the brain, then transferred slowly to long-term storage in the neocortex (Moll and Miikkulainen 1997). The result is a "seemingly unlimited storage for everyday experiences, and a retrieval system that allows us to access the experiences with partial activation of their components" (Moll and Miikkulainen 1997). Stories are clearly episodic in nature. To the extent that the storyteller is able to provide a sufficiently vivid account for the listener to vicariously experience the story, many features of the story will be encoded in memory and will be readily available for retrieval.

The evidence from cognitive psychology, then, is quite consistent. To the extent that stories promote elaborations such as connections to the listener's personal experience, or evoke clear visual images, they will be more memorable and, hence, more effective carriers of knowledge than less vivid, purely listed information. More important, rich narratives are more likely judged as true or likely to occur. "If you want people to remember information and believe it, your best strategy in almost every case is to give that information in the form of a story" (Solovy 1999). Denning (2000) has written a fascinating, first person account about his discovery of the persuasive merits of stories over rhetoric in transforming the World Bank to a knowledge-conscious organization.

Managerial Implications

We suggest in this chapter that skills, managerial systems, and norms and values, woven into interdependent systems of knowledge termed core capabilities, are critical to any organization. These types of knowledge, and especially their tacit dimensions, are conveyed through processes of socialization and internalization. Two mechanisms key to those processes are mentoring and storytelling. Managers need to be aware of and understand the cognitive processes underlying these types of informal learning. Our review of the management and cognitive psychology literatures on the two processes leads to a number of managerial implications. In Table 12.1, we summarize the major research findings (column 1) and draw implications from each finding (column 2). Each of these in turn suggests specific managerial actions (column 3). Note that column 3 represents only a sample of possible actions—many more could be developed.

Most mentors are in a position to teach because they have developed expertise through years of practice in a particular field or organization—not because they desire to teach or have expertise in mentoring. The potential behaviors suggested in Table 12.1, derived from research on how people learn, are not necessarily obvious—and they are neither quick nor easy to implement. Nor are they efficient in the short term. Mentors who follow these suggestions will be superior teachers, but will managers reward them for working at transferring their expertise? Even one of the easiest, allowing a protégé to shadow a mentor, requires the presence of two people where only one is strictly required. Shadowing activities are not billable in most companies.

Moreover, not all experts know how to bridge the gap between their own knowledge and the fragmentary or incomplete experience base of the novice— even assuming that they are willing to try. The larger the gap, the more effort is

Table 12.1 Selected Managerial Implications of Cognitive Science Research

Cognitive Principle	Implication	Examples of Potential Behaviors
Active engagement in one's own learning improves learning.	Providing opportunities for active learning will enhance learning.	Mentors design active learning exercises. Give protégés responsibility for projects.
Lack of receptors (knowledge base) makes it difficult for inexperienced people to learn.	The wider the knowledge gap between mentor and protégé, the more difficult the knowledge transfer.	Apprentices and journeymen can be mentors for novices. Experts may need tutoring in how to teach.
Self-monitoring and self-reflection on one's own learning progress leads to better learning.	Protégés will learn better if they are self-reflective about their learning.	Mentors should assist protégés in becoming self-reflective, providing feedback about protégé's progress that is specific to tasks (rather than personal).
People learn from observing models of behavior, particularly admired or powerful models.	Learning may be informal. Teaching may be unintentional.	Protégés should be allowed and encouraged to "shadow" their mentors.
Developing expertise takes years and much practice.	There are no rapid shortcuts, but there may be superior routes to knowledge transfer.	If time pressures are not to drive it out, mentoring has to be rewarded and built into the organizational systems.
The hallmark of expertise is the ability to recognize patterns and draw inferences from them.	In order to become experts, protégés have to accumulate many experiences from which they can derive patterns.	Mentors need to provide real experiences or many simulations and cases for protégés.
If information is expressed in memorable form, it will more likely influence attitudes and behavior.	Stories are more effective than statements in transferring knowledge. Confronted with a published norm and a contradictory story, people will tend to believe the story.	Managers need to mine organizational culture for stories that support values, norms, and managerial systems important to the organization's core capabilities.

required to close it from both mentor and protégé, and the more frustration in incomplete communication is likely on both sides. In our own research, we saw some experts who were extraordinarily patient with novices and skilled at assessing the protégé's level of understanding so that the necessary knowledge could be fed in calculated dosages and couched in accessible language. In other cases, experts were highly frustrated at the discovery of how basic was the knowledge that the protégé lacked. As suggested in Table 12.1, mentoring systems could include teaching by those with proximate knowledge (e.g., apprentices teaching novices) in order to better close knowledge gaps. We also observed in the field newly minted entrepreneurs—apprentice level in their understanding—mentoring novices with apparent success.

An inescapable implication of this research is that mentoring takes time and continuity. Two forces militate against the transfer of expertise from a mentor to a protégé: the time pressures in organizations, both business and nonprofit, and the increasing tendency for individuals to work in many different organizations, picking up experience and expertise from many different individuals. However, these trends in society may in fact create higher demand for mentoring relationships, not only because people will have less time to "come up to speed" on their own, but because individuals will need to be active and continuous learners as they move from one organization to another. As higher value is placed on expertise, managers will need to become increasingly skilled at recognizing the potential for apprentices and journeymen to teach and encouraging knowledge flows between individuals further down the ladder of experience depicted in Figure 12.1.

Mentoring requires a light—and sophisticated—managerial hand. Therefore, merely setting up a formal mentoring program may accomplish little, especially if the mentors are uninterested and neither rewarded nor skilled in teaching. Rather, managers need to consider how to structure incentive systems so that mentoring is rewarded and recognized as a valuable contribution to the organization. Mentors and protégés who select each other will be more successful than will those who are appointed. Moreover, mentors should be given some help in becoming more effective teachers.

There are also implications from our study of storytelling. Managers concerned with knowledge flows have not traditionally involved themselves with seemingly irrelevant myths and gossip. Yet, as we have seen, stories are powerful conveyors of meaning and tacit knowledge. Most stories told informally in organizations are negative. Therefore, managers interested in how knowledge accrues in the organization cannot ignore these important transmitters. Stories that dramatize or illustrate managerial systems, values, and norms are more likely to be believed and acted upon than mere statements of policies and norms. Therefore, managers should mine organizational lore for stories that support the goals and mission of the organization.

Like mentoring, storytelling is an activity to be influenced rather than directly manipulated. One possible managerial behavior that follows from recognizing the power of stories is the *construction* of stories to make strategic points about an organization:

> We can also use the ability of a good story to generate imitative examples to discover new knowledge and capability that we possess but do not use. The creation of scenarios based on this new view of reality will improve our forward planning and implementation. (Snowden 1999, p. 5)

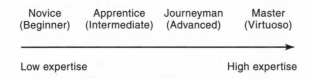

Figure 12.1 Continuum of expertise.

We suggest that artificially constructed stories ultimately will be less effective than true ones. Employees are already frequently suspicious of management. Should word of the "created scenarios" leak out, that could itself become the basis of a story ("The Big Boss is human, all right—he lies") and fan the flames of cynicism. If the values and norms of the organization are truly held, there should be stories somewhere about behaviors that support those views. If there are only stories to the contrary, that is a strong message to management.

Finally, the insights from the literatures speak to the design and use of information technologies. While it is beyond the scope of this chapter to explore this issue in depth, some implications spring to mind. If stories are powerful in verbal form, their effect can be enhanced through the use of multimedia. Consistent with the elaboration effect, seeing and hearing the storyteller can add weight and detail to the story,[13] as can visuals about the environment in which the story occurred. Information technologies similarly can add power to mentoring. Simulations can extend the reach of the expert by providing opportunities for learning by doing in artificial environments. And computer systems can help the apprentice teach the novice (or the journeyman, the apprentice) by providing access to repositories of knowledge that may have little meaning to the uninitiated, but can be interpreted by someone with more experience. Information technology similarly is an indispensable tool for peer mentoring, as groups of physically dispersed individuals come together virtually to share knowledge in communities of practice.

Whether or not internalization and socialization are mediated with technology, managers are better equipped to build critical knowledge assets if they understand *why* and *how* people learn informally—not just that informal learning occurs. Moreover, the knowledge-sharing mechanisms of mentoring and storytelling can be enhanced by informed managerial action.

Acknowledgments: The authors gratefully acknowledge the support of the Institute for Knowledge Management, the Office of the Vice President for Arts, Sciences and Engineering at Tufts University, and the Division of Research, Harvard Business School.

Notes

1 The initial report on this research appears in Leonard and Swap (2000).

2 For Nonaka and Takeuchi (1995), "First, knowledge, unlike information is about *beliefs* and *commitment*. Knowledge is a function of a particular stance, perspective, or intention. Second, knowledge, unlike information, is about *action*. It is always knowledge 'to some end.' And third, knowledge, like information, is about *meaning*. It is context-specific and rational" (p. 58). In their full definition, Davenport and Prusak (1998) observe that knowledge "provides a framework for evaluating and incorporating new experiences and information. It originates and is applied in the minds of knowers. In organizations, it often becomes embedded not only in documents or repositories but also in organizational routines, processes, practices, and norms" (p. 5).

3 Interview with Fred Luconi by the two senior authors.

4 While "mentor" seems to have achieved general acceptance in this context, there is no commonly accepted term for the person being mentored. "Mentee" is contrived

and can be confusing when used alongside "mentor," while "protégé" connotes a molding in the mentor's image, which some might resent. However, for purposes of this article, lacking a better term we defer to the generally used "protégé."

5 Self-selected mentor-protégé teams tend to be more effective than appointed teams. However, since people tend to select individuals who are similar to themselves, formal mentoring programs are sometimes necessary in order to provide mentors to minority populations in the organization (Ragins and Cotton 1991).

6 Kram (1983) divides mentoring functions into Career Function (sponsorship, exposure and visibility, coaching, protection, challenging assignments) and Psychosocial Functions (role modeling, acceptance and confirmation, counseling, and friendship). Most of these functions channel information if not knowledge—but only a few of them do so directly. Although protégés certainly learn from exposure, challenging assignments, and confirmation, knowledge flows most obviously through coaching, role modeling, and counseling. Benabou and Benabou (1999) divide mentoring functions into three: professional, political (which is subsumed in Kram's career function), and psychosocial.

7 Leonard-Barton (1995) suggests four dimensions, only three of which are relevant here: critical skills, managerial systems, norms and values. The fourth is physical systems, in which knowledge can be embodied, for example, proprietary software or special equipment.

8 Not all supervisors regard themselves as mentors, and some researchers even have suggested that supervisors should *not* serve as mentors (Kram 1983). Still other researchers have found supervisors to be the best mentors (Burke, Mckeen, and McKenna 1993).

9 Morrison (1993) includes peer mentors in her study and found that newcomers were initially more likely to seek such information from peers than supervisors, but the difference disappeared by the second wave of research in the six months covered.

10 Although norms and values are similar concepts, they differ in important ways. *Norms* (standards for appropriate behavior) guide individual decisions within organizations. For example, norms can dictate how to dress, or what kinds of details are appropriate in product design. Norms can facilitate knowledge acquisition, for example, by providing guidelines for how knowledge should be shared across boundaries. Norms can also inhibit knowledge flow. For instance, an implicit norm of "Don't rock the boat" can discourage employees from taking risks by challenging accepted wisdom. *Values* are deeply held beliefs about what is of greatest importance to the organization. For example, the founders of Johnson & Johnson and Hewlett-Packard left a heritage of ethos that directs the companies' interaction with society even today.

11 It is certainly possible to imagine, however, a context in which critical skills *could* be transferred through stories, particularly when those skills are heavily laden with tacit knowledge. For example, the critical skills used by a psychiatrist or clinical psychologist to form relationships with patients might be transferred, in part, through stories told by experienced practitioners about their cases.

12 This example comes from the second author's consulting practice.

13 Part of the "HP Way" is to respect employees as individuals. When Hewlett-Packard decided not to offer benefits to partners of gay and lesbian employees, those employees felt there was an inconsistency with the core values of the company. Stories about the actual experiences of these employees were collected and presented before management at a "Reader's Theater." Confronted with this vivid narrative evidence, management reversed its decision (Leonard and Swap 1999 p. 70).

References

Anderson, J. *Cognitive Psychology and Its Implications*, 4th ed. New York: W. H. Freeman and Company, 1995.

Bandura, A. *Social Learning Theory*. Englewood Cliffs, NJ: Prentice Hall, 1977.

Benabou, C., and Benabou, R. Establishing a formal mentoring program for organization success. *National Productivity Review, 18*, 2 (1999), 7–14.

Brown, J. S.; Collins, A.; and Duguid, P. Situated cognition and the culture of learning. *Educational Researcher, 18*, 1 (1989), 32–42.

Burke, R. J.; McKeen, C. A.; and McKenna, C. Correlates of mentoring organizations: the mentor's perspective. *Psychological Reports, 72*, 3 (1993), 883–896.

Cohen, D., and Prusak, L. *In Good Company: The Role of Social Capital in Organizations*. Boston: Harvard Business School Press, 2000.

Covaleski, M. A.; Dirsmith, M. W.; Heian, J. B.; and Samuel, S. The calculated and the avowed: techniques of discipline and struggles over identity in Big Six public accounting firms. *Administrative Sciences Quarterly, 43*, 2 (1998), 293–328.

Dahle, C. Women's ways of mentoring. *Fast Company, 17* (September 1998), 186–195.

Davenport, T. H., and Prusak, L. *Working Knowledge: How Organizations Manage What They Know*. Boston: Harvard Business School Press, 1998.

Denning, S. *The Springboard: How Storytelling Ignites Action in Knowledge-Era Organizations*. Woburn, MA: Butterworth-Heinemann, 2000.

Ericsson, K. A. The acquisition of expert performance: an introduction to some of the issues. In K. A. Ericsson (ed.), *The Road to Excellence*. Mahwah, NJ: Lawrence Erlbaum, 1996, pp. 1–50.

Geiger, A. H. Measures for mentors. *Training & Development, 46*, 2 (1992), 65–67.

Ibarra, H. Making partner: a mentor's guide to the psychological journey. *Harvard Business Review, 78*, 2 (March–April 2000), 146–155.

Itami, H., with Roehl, T. *Mobilizing Invisible Assets*. Cambridge: Harvard University Press, 1987.

Kluger, A. N., and DeNisi, A. The effects of feedback interventions on performance: a historical review, a meta-analysis, and a preliminary feedback intervention theory. *Psychological Bulletin, 199*, 2 (1996), 254–284.

Kram, K. E. Phases of the mentoring relationship. *Academy of Management Journal, 26*, 4 (1983), 608–625.

Kram, K. E. *Mentoring at Work*. Glenview, IL: Scott, Foresman, 1985.

Kram, K. E., and Isabella, L. Mentoring alternatives: the role of peer relationships in career development. *Academy of Management Journal, 28*, 10 (1985), 110–132.

Leonard-Barton, D. *Wellsprings of Knowledge*. Boston: Harvard Business School Press, 1995.

Leonard, D., and Sensiper, S. The role of tacit knowledge in group innovation. *California Management Review, 40*, 3 (1998), 112–132.

Leonard, D., and Swap, W. *When Sparks Fly: Igniting Creativity in Groups*. Boston: Harvard Business School Press, 1999.

Leonard, D., and Swap, W. Gurus in the garage. *Harvard Business Review, 78*, 6 (2000), 71–82.

Lunding, F. S.; Clements, C. E.; and Perkins, D. C. Everyone who makes it has a mentor. *Harvard Business Review, 56* (July/August 1978), 89–101.

Martin, J. Stories and scripts in organizational settings. In A. Hastorf and A. Isen (eds.), *Cognitive Social Psychology*. New York: Elsevier, 1982, pp. 255–305.

Martin, J.; Feldman, M.; Hatch, M. J.; and Sitkin, S. The uniqueness paradox in organizational stories. *Administrative Science Quarterly, 28,* 3 (1983), 438–453.

Moll, M., and Miikkulainen, R. Convergence-zone episodic memory: analysis and simulations. *Neural Networks, 10,* 6 (1997), 1017–1036.

Morrison, E. W. Newcomer information seeking: exploring types, modes, sources and outcomes. *Academy of Management Journal, 36,* 1 (1993), 557–589.

Mullen, E. J. Framing the mentoring relationship as an information exchange. *Human Resource Management Review, 4,* 3 (1994), 257–281.

Mullen, E. J., and Noe, R. A. The mentoring information exchange: when do mentors seek information from their protégés? *Journal of Organizational Behavior, 20,* 2 (1999), 233–242.

Neuhauser, P. *Corporate Legends and Lore: The Power of Storytelling as a Management Tool.* New York: McGraw-Hill, 1993.

Noe, R. A. Women and mentoring: a review and research agenda. *Academy of Management Review, 13,* 1 (1988), 65–78.

Nonaka, I., and Takeuchi, H. *The Knowledge Creating Company: How Japanese Companies Create the Dynamics of Innovation.* New York: Oxford University Press, 1995.

Paivio, A. A dual coding perspective on imagery and the brain. In J. W. Brown (ed.), *Neuropsychology of Visual Perception.* Hillsdale, NJ: Lawrence Erlbaum, 1989, p. 33.

Pfleeger, S., and Mertz, N. Executive mentoring: what makes it work? *Communications of the American Academy of Management, 38,* 1 (1995), 63–73.

Prahalad, C. K., and Hamel, G. The core competence of the corporation. *Harvard Business Review, 68,* 3 (1990), 79–91.

Ragins, B. R. Diversified mentoring relationships in organizations: a power perspective. *Academy of Management Review, 22,* 2 (1997), 482–521.

Ragins, B. R., and Cotton, J. L. Easier said than done: gender differences in perceived barriers to gaining a mentor. *American Management Journal, 34,* 4 (1991), 939–951.

Ragins, B. R., and Cotton, J. L. Mentor functions and outcomes: a comparison of men and women in formal and informal mentoring relationships. *Journal of Applied Psychology, 84,* 4 (1999), 529–550.

Scandura, T. A. Mentoring and career mobility: an empirical investigation. *Journal of Organizational Behavior, 13,* 2 (1992), 169–174.

Schacter, D. L. *Searching for Memory.* New York: Basic Books, 1996.

Schank, R. C. *Tell Me a Story: Narrative and Intelligence.* Evanston, IL.: Northwestern University Press, 1990.

Simon, H. A. Problem solving and education. In D. T. Tuma, and R. Reif (eds.), *Problem Solving and Education: Issues in Teaching and Research.* Hillsdale, NJ: Lawrence Erlbaum, 1980, pp. 81–96.

Simon, H. A., and Chase, W. G. Skill in chess. *American Scientist, 61,* 4 (1973), 394–403.

Simonetti, J. L.; Ariss, S.; and Martinez, J. Through the top with mentoring. *Business Horizons, 42,* 6 (November–December 1999), 56.

Snowden, D. J. The paradox of story: simplicity and complexity in strategy. Unpublished manuscript, 1999.

Solovy, A. Once upon a culture. *Hospitals and Health Networks, 73,* 5 (1999), 26.

Soraci, S. A.; Franks, J.; Bransford, J.; Chechile, R.; Belli, R.; Carr, M.; and Carlin, M. Incongruous item generation effects: a multiple-cue perspective. *Journal of Experimental Psychology, 20,* 1 (1994), 67–78.

Starcevich, M., and Friend, F. Effective mentoring relationships from the mentee's perspective. *Workforce* (July 1999), 2–3.

Szulanski, G. Exploring internal stickiness: impediments to the transfer of best practice within the firm. *Strategic Management Journal, 17* (Winter 1996), 27–43.

Teece, D. J.; Pisano, G. P.; and Shuen, A. Dynamic capabilities and strategic management. *Strategic Management Journal, 18,* 7 (1997), 509–533.

Tulving, E. Episodic and semantic memory. In E. Tulving and W. Donaldson (eds.), *Organization of Memory.* New York: Academic Press, 1972, pp. 381–404.

Tversky, A., and Kahneman, D. Availability: a heuristic for judging frequency and probability. *Cognitive Psychology, 5,* (September 1973), 207–232.

Van Collie, S.-C. Moving up through mentoring. *Workforce, 77,* 3 (March 1998), 36–39.

Vygotsky, L. S. *Mind in Society: The Development of the Higher Psychological Processes.* Cambridge: Harvard University Press, 1978.

Walsh, A. M., and Borowski, S. C. Cross-gender mentoring career development in the health care industry. *Health Care Management Review, 24,* 3 (June 22, 1999), 7–17.

Wilkins, A. The creation of company cultures: the role of stories and human resource systems. *Human Resource Management, 23,* 1 (1984), 41–60.

Wilson, J. A., and Elman, N. S. Organizational benefits of mentoring. *Academy of Management Executive, 4,* 4 (1990), 88–94.

13

Narrative Patterns: The Perils and Possibilities of Using Story in Organizations

DAVID J. SNOWDEN

Organizations are finally waking up to the power of stories. As managers and executives experience the opportunities revealed through the use of stories within their organizations, they have become more open to moving from the use of storytelling in the context of communication, to the wider opportunities provided by narrative techniques in the fields of organizational change, knowledge management, and strategy. Stories in organizations reveal patterns of culture, behavior, and understanding in a different and frequently more effective way than interviews and questionnaire-based approaches. The stories told in an organization, formally in presentations, around the water cooler, in project reviews, indeed in all aspects of organizational life, reveal the ideation patterns of that organization. Narrative techniques both reveal the patterns of an organization and are in turn the means by which it can be patterned. Narrative is a powerful tool within organizations, but it is not susceptible to the engineering approaches that have dominated management practice in the last few decades. As we will see, managers need to create an environment in which the patterns of narrative meaning and the patterning capability of narrative interventions are managed in the way a gardener manages a garden, not the way an engineer designs a machine.

Narrative is an art and a science; an overemphasis on either aspect is wrong. Neither is narrative a silver bullet that can solve all the problems that an organization faces. One temptation to which many an organization has succumbed is to use stories to propagate ideal behavior. This can result in "Janet and John" stories. Janet and John are the two central characters of a series of books used to teach reading to British four- and five-year-olds (in the United States, their counterparts are "Dick and Jane," in Canada "Bob and Betsy," in Wales "Sion a Sian"; all cultures seem to have an equivalent). The trouble with Janet and John is that they are just too good; they make any self-respecting and intelligent child sick. All Janet and John stories end happily as any naughty behavior receives inevitable punishment and moral or noble actions receive reward and recognition. Most "official" communication in organizations takes a Janet and John approach, attempting to tell things in some idealized vision of cooperative behavior and sacrifice to achieve corporate goals. Stories of best practice hold up a team or division as a role model for others to copy, as they are portrayed fulfilling the chairman or CEO's vision, embodying the organization's core values of customer satisfaction, hard work, and so on. Within the context of senior management, they may even be seen to have been successful, partly because senior managers are often only told the stories they want to hear, are insulated from negativity, or simply succumb to the very human tendency to hear what we want to hear.

The field of narrative is not best served by the naïveté represented by the Jane and John story or by the attempt to transfer skills developed for another context without substantial amendment and augmentation. It requires greater sophistication and realism by senior management. The field of narrative in organizations is a new discipline that draws on many traditional sources but is neither confined nor represented by those traditions. This brief chapter aims to provide some cautionary comments and a high-level overview of some of the newly developing areas of narrative work. It reflects the experience of the Institute for Knowledge Management and, more recently, the Cynefin Centre for Organizational Complexity in developing and patenting methods, tools and techniques for narrative work in organizations.

Dangers and Limitations of Just Telling Stories

All organizations have messages that they wish to convey both internally and externally; however, there are a number of issues that organizations must be aware of before they begin to use storytelling as a way to convey these messages. Conventional communication is often stale and the stories created predictable; effective communication needs a story to be told in a convincing and attention-grabbing/retaining way. Consequently, it is not surprising that the novelty of an Irish Seanachie at a company event, or a group of actors using techniques such as the forms of medieval morality plays, can have a considerable impact on audiences jaded by a surfeit of corporate videos, tightly scripted messages, and idealized examples of "best practice." However, novelty is, by definition, short-lived in its impact, and companies adopting such techniques often end up pursuing novelty for its own sake.

As a result, it is not infrequent for employees to dismiss storytelling as just another consulting or management fad, and regrettably there is an element of truth in this belief. Organizations must be aware that it is not enough to just employ a journalist, scriptwriter, actor, or even a traditional storyteller. All these people have valuable traditional skills within the context for which they were developed: newspaper, films, the theater, and the campfire. However, their skills do not necessarily transfer into the organizational context intact. All too frequently, there may be resistance in the audience to being "told a story." A fictional or allegorical story may just engender cynicism or dismissal: "So now they are telling us fiction," or "That was very entertaining, but why can't they just say what they mean?" A factual story is even more fraught with peril: to tell the truth, the whole truth, and nothing but the truth requires both a prestigious feat of memory and a suspension of the normal human tendency to reinvent history to conform to the requirements of the present. More important, the bare facts are often boring and do not make for a compelling story.

We refer to this approach of directly retelling events to others as "anecdote enhancement," and it includes much of what is known as "storytelling" within organizations. While it can be useful, particularly in training, it presents problems in sustainability and impact. Practitioners who focus on anecdote enhancement select the most compelling of the facts and provide appropriate emphasis: create tension, introduce clear protagonists, build a proper context, and spell out the message. The danger here is that the story creator's emphasis and selection may not correspond to the experiences of other people in the organization. It takes only one person to say "but that's not what really happened," or "but that's not the complete story," and the whole process is undermined. This is particularly true when organizations have just spent large sums of money on a communications or cultural change program. Several years of using anthropological techniques to capture water cooler stories after some official communication show a near-universal occurrence of *anti-story:* the cynical and naturally occurring counter-reaction to an official story of goodness that fails to reflect the reality of the audience's experiences. Narrative patterning is about the creation of sustainable interventions for cultural change, knowledge management, communication, and a host of other organizational objectives. The remainder of this chapter provides an overview of the depth of narrative; as such, it includes aspects of storytelling but is not limited to anecdote enhancement.

Creating and Managing the Flow of Narrative within an Organization

A common scenario, the creation of a new organizational mission or set of values, can illustrate the way in which narrative is much wider in its application than anecdote enhancement. The process of developing value statements begins when a group of executives spends many weeks or months gathering and interpreting the results of consultative exercises, garnering the expertise of external consultants, identifying and resolving differences, clarifying the precise meaning of language, and sharing and merging experiences. At the end of this process a freshly minted set of corporate values is produced that the executives believe reflects the priorities, culture, and strengths of the organization, for example, "putting customers first." Slides sets and briefing packs are created, workshops are held for employees, cards are printed with the new values for employees to carry around in their top pocket, articles are published in internal journals and Web sites, posters are tacked onto notice boards. However, rather than embracing the vision statement, an anti-story begins to develop among the employees. In response to the values statement just mentioned, anti-stories arise: "They've just spent all that money to decide we need to be nice to customers. I could have told them that for nothing, and a decent pay raise would have been more welcome."

The main reason for anti-story is that, while the "vision statement" has profound significance for the executives who lived the journey of its creation, it has little resonance (other than negative) with the employees who have not yet undertaken that journey. For the executives, the value statement is replete with the significance of the many conversations and discussions and stories that they engaged in. Yet the employees have yet to engage at such a level. In fact, it may be worse, as the language used may trigger memories of past initiatives that failed to deliver on expectations or may be perceived as being hypocritical when measured against the past perceived behavior of those executives. For staff to buy in to such initiatives with more than token compliance, they have to relive the journey of the executives. This reliving of others' experience is the historic role of storytelling in society in providing context for human action. To help individuals build this shared context, there are three narrative methods that can be used, either together or in combination: fable, myth management, and the story virus. These methods are the foundations of organizational storytelling as well.

Fable-Form Story

Fable-form stories are moral tales designed to create a context in which a message can be delivered. They are long, complex stories that are difficult to repeat verbatim but have a memorable message or moral. All cultures have such stories that are told by each generation to their children to inculcate common values. Like all good stories they do not attempt to deliver the message until the story itself has provided the context that will make the message acceptable. This building of context is key to the effectiveness of the story, from the elaborate stories told by traditional storytellers to the picture books that provide the first bedtime stories for children. The message of "Beauty and the Beast" is that innocence can be corrupted by evil but redeemed by innocence. The message is not stated up front, but the story gradually builds to the point where the message is inevitable, understood, and incorporated into the underlying value system of the audience.

Fable is rooted in ancient practices of story. The Celtic bards who were welcomed in any household for their ability to hold audiences spellbound with stories of Pwyll, Branwen, Math, and the Dream of Rhonabwy memorized not every word but the overall structure and rhythm such that they could extemporize in the context of their particular audience. The nonrepeatability of the story is not accidental; good storytellers will weave variation into each retelling of the story so that they maintain power over the story and its telling, and thereby maintain control over the delivery of the message. Exactly the same skill is required of the modern executive. The range and complexity of corporate stories is not as great as in the Mabinogion (an ancient collection of Welsh stories referenced earlier), and the process of their creation in an organizational setting can be achieved through a process of telling and retelling, which is described later in this chapter.

As stated, in fable, the message is delivered at the end of the story, by which time the story has created a context in which the message is inescapable or at least unarguable. We like to learn in this way; how many stories state the ending at the beginning? How many endings make sense only when you have heard the whole story? This contrasts with most corporate communications, where the message is delivered at the start and then explained or justified. The fable structure prevents the problems associated with starting a communication with the message, where the audience makes up its mind early in the process and decides up front whether it will accept the message.

Unlike anecdote enhancement, a fable can contain elements from multiple anecdotes from the organization and is not dependent on a single original story to deliver its message. This makes it far less susceptible to the problems of selection and enhancement. The story *emerges* in a workshop through a process of telling and retelling that replicates the natural conditions in which powerful stories generate individually and collectively. The intention is to get to a position where, without slide sets or scripts, executives can communicate the message through a naturally told story.

The process is fairly simple and does not require skilled facilitation, which is a normal dependency of anecdote enhancement. The executives begin by familiarizing themselves with a fable template, an example of which can be found in Box 13.1; this example has seven sections assembled in a nonlinear sequence (the numbers in the right-hand column indicate the assembly sequence). The familiarization is achieved by being told a story and then having the template explained in the context of that story.

The executives then populate the fable form using anecdotes from their own experience or that of their fellow workshop attendees section by section, in the order signified in Box 13.1. At each telling the story is refined through the telling and the response of the audience. This imitates the process by which stories are naturally developed by individuals, through telling and retelling with different audiences. Favorite dinnertime stories, the stories told to new members of an organization—all evolve in this way. The personalization of the form is very important, for while it takes a very gifted storyteller to tell someone else's story, an individual can easily be guided on how to tell a story with credibility and ease if it is based on his or her own experience. The ease in this process enables a large number of people to learn and internalize their own fable. This is practical, achievable, and sustainable; training executives to be skilled storytellers, journalists, or scriptwriters in a two-day course is not. It also contrasts favorably with the staged delivery of a written speech or a standard slide set using someone else's language.

In one case, thirty executives were trained over two half-day workshops to construct fables based around a new corporate mission statement. As a result, the organization had thirty people telling different stories based on their own experience and anecdotes already gathered from the organization, but each delivering precisely the same message. The multiple elements of the fable form can effectively

BOX 13.1

Context	Storyteller creates a relationship with the audience and sets up the message without revealing it. Self-depreciation can help here, as the storyteller must not appear to preach or to be too arrogant. A mistake or act of commonplace foolishness that has relevance to the story would serve. Irony and cynicism, if not carried too far, can also be very effective.	7
Context Three	Three anecdotes assembled in ascending sequence of impact, drawn from the organization's history, which in no way reveal the message but which draw the audience into the context of the story to prepare them for the message. It is very important that the anecdotes do not deliver the message or provide a clue as to that message. Threes are also common to stories: three goals, three princes etc., etc. We expect three, two disappoints, and a fourth is not heard. The children's story of the "Three Billy Goats Gruff" has three goats encountering a troll at a bridge; we start with the smallest, continue to the middle-sized one, and then to the largest, after which the story can be resolved. Each anecdote (or in the case of the goats, troll encounters) builds experience and increases the anticipation of the audience.	2
Turning Point	The story turns; a clear incident signals to the audience that the story is moving from context to message. This can be done with tone of voice or the use of another anecdote that turns from humor to seriousness: there has to be a transition.	4
Message Three	Three anecdotes assembled in ascending sequence of impact, which deliver the message through successive revelation without revealing the message itself. Delivering the message too quickly is a mistake; by gradually building the message through a series of revelations, the point is driven home with far greater effectiveness.	3
Message	The underlying message which permeates the story itself and which does not always have to be precise. The message itself is never formally stated, and there is no need to get a precise statement identified in the workshop as that will refine during the process of telling and retelling.	1
Slogan	A simple phrase such as "social context, social obligation," which is easily memorized. This phrase should be seeded in the earlier parts of the story, including context three, so that it has become familiar to the audience and will suddenly make sense as it is revealed in the context of the message.	6

(continued)

| Reverse and Resolution | An old story trick: the message is thrown into sharp relief when the resolution appears to be achieved but is suddenly cast into doubt before being restored. This reminds the audience of the core message. It is a common trick in films. Think of *Fatal Attraction*: just when we think the villain of the piece is drowned and the hero is safe, she rises out of the bath in one last mad attempt to kill him. Without this reversal the story would not have bite. The reverse acts to remind us of the start of the story; it builds the message back into the context. | 5 |

re-create the context in which the values or mission statements were formulated so that they are not pious platitudes but the natural and accepted consequence of hearing the story. The story can also adapt itself with different anecdotes used for different audiences and with changing circumstance. It is a natural story that has evolved, albeit a forced evolution, through telling, retelling, and example.

A final point that involves fable creation needs to be addressed. While happy endings may seem to be a good idea, more often than not they generate anti-story. Most people, however loyal, react against a Janet and John message no matter how well intentioned. The best form of fable has an ironic end, in which the audience realizes without the need for articulation how a happy ending could have come about. For example, a story designed to encourage knowledge sharing might be illustrated by three anecdotes of foolish wasted effort reinventing the wheel, to set the context, followed by three *understated* anecdotes of success that could only be achieved by the desired behavior. The final anecdote could show an example of where copying past success was the wrong thing to do, as it prevented a new idea being generated. This is an ironic end; it is much more effective. The audience is not being preached to; listeners can fill in the gaps and make the correct judgements for themselves.

Myth Management

Myths are timeless. In all societies, national, tribal, and organizational stories are told and retold, creating and reinforcing themes. Characters often emerge from those stories or generate them in the first place. In IBM, stories about Thomas J. Watson Jr. are still told many years after he left the company; "Richard" stories abound in the Virgin Group. This is the same phenomenon, formed in the same way that over longer periods and with larger populations produced the mythologies of ancient society. Think of the wartime myths of Britain and compare them with those of the former Soviet Union. Examine the stories of the American Civil War that still provide evidence of a cultural divide between the descendants of the two sides.

Although myths in organizations do not have the same longevity as myths in society as a whole, their impact on people's lives can be as strong. In the context of an organization, myths consist of self-similar stories that are told and retold around certain common themes. Sometimes these themes can be so strong and clear that they achieve the status of an organizing or governing principle. Just as the myth structure of society permits acceptable and unacceptable behavior, so the myth structure of an organization can bound its capabilities and perception.

The myth stories that are told in an organization bear an interpretive relationship to facts; which facts are told, and which aspects are emphasized, exaggerated, or satirized can tell us much about the organization and enable an understanding of the myth structure that pervades it. The myth stories create an unconscious perspective lens, a filter through which reality is both perceived and created. Managers must therefore keep in mind as they attempt to initiate change or rewrite the myths of the organization that the organization is not a blank slate; there will often be an existing group of myths in place at an organizational (and frequently suborganizational) level that are powerfully entrenched and that also provide the interpretive framework through which any new messages will be perceived. This is a part of the pattern entrainment that forms a key aspect of human intelligence. Decisions are not made on the basis of a rational evaluation of carefully considered alternatives, but through a first-fit pattern matching with past experience, and much of that experience is the indirect experience we receive through stories. Pattern entrainment allows humans individually and collectively to make rapid decisions under conditions of uncertainty; that is the upside. The downside is that whole communities fit what they see to match those preexisting patterns.

A new set of values or a mission statement is an attempt to refocus or redirect the organization to achieve goals encapsulated in those values, but any communication will be filtered through the current mythology of that community. Understanding that mythology is therefore key to success. The way in which facts from the past have been interpreted can tell us how the values will be interpreted, both in the present and in the future. It can also indicate the degree to which the message, supported by action, will have to be radical if it is to break an ingrained pattern of interpretation that dominates that organization. If the new values conflict with the value system reinforced by the myths, then their implementation is more likely to engender anti-story. However, if the values build on, or seek to modify, existing corporate myths, adoption of the new values or mission is more likely.

Myth management offers the opportunity to evolve and disrupt negative patterns as well as reinforce weak but positive patterns. It is one of the newest and at the same time one of the oldest methods for cultural change, organizational alignment, innovation, and many other apparently intractable problems. In this case we are looking at one aspect of myth management, namely, the instantiation of a new value system. Most organizations have finely tuned hypocrisy triggers in their informal networks and that produce anti-stories that can trap the innocent as well as the guilty. One of the simplest methods of myth management is to research the anti-stories that are likely to be triggered by this shift in values. For example, in one organization executives were asked to nominate members of their staff with high potential who were often considered to be cynical or negative. These individuals were then taken on a weekend leadership development program. While a good program was delivered, the real purpose was to test different corporate messages on a naturally cynical audience, to flush out potential anti-stories in advance, and understand what triggered these stories. This simple exercise was used in two ways: first, to inform a conventional communication campaign, providing a series of checkpoints against which written material, posters, and briefing notes for senior managers could be tested; second, in a fable construction workshop for senior managers who had to test their stories against the range of anti-story and revise those stories to ensure that the worse anti-stories were not generated. These two examples are avoidance techniques; story virus techniques (described later) were also used to prevent the generation of anti-stories

More advanced techniques involve gathering large volumes of anecdotal material from the organization and then using statistically selected groups of staff in a workshop process to allow the underlying themes of the organization to emerge. This process might be carried out with one group selected to represent the demographic characteristics of the organization as a whole, or different groups such as senior managers, middle managers, salespeople, and so forth might be selected so that contrasting themes could be identified. Emergence is an interesting new technique in organizational change that is neither qualitative nor quantitative. Emergence is an aspect of complex systems in which the interactions between agents in the system produce patterns. Think of the formation of a snowflake or the flocking behavior of birds; in both cases complex patterns emerge from large group interactions. Emergence for clarity relies on groups of people with tacit knowledge of the organization identifying subject areas (typically several hundred) from a large body of anecdotal material. The subject areas are then clustered, and for each cluster positive and negative attributes are brainstormed and then clustered to turn to identify themes. This is a nonanalytic, two-stage, lightly facilitated process, which reduces the potential impact of the researcher.

Two examples, one related to the emergent process and one to the anti-story elicitation technique, will serve to summarize this section.

1. In one large organization, a dominant theme that emerged from eight different sample groups was "don't buck the process." A large body of anecdotes comprised stories of stupidity arising from a slavish adherence to standard process, with amusing stories about how each new member of staff had learned the lesson the hard way. In this organization, a particular form of formal process had come to mean "the organization takes this seriously," and the absence of such a process led to dismissal of initiatives designed to reduce bureaucracy and cost. Despite the intent, the myth structure of the organization prevented change. In this case, the clear strength of the myth would require a highly disruptive technique to achieve change, which was a step too far for the organization concerned, as the dependency on process control was pervasive across all levels of

management. This type of theme, if negative, is perverse, self-reinforcing, and extremely dangerous, but regrettably common. Its one of the reasons that large companies fail to adapt to radically changing markets.

2. In another case, the anti-story elicitation approach described earlier identified that an executive was about to, in all innocence, use a form of words in a corporation-wide announcement that had been used by another CEO in a recently acquired subsidiary some years ago. These words had been delivered immediately prior to a massive downsizing operation. There was no way that he could be aware of this, and the form of words seemed innocent, even motivational, but they triggered a resonant meaning within a part of the organization that quickly infected the rest. The existence of myth monitoring meant that the impact was recognized far earlier than normal channels and permitted a tightly targeted intervention.

Organizations need to realize that all communication takes place in the context of multiple pasts of which we can never be fully aware. Myths exist in organizations and have the same impact as myths on society as a whole: they define what we are, and how we view things.

Story Virus

If an anti-story has become dominant in an organization, factual rebuttal will rarely dislodge it. A number of techniques can begin to counter the effects of an anti-story; these are referred to as "story viruses." Readers should understand that this is a specialized form of narrative work and needs to be approached with care, but it is one of the most useful and can be trained to the point where it is a natural process. Among the types of story virus techniques that can be used are the following:

1. *Socratic dialogue.* In this situation, the anti-story or the person telling it is questioned to the point of destroying his or her own story. The storyteller does not have to be attacked directly (and it would be rare to know who was spreading the rumor in the first place) but can be challenged through rhetorical questions. This is a form of dialectic reasoning in which the intention is not to win the argument but to inject a question in order that the anti-story moves on to a safe place. Mark Anthony does this in the famous funeral oration, ending each statement with "I come to bury Caesar, not to praise him," this posing a question to the crowd that turns it to his favor. An executive can do the same, posing a question that he or she does not answer, but the employees will come to answer in a favorable manner.

2. *Reductio ad absurdum* means to reduce to the absurd. Here the anti-story is managed by picking on various aspects of it and through a process of logical argument showing that its premises lead to absurdity. At the heart of this technique is picking on one vulnerable aspect of the anti-story and elevating its importance before progressively making the statement ridic-

ulous. Examples of this type of virus are long and drawn out; they may involve careful communication and "myth monitoring" over a period of weeks or months.

3. *Metaphor* is an established way of getting people to see things differently. We generally understand new things by metaphorical reference to something that is already understood. By creating an association with another well-known story, we can demonstrate how the errors in the metaphor are similar to the errors in the anti-story. This is an old technique that popular speakers use in dealing with hecklers; they associate the concept of criticism with a ridiculous image. One, admittedly unfair, example was used by the author when facing an attack from an overenthusiastic supporter of the tool known as appreciate inquiry, which has some use in narrative but which focuses on positive stories and tries to reduce negativity. Now the Cynefin narrative techniques encourage negative storytelling; indeed, capturing and distributing stories of mistakes, a "worst practice" system, is seen as more valuable than an idealized "best practice" system. Rather than engage in a detailed debate that would have lost the audience, appreciate inquiry was handled as follows: "Appreciate inquiry, that's the technique that focuses on positive stories? It always reminds me of the final scene of the Monty Python film *Life of Brian* where they are all swing backward and forward on the crosses singing 'always look on the bight side of life.' " Now that was unfair, and took place in the context of a warm audience, sharing cultural roots with the speaker, but it illustrates the technique, which need not be culturally specific.

4. *The killer fact* can be effective, but often an anti-story is made worse by arguing with the facts. We see this a lot in scientific communities, whose arguments would convince other scientists but have the opposite effect on others. For example, scientists had proved the river Thames in London was clean and quoted low levels of cadmium to prove it, but all this statement did was create new fears. However, when a salmon was later caught in the river, everyone believed the river was clean. The presence of a salmon turned out to be the killer fact; the detailed scientific proof was not.

5. *Exaggeration* of a key element or aspect of the story to make it laughable, ideally in a good-humoured way. In one case at IBM an urban myth within one of the sales teams (a specialized form of myth story that arises to explain or excuse) about the terrible consequences to clients of not buying an IBM solution was destroyed for over three years. This was done using a story that gradually transformed from a hero story in which IBM knowing best did result in client failure, but the level of failure and the clients' rectification of their sin were so ridiculous as to be laughable, and anyone attempting to use the urban myth as an excuse was made ridiculous by association. The key here is to take the strength of the undesired story and exaggerate it until it becomes ridiculous—no direct contradiction.

6. *Direct contradiction* has value but often makes things worse, not better, because it may take the anti-story seriously and increase its credibility and

pervasiveness. In general the advice is, if you do not have a killer fact that will be understood and that will gain resonance with the audience, this approach should not be used.

The need to use story virus can be reduced by gaining a proper understanding of how anti-story arises within the context of a particular organization. By using fables and myth management earlier in the process, the need for story viruses can be minimized.

A Wider Perspective on Narrative

A combination of fable, myth, and story virus complements more traditional communication methods and represents a more sophisticated approach to managing the flow of communication and understanding within an organization. However, it should be understood that whereas storytelling is an important aspect of narrative, it is not the whole of it. The many forms of narrative can also act as a source of understanding, disrupt ingrained thinking, provide a repository of learning, replace user requirement specifications, and enable confession of failure without attribution of blame. It seems as if determining the pattern language of the organization is about gathering information, which can be as much a form of communication as disseminating ideas is about disseminating information. Narrative does this by making clear the patterns that exist, shifting perspectives about those patterns, and, when necessary, disrupting or challenging those patterns within the organization.

Pattern Perspectives—Revealing Meaning and Enabling Understanding

Human knowledge is deeply contextual and requires stimulation if it is to be revealed. Telling stories, both fact and fiction, is a powerful way of achieving that stimulation. A theme in the story is an *emergent* property of anecdotes captured within an organization. Identifying the pattern of themes that underpin water cooler stories provides valuable insights to the reality of an organizational culture.

Another valuable source of pattern identification and understanding comes from the development of archetypes. Archetypal characters are common to all storytelling. As people tell stories about their situation, characters emerge from those stories. As stories are told about the characters, they become more extreme until each represents one aspect of that society, and collectively they represent the culture as a whole. Archetypes used in organizations are not universal but are unique to the context of each organization, and therein rests their value. Like themes, they emerge indirectly from the workshop process described earlier. The same effect can also be achieved through virtual facilitation, but it does require interaction (i.e., emergence), not an analytical approach that will be polluted by the analyst in terms of meaning. Often, this requires using large volumes of anecdotes from the organization, starting with characters or stereotypes, and then clustering the many positive and negative attributes of those characters to create archetypes. Archetypes have been used to provide measures of employee and customer satisfaction, and in the latter case also provide an interesting new perspective on brand. To take an example, school students were used to collect anecdotes from customers as they left an out-of-town hypermarket. Those stories were used with a sample of customers to create a set of stereotypes and archetypes that were realized by a political cartoonist. The same process was repeated with store staff, using informal capture methods not involving direct questioning, to get their stereotypes and archetypes of their customers. The two sets were then shown to senior management, who could see instantly what was going wrong and had the means of rectification to hand. Both sets of cartoons were put up in every staff room with a banner that said, "This is what they think of you, and this is what you think of them." This technique is one of descriptive self-awareness in which the consultant does not analyze or prescribe, but creates the conditions for descriptive self-awareness; a mirror is held up to the soul of the participant. Archetypes that emerge as patterns from stories told naturally can be a more valuable measure of reality than quantitative or qualitative techniques that inevitably see only what they have been designed to see, and are less open to new discovery and too dependent on expert analysis. The identification of organizational archetypes becomes an even more valuable tool when combined with demographic data to create "villages of persona," which have provided a radical and more creative alternative to developing user requirement specifications for intranet design.

The same techniques, along with disruptive metaphors and other knowledge management techniques such as social network stimulation, can be used when two companies merge or in an acquisition. Although both firms may use the same language, the parties have different histories, and these past experiences profoundly influence the use of language. The same phrase may be positive in one company but trigger anti-story in the other. The coming together of two organizations will increase the number of strong frequently told stories (sometimes known as identity stories) told by each party, and, if anything, differences will be exaggerated. Over time, though often far too late, the language and the stories will merge. Narrative techniques such as fable construction, archetypes, and myth management allow us to accelerate this natural process by creating new common stories, mixing anecdotal material, archetypes, and values to communicate a new common culture by changing the myth structure that underpins it. Narrative allows us to accelerate the creation of common understanding and purpose in a nondirective, and thereby more sustainable, form.

Pattern Disruption

Organizations (and societies, for that matter) develop "scripts," or controlling stories that punish deviation. These develop and are reinforced by ordinary people; they are rarely imposed from the top and as a result cannot be changed by diktat. While scripts increase the predictability of human interactions, they stifle innovation and prevent both insight and descriptive self-awareness. However, as in most aspects of human behavior, ingrained behavior is difficult to change by direct challenge.

Departure from a script is not an easy thing for an individual or a community. For example, a dominant script in many organizations is the need for continued success and the avoidance of failure. This means that in many knowledge management efforts, getting people to tell stories of failure is difficult, if not impossible. In this situation, exhortations that this is a "no blame" culture are more likely to generate anti-story than genuine sharing. Trust enables sharing of failure, but trust is won over years and lost in seconds. Some trust is contextual, as members of a fire-fighting crew will trust each other during a fire, but that same level of trust cannot be induced in an office environment and will not sustain itself within the fire crew in a different context. Historically, many cultures have developed archetypal story forms that are used as a confessional device or as a means of criticism without the pain of direct contradiction. This is already commonplace in most organizations in the form of "Dilbert" cartoons pinned to a wall. The Sufi tradition has an archetypal character that is used as a substitute for "I" in telling stories of failure. Once a set of archetypes has emerged from the anecdotes of a community, they can be used as confessional devices to allow stories of failure to be told without attribution of blame. In knowledge management initiatives, stories of failure are more valuable than those of success. The indirect nature of an archetype allows us, through these archetypes, to tell stories about ourselves without the pain of public confession.

Metaphors not only are a useful form of story virus but also can be used as a way for reframing problems. For example, a major challenge in the eighteenth century was to discover a way to measure longitude while on a ship, which is well documented in Dava Sobel's popular book *Longitude*. The eventual solution was a clock that kept accurate time on shipboard. However, it took the experts several decades to acknowledge this solution, and their treatment of the clockmaker who came up with this novel approach was nothing short of shameful. He was not a scientist in their sense of the word, and his ideas did not conform to the dominant science of the day, namely, astronomy. Most innovators in history, and in organizations today, suffer from the same neglect.

Asking a group of research scientists or managers to read Sobel's book prior to an innovation workshop allows a metaphorical question to be asked: "Give me an example of how you have treated your staff in the way that the scientists treated that clockmaker." This is a question that can be answered because the metaphor creates a safe space in which the question can be addressed. Asking the same group for examples of where they had ignored the radical thinking of organizational mavericks would not achieve the same result. This use of metaphor is a powerful way of breaking up scripts. Films, children's books common to the culture of the day, and cultural icons such as Shakespeare or Cervantes all provide source material that can be used to generate discussions. By having a conversation in a metaphorical setting, much of the pain of abandoning cherished beliefs or unarticulated prejudice can be more easily handled. Pattern disruption techniques are of particular use when we have two cultures merging, or an old culture that needs to change but is resisting doing so. This includes, but is not limited to, merger and acquisition work.

Storing and Revealing Patterns—Narrative Databases

The stories that people tell are a wonderful source of material for understanding culture and discovering examples of knowledge and learning. Storytelling originated in the need to re-create the circumstances of knowledge use, thus creating an early knowledge asset register and map. Today, any member of staff coming off a project can easily record in an hour, or even ten minutes, what it might otherwise take three weeks to get around to spending half a day writing up (if it is ever done). Both the written record, which is reflective, and the spoken record, which is immediate, can provide different sources of value. However, most current knowledge management practice focuses on written material. This is time-consuming and often results in lost experiential knowledge. Narrative databases not only allow us to capture large volumes of oral material at little cost but also critically allow us to index those records on a single screen to give current and future staff access to "the wisdom of the elder."

Narrative databases work on the basis of serendipitous encounter. Given a choice between drawing down best practice from an intellectual capital management system and hearing the stories of eight or nine people with relevant experience, the natural choice is the stories. Narrative databases work in the same way by allowing abstract searches by archetypes, themes, intention, emotional level, and perspective in such a way that multiple stories are encountered from which listeners can synthesize their own meaning. The more traditional intellectual capital management system still has value but is far more effective when linked to a narrative database. The additional value of narrative is that it can create a supporting "worst cases system" in which encountering stories of failure is more likely to foster success in the future.

For organizations undergoing downsizing or experiencing high levels of turnover, oral history databases provide a radical, comparatively cheap, quick, and effective solution to creating knowledge and learning repositories. Oral history databases also provide a means by which we can look at an issue from many perspectives. Their use in advanced decision support systems, as an alternative to scenario planning, is a current subject of research within the Cynefin Centre.

Conclusion

Narrative is both a science and an art, and to neglect one at the expense of the other is not only foolish but also dangerous. In playing with people's stories, you are playing with their souls, and that requires a high level of responsibility. A Seanachie, the Irish word that means far more than "storyteller," will spend many years as an apprentice; organizational work on story and narrative requires a similar level of personal commitment. The danger is that in attempting to enter the field, a practitioner will either trivialize it (anyone can tell a story) or assume a false commonality with entertainment and journalism. Narrative, at its best, is a simple way to convey complex ideas and to create an understanding of culture and learning within communities. It will not do to confuse something that is simple but which requires profound understanding with something that is just easy to do and provides a quick hit. Storytelling is simple but not simplistic, but above all a profoundly human technique that rejects the mechanical and authoritarian practice of too many management scientists and consultants.

Index